POSTWAR AIR WEAPONS
1945–PRESENT

**THE ESSENTIAL
WEAPONS IDENTIFICATION GUIDE**

POSTWAR AIR WEAPONS

1945–PRESENT

THOMAS NEWDICK

amber
BOOKS

This edition published in 2011 by
Amber Books Ltd
Bradley's Close
74–77 White Lion Street
London N1 9PF
United Kingdom
www.amberbooks.co.uk

A catalogue record for this book is available from the British Library.

ISBN: 978-1-907446-59-7

Project Editor: Michael Spilling
Design: Brian Rust
Picture Research: Terry Forshaw

Printed in China

PICTURE CREDITS
Art-Tech/Aerospace: 26, 28
Art-Tech/MARS: 12, 13, 15, 16, 18, 20, 42, 70, 76, 83, 102, 105, 167
DACT/Katsuhiko Tokunaga: 8
Eurofighter: 132
Gripen: 90
Press Association: 114
Public Domain: 183
U.S. Department of Defense: 6, 7, 34, 37, 44, 56, 59, 62, 66, 89, 92, 98,
    101, 111, 120, 130, 136, 143, 144, 145, 150, 153, 154, 158, 164, 169, 174

All artworks Mark Franklin © Amber Books

Contents

Introduction

Since the first aircraft took to the air for combat, warplanes have served primarily as platforms for carrying weapons: be it ordnance intended to be delivered against a ground target, or the means of destroying the opposition in the air. The years after World War II saw great advances in the fields of destructive power and accuracy, leading to the era of the 'smart' weapon.

THE FIRST WEAPONS to be used in the air included small arms, grenades and artillery shells. By World War I, aircraft were being equipped with purpose-designed aerial bombs, while machine guns soon superseded infantry weapons and handguns.

In the arena of air-to-air combat, the aerial gun – whether the machine gun or more powerful cannon – long remained the dominant fighter weapon. This situation only began to change after 1945 as first unguided rockets, and then guided air-to-air missiles, were developed to defeat aircraft that were becoming ever more capable in terms of performance.

Early guided weapons

The first practical air-launched guided weapons began to be studied in earnest during World War II but were handicapped by their primitive guidance systems, which typically relied upon a trailing wire to carry signals generated by the operator in the launch aircraft. The subsequent breakthroughs in radar technology, infrared detection, and electro-optics finally permitted more advanced guidance systems to be employed, increasing reliability and accuracy and relieving the burden on the pilot or crew. Ultimately, guided weapons offered a 'fire and forget' capability, although it was to take many years before this technology was refined.

At the same time that guided missiles began to supplant aircraft guns for aerial combat, guided weapons also began to make their mark as bomber armament. Initially, however, the size of early nuclear

▼ **Bombs away**
Free-fall or 'dumb' bombs are among the most primitive air-to-ground ordnance, but still have a role to play in modern warfare. Here, a USAF F-111 drops four inert 2000lb (907kg) Mk 84 bombs over a target range.

weapons – the *raison d'être* of the strategic bomber after 1945 – prohibited their carriage by all but the largest air-to-surface missiles, but the reduction in the size and weight of warheads later permitted smaller free-fall and guided nuclear weapons to be carried by tactical fighters and even helicopters.

The potential of the guided missile to destroy hardened, pinpoint and high-priority targets was quickly recognized, and led to the introduction of air-launched missiles designed for use against particular objectives, whether warships, tanks or radars. Anti-ship missiles were fielded in World War II and represent an entire field of development, requiring specialist launch modes, guidance systems and warheads. Similarly, the realities of armoured warfare experienced a paradigm shift with the introduction of guided weapons, soon adapted for air launch.

Modern aerial firepower

Today, air force commanders expect more from their armoury of air-launched weapons than ever before. Whether assigned to the air-to-air or air-to-ground role, modern air-launched weapons must combine destructive power with accuracy, reliability, ease of operation and low cost. The last factor has driven the development of precision-guidance kits that can be strapped on to existing free-fall ordnance to create

▲ **Multi-role war load**

A USAF F-15E Strike Eagle over the mountains of Afghanistan. The aircraft carries a typical mixed war load, including three AIM-120 AMRAAMs and an AIM-9 Sidewinder for the air-to-air mission, with 227kg (500lb) laser-guided bombs and GBU-38 Joint Direction Attack Munitions, plus LANTIRN navigation pod and the Sniper targeting pod, for the offensive role.

economic and reliable offensive weapons. In the realm of air-to-air combat, priority is focussed on the capability to destroy targets that may range from agile, stealthy, high-performance warplanes to simple drones and cruise missiles. As well as defeating airborne threats at standoff distances (before the enemy has a chance to deploy his own weapons), the realities of modern air warfare also demand weapons with the flexibility to destroy targets at close quarters – perhaps in a dogfight, or otherwise in a situation where the rules of engagement demand a positive visual identification.

In the future, air-launched weapons will likely increasingly stress multi-role capability, allowing a single guided missile to be used against a wide spectrum of targets, both in the air, or on the ground. However, there will likely remain a place for the free-fall bombs and rockets that were the primary offensive air-launched weapons from the earliest days of air combat.

Chapter 1

Air-to-Air Missiles

For a period in the 1950s, the air-to-air missile (AAM)
appeared to be the 'silver bullet' of air combat. A new
generation of interceptors, optimized to destroy high-flying
enemy bombers, relied on an all-missile armament, fighter
designers doing away with the aircraft gun altogether.
Successive wars in the Middle East and Southeast Asia,
however, demonstrated that the AAM was not always the
best option in modern air combat, particularly in the low-
level, close-quarters dogfight. Therefore most modern fighter
aircraft now carry a gun for close-in dogfighting, although
the guided missile remains the key weapon in the air-to-air
arena. Israeli and Soviet developments in the field of super-
agile, short-range AAMs in the early 1980s spurred the
introduction of a new generation of weapons in the following
two decades that offer a combination of both
manoeuvrability and, increasingly, standoff range.

◄ **Modern fighter power**
Representative of the latest generation of air dominance fighters, this French Air Force Dassault Rafale
carries a typical air-to-air weapons load of six Missile d'Interception, de Combat et d'Autodéfense (MICA)
missiles, supplemented by three 1250-litre (275-gallon) external fuel tanks. The AAMs include examples of
both the radar-guided MICA EM and the infrared-guided MICA IR, the latter being carried on the wingtip
weapons stations. In future, the Rafale will add the ramjet-powered Meteor AAM to its arsenal, further
increasing its capability to destroy agile targets at extended ranges.

Early Cold War AAMs

Inspired by wartime German efforts, development of the first generation of air-to-air guided missiles began in the late 1940s, these being primarily intended to destroy bomber-size targets.

THE DEVELOPMENT OF a first-generation AAM for the US military began in 1946, with a US Air Force (USAF) requirement for a radar-based interceptor fire-control system and guided missile in order to tackle Soviet bombers. Initial testing began in 1949, with the missile carrying the preliminary designation AAM-A-2. The original plan foresaw a defensive AAM for carriage by bombers, before the launch platform was switched to fighters – initially the F-89H/J Scorpion and F-102A Delta Dagger. The missile itself was designated F-98 (in the 'Fighter' series).

The initial production model was the GAR-1 Falcon, which became the first weapon of its type to enter operational service anywhere in the world, in 1956. Production of the semi-active radar homing GAR-1 (later redesignated AIM-4 under the Tri-Service Aircraft Designation System introduced in

1962) began in 1954, and the missile was produced in both infrared (IR) homing and semi-active radar homing (SARH) variants. Typically, examples of the IR and SARH missiles would be ripple-fired, to increase kill probability, in a method that would later be adopted for most medium-range Soviet AAMs.

The first IR-homing 'fire-and-forget' version of the Falcon was the GAR-2 (later AIM-4B), while the GAR-3 was an improved SARH model. Among the first generation, the more agile GAR-1D (AIM-4A) became the major production model with SARH, and also served as the basis for the GAR-2 and the GAR-2A (AIM-4C) with a more sensitive IR seeker.

Specifications

Wingspan: 940mm (37in)	Range: 10km (5.4nm)
Length: 3740m (147.3in)	Propulsion: Aerojet 1.8KS7800 solid rocket
Diameter: 203mm (8in)	Warhead: 20kg (45lb)
Weight: 143kg (315lb)	Guidance: radar beam riding
Speed: Mach 2.5	

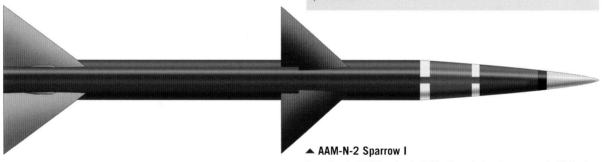

Specifications

Length: 3099mm (12ft 2in)	Maximum range: 7km (4.35 miles)
Wingspan: 1000mm (40in)	Maximum altitude: 17,980m (59,000ft)
Diameter: 260mm (10.24in)	Guidance: semi-active radar homing
Weight: 148kg (397lb)	Powerplant: 1.3 tonne (3530-lb) thrust
Warhead weight: 20.5lb (55lb) high explosive	Hotchkiss-Brandt solid-fuel rocket motor
Maximum speed: Mach 1.8	

▲ **AAM-N-2 Sparrow I**

Becoming the AIM-7A under the 1962 military designation system, the US Navy's Sparrow I used a primitive beam-riding guidance system combined with an optical sight that limited the missile to engagements within visual range.

▼ **Matra R.511**

Although considered as interim equipment, the R.511 survived in service with French Air Force Mirage and Vautour fighters into the early 1970s. The Hotchkiss-Brandt warhead was detonated by command signal from the homing head.

▼ RS-2U (AA-1 'Alkali')

In its improved RS-2U guise, the 'Alkali' was optimized for use by the MiG-19PM all-weather interceptor. The weapon illustrated has the optional tracers fitted on the fin tips to enable guidance. The aerial at the rear received the radar signals.

Specifications

Length overall: 2500mm (8ft 2in)	Warhead weight: 13kg (28.7lb)
Fuselage diameter: 200mm (7.9in)	Range: 2–6km (1.2– 3.8 miles)
Wingspan: 654mm (26in)	Speed: 2880km/h (1790mph)
Launch weight: 82.7kg (183.3lb)	Guidance system: Beam riding

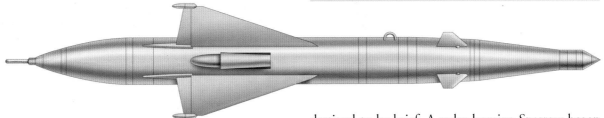

An improved derivative, the Super Falcon, arrived in 1958, beginning with the SARH GAR-3 (AIM-4E). This used a longer-burning motor for increased range and was soon followed by the GAR-3A (AIM-4F) with dual-thrust motor and improved guidance. The IR version of the Super Falcon was the GAR-4A (AIM-4G).

Sparrow and Sidewinder

Begun as a US Navy programme in 1947, the initial version of the prolific Sparrow was the AAM-N-2 Sparrow I (AIM-7A) that originated under Project Hot Shot, the aim being to combine an aerial rocket with a beam-riding guidance system. Unpowered flight tests commenced in 1948, with a first successful aerial interception achieved in 1952, after which the Sparrow I entered service in 1956 on F3H-2M Demon and F7U-3M Cutlass carrier fighters. However, the beam-riding guidance proved problematic, and the service life of the Sparrow I was

destined to be brief. A radar-homing Sparrow began to be studied in 1950, as the AAM-N-3 (AIM-7B) Sparrow II. By the mid 1950s, the Sparrow II was adapted for active radar guidance, to arm the F5D Skylancer and Canadian CF-105 Arrow interceptors. Both these aircraft were cancelled, and in 1958 the Sparrow II was abandoned in favour of the Sparrow III with SARH guidance.

Development of the Sparrow III began in 1955 with the AAM-N-6 (AIM-7C), which entered US Navy service in 1958 and served as the basis for the many variants that followed. In 1959 an improved version appeared, as the AAM-N-6a (AIM-7D), with increased altitude and range parameters.

The origins of the AIM-9 Sidewinder, the world's most successful AAM, date back to 1950, and a project of the US Naval Weapons Center. Developed as a simple heat-seeking missile, the Sidewinder utilized a lead sulphide IR seeker and characteristic 'rolleron' stabilizers on the tailfins. A first IR-guided Sidewinder scored a test kill in 1953 and the first production examples were delivered to the US Navy

▼ AIM-4F Falcon

Originally designated as the GAR-3A, the AIM-4F of 1959 was part of the Super Falcon series, with SARH guidance. Replacing the AIM-4A, the AIM-4F used a new dual-thrust rocket motor and the guidance system was upgraded for increased accuracy and improved ECM resistance.

Specifications

Length overall: 2180mm (78ft 1.8in)	Range: 11.3km (7 miles)
Fuselage diameter: 168mm (6.6in)	Speed: Mach 4
Wingspan: 610mm (24in)	Powerplant: Solid-fuel rocket
Launch weight: 68kg (150lb)	Guidance system: SAHR
Warhead weight: 13kg (28.7lb)	

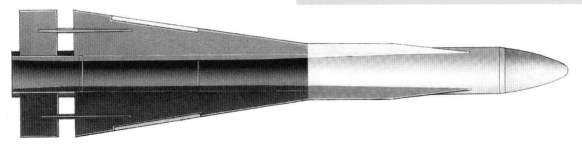

in 1956. The first version to enter service was the AAM-N-7 Sidewinder I (AIM-9A), soon superseded by the series-production AAM-N-7 Sidewinder IA, initially known as the GAR-8 in USAF service, and later as the AIM-9B.

British, French and Soviet developments

Developed by Fairey Aviation, the Fireflash beam-riding missile entered limited service with the Royal Air Force (RAF) for test and evaluation purposes, being carried by the Swift F. Mk 7. The weapon's guidance system precluded the use of an internal rocket motor, and so it was powered by two jettisonable boost motors. The first British AAM to enter full-scale squadron service was the IR-guided Firestreak, developed by de Havilland Propellers (later de Havilland Aircraft) from 1951 under the codename Blue Jay. The Firestreak provided the armament for RAF Javelin and Lightning and Royal Navy Sea Venom and Sea Vixen fighters. The first firings by an operational unit were recorded by No. 893 Naval Air Squadron Sea Venoms in 1958.

In France, development of guided missiles was pursued along two different paths by Matra (Mécanique Aviation Traction) and Arsenal de l'Aéronautique. While Arsenal favoured wire or radio guidance, Matra elected to incorporate autonomous

homing. The first French AAM effort was a copy of the wartime German X-4, the AA.10, retaining the wire guidance and liquid-fuel motor of the original. Tests began in 1947 before the weapon was revised in 1951 as the AA.20 (later Nord 5103) with simple radio command guidance. A contract for this weapon was placed in 1953 and it entered operational service in 1956 for carriage by the Aquilon, Mystère IVA, Super Mystère B2, Vautour IIN, Mirage IIIC and Etendard IVM. With around 8000 units produced, the Nord 5103 was France's first fully operational AAM. An improved model, the Nord 5104 (AA.25) added radar command guidance to the Nord 5103 airframe for compatibility with the Cyrano radar of the Mirage IIIC. Ultimately, the Nord 5104 lost out to Matra's rival R.530 (AA.26) with SARH in 1959.

Matra's AAM studies began in 1949. The experimental R.051, tested in 1955–56, led to the R.510, which used an optical-homing guidance method and was first flown in 1957, with a pre-series batch ordered for evaluation by the French Air Force. Capable of only clear-weather operations, the R.510

was followed by the R.511 of 1958. The first European AAM with SARH guidance, the R.511 provided an all-weather capability and entered operational service when it was issued to French Air Force Vautour IIN and Mirage IIIC units, and also saw use on French Navy Aquilons. Development of the R.510 and R.511 continued with experiments using IR seekers, although these yielded limited success and had been discontinued by 1958. The R.511 remained in service until 1973, when it was replaced by the much-improved R.530.

The first Soviet AAM to enter production and service was the K-5 (which received the NATO/Air Standardization Coordinating Committee reporting name AA-1 'Alkali'). Development of the K-5, which received the missile service designation RS-1U, was sanctioned in 1953 and the missile was tailored for tail-chase engagements against enemy bombers. Incorporating radio command guidance, the RS-1U armed the MiG-17PFU, MiG-19PM and Yak-25K interceptors and was followed by the RS-2U with improved performance, for use on the MiG-19PM. The ultimate derivative was the RS-2US that was optimized for carriage by supersonic interceptors and armed the MiG-19PM, MiG-21 and Su-9.

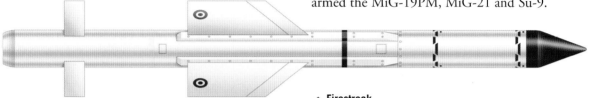

▲ Firestreak

The first operational British AAM was the IR-homing Firestreak. According to contemporary accounts, firing trials of the Firestreak confirmed a success rate of 85 per cent, with 50 per cent of launches resulting in a direct hit.

▼ Lightning strike

A Firestreak IR-homing AAM is loaded carefully on to an RAF Lightning fighter by British groundcrew.

Specifications

Length overall: 3190mm (10ft 5.6in)	Range: 6.4km (4 miles)
Fuselage diameter: 223mm (8.75in)	Speed: Mach 3
Wingspan: 750mm (2ft 5in)	Powerplant: Magpie solid-fuel motor
Launch weight: 136kg (300lb)	Guidance system: Rear-aspect infrared
Warhead weight: 22.7kg (50lb)	

AAMs in the Taiwan Crisis

The world's first successful combat use of AAMs occurred during the 1958 'Taiwan Crisis', when Chinese Nationalist and Communist forces clashed over the islands of Quemoy and Matsu.

THE WORLD'S FIRST successful use of an AAM in combat occurred on 24 September 1958, when a pair of F-86F Sabres flown by Li Shu-Yuan and Qian Yi-Qiang of the Chinese Nationalist Air Force (CNAF) each used an AIM-9B Sidewinder to down MiG-15s of the People's Liberation Army (PLA) Air Force. During the so-called 'Taiwan Crisis', the US Marine Corps (USMC) supplied Chiang Kai-shek's Nationalists with AIM-9Bs, and these missiles were credited with destroying four MiG-15s, all shot down in the course of fighting on 24 September. At least two other MiGs were damaged by Sidewinders on the same day, while another four fell to the Sabres' machine guns.

Live firing trials of the Sidewinder had only begun in 1951, with the first successful engagement of a drone on 11 September 1953. The missile's combat debut in the Taiwan Crisis five years later proved its ready adaptability to fighter aircraft and its simplicity of use. The Sidewinder's success rate in the conflict is all the more impressive when one considers that the early models were limited to close-quarters, tail-chase engagements against targets at high altitude (above 9144m/30,000ft), and under conditions of good visibility. In non-combat scenarios, early Sidewinders demonstrated a single-shot kill probability of around 70 per cent.

The background to the Taiwan Crisis was the blockade of the Nationalist-held islands of Quemoy and Matsu. The first aerial combats occurred in August 1958, in the course of which the CNAF posted claims for six MiGs destroyed by gunfire, with a further dozen or so shot down (again with the F-86F's machine guns) before the arrival of the AIM-9B in combat on 24 September. The success of the CNAF Sabres in the air – and the shock appearance of the Sidewinder – was enough to dissuade the Communists from launching more concerted efforts to retake the islands, and Nationalist air superiority was reflected in only two confirmed losses (both F-84G Thunderjets) in July. In total, six AIM-9Bs were launched in combat during the Taiwan Crisis, resulting in four confirmed kills.

In enemy hands

One unexpected outcome of the air combat over the Formosa Straits was to kick-start Soviet efforts to develop a heat-seeking AAM comparable to the Sidewinder. When in 1958 a US Navy fighter was shot down over the Chinese mainland, the remains of an AIM-9 among the wreckage were shipped to the Soviet Union, and here they were used to inform the development of the R-3S (AA-2 'Atoll'). By 1959 the Soviets had produced a reverse-engineered version of the Sidewinder, and the R-3S went on to form the basis of the original missile armament for the MiG-21F-13 fighter. Both the AIM-9 and AA-2 would go on to see much combat in the years that followed.

Specifications

Length overall: 2850mm (9ft 4in)	Range: 1–18.2km (0.6–11.3 miles)
Fuselage diameter: 127mm (5in)	Speed: Mach 2.5
Wingspan: 630mm (24.8in)	Powerplant: Solid-fuel rocket
Launch weight: 86.2kg (190lb)	Guidance system: Infrared
Warhead weight: 9.4kg (20.8lb)	

▲ **AIM-9B Sidewinder**

The USMC-led project to provide the CNAF with the AIM-9B was conducted under conditions of great secrecy. Its installation on the CNAF F-86F made use of an adapted High-Velocity Aircraft Rocket (HVAR) launch system. A total of 20 Sabres were initially modified with the Sidewinder, although reportedly only four of these aircraft saw combat during the Taiwan Crisis.

AAMs of the 1960s and 1970s

While the 1950s had seen a number of fighter aircraft fielded with missile-only armament, early combat experience demonstrated that the AAM was still some way short of maturity.

THE 1960s saw the emergence and development of two distinct classes of AAM – smaller types, normally with IR guidance, for close-range air combat, and larger types with SARH in order to destroy targets at longer ranges. In the Soviet Union, AAMs were typically designed as part of 'weapons complexes' that comprised interceptor, fire-control system and missile, while in the West the focus was on continued development of established AAM families, headed by the AIM-7 and AIM-9.

Development of the prolific Falcon family also continued into the early 1960s, with the GAR-2B

(AIM-4D) being the ultimate IR version of the missile. This AAM allied the airframe of the GAR-2A with the updated seeker from the GAR-4A. Optimized for fighter combat, the AIM-4D entered service in 1963. Ultimately, the last Falcons in USAF service were the AIM-4F/G, which armed F-106A interceptors into the mid 1980s.

A unique version of the Falcon series was the GAR-11 (AIM-26A) that carried a 1.5-kiloton nuclear warhead and which armed Air Defense Command interceptors. Larger and heavier than other models, the nuclear-armed version was to be

▲ **Long-range striker**
US Navy ground crew use loading equipment to fix a AIM-54 Phoenix long-range AAM under the wing of an General Dynamics F-111B during a demonstration at the Hughes Aircraft Company, June 1967.

used in head-on attacks against enemy bombers, under radar guidance. Operational in 1961, it was complemented by the conventionally armed GAR-11A (AIM-26B), which was also used by Swedish Air Force J 35 Drakens as the Rb 27.

In 1960, the AAM-N-6a Sparrow III was adopted by the USAF for its F-110 Spectre (later F-4 Phantom II) fighter. An improved version of the Sparrow, the AAM-N-6b, entered service in 1963 and was soon redesignated as the AIM-7E, this model introducing a new rocket motor to boost range and performance. With more than 25,000 examples built, the AIM-7E was the major production version of the missile and also served as the basis for a naval surface-to-air missile (SAM), the Sea Sparrow.

The much-improved AIM-7F entered production in 1975, this weapon being optimized for use by the F-15 Eagle and F/A-18 Hornet. The 'Foxtrot' was equipped with a dual-thrust motor for increased range, while the guidance system was adapted for compatibility with pulse-Doppler radars.

▼ **Killer Sparrow**
An USAF F-15A Eagle fighter displays its four AIM-7F Sparrow missiles on a mission, November 1975.

In the UK, the Firestreak was followed by the Red Top, which armed the RAF Lightning and Royal Navy Sea Vixen interceptors. Like its predecessor, the Red Top was IR guided, but while the Firestreak was limited to pursuit-course engagements, the Red Top was designed to be fired from all aspects, including collision course or from dead ahead against supersonic targets. In practice, the Red Top was generally limited to tail-chase scenarios. After entering squadron service in 1967, the Red Top survived in use until the final RAF Lightnings were retired in 1988.

Early Sidewinders

Back in the US, early versions of the Sidewinder were limited to rear-aspect attacks from close range, in good visibility, with a reported single-shot kill probability of 70 per cent. A SARH version, the AIM-9C, saw service with the US Navy, arming the F-8 Crusader fighter. This was followed by the AIM-9D, based on the AAM-N-7, but which returned to IR guidance. Both the AIM-9C and D used a new rocket motor to increase speed and range, and had a larger warhead and redesigned fins. The AIM-9D utilized a new nitrogen-cooled seeker, which gave an expanded engagement envelope.

While the Sidewinder had begun as a US Navy programme, in 1955 the USAF tested the weapon against its own GAR-2, and found the Navy's weapon superior. After deliveries of the AIM-9B, the USAF then received the AIM-9E, the first model tailored to its own requirements. Based on the AIM-9B, the 'Echo' missile featured a new seeker with thermoelectric cooling for improved tracking rate. The AIM-9E was also built in Germany for NATO service as the AIM-9F, which entered service in 1969.

Navy variants

Next in line was another US Navy variant, the AIM-9G, essentially an AIM-9D with further expanded acquisition envelope, which entered production in 1970. Appearing in 1972, the Navy's AIM-9H added solid-state electronics and improved seeker tracking rate. Meanwhile, the USAF was also demanding improved versions of the Sidewinder, the AIM-9J being fielded from 1972 as an updated AIM-9E with some solid-state electronics, increased endurance and double-delta canard control surfaces. Built mainly for export, the AIM-9N was an improved AIM-9J with an upgraded seeker.

Arguably the ultimate AAM to be developed in the West during the Cold War was the very long-range AIM-54 Phoenix, which was introduced from 1960 and intended as the armament for the US Navy's abortive F-111B fleet interceptor, with the designation AAM-N-11. Operating in conjunction with the AWG-9 pulse-Doppler fire-control system, the F-111B/AIM-54 combination made it as far as live firing trials, which commenced in 1966. However, the Phoenix eventually provided the armament for the US Navy's F-14 Tomcat, for which production of the initial AIM-54 commenced in 1973, the missile entering service the following year.

Defender of the fleet

The AIM-54 was intended to defend a carrier battle group against Soviet Navy bombers and anti-ship missiles, a single Phoenix-armed aircraft providing the outer tier of a layered defence that extended over an area of 31,079 square km (12,000 square miles). The missile typically used SARH for its cruise phase, before switching to its own pulse-Doppler radar for the active-homing terminal phase. The AWG-9 radar could track 24 targets simultaneously at ranges of up to 130 nautical miles, and an F-14 could engage six of these simultaneously with AIM-54s.

The AIM-54B appeared in 1977, with some modifications, before the emergence of the definitive AIM-54C. Development of the latter was undertaken in order to account for any technical details that had been passed to the Soviet Union by Iran, the only export operator of the AIM-54. Compared to its predecessors, the AIM-54C offered solid-state radar, all-digital electronics, a strap-down inertial navigation system and improved electronic counter-countermeasures (ECCM).

Deliveries of the AIM-54C began in 1981. More than 5000 AIM-54 missiles were completed, and

▼ **Red Top**

When the British Red Top was introduced in the mid 1960s, it was heralded as the world's first all-aspect AAM, the seeker being sensitive enough to detect the much lower heat signatures generated by the target aircraft's flight surfaces warmed by kinetic heating. The Red Top was exclusively carried by the Lightning interceptor.

Specifications	
Length overall: 3320mm (10ft 8in)	Range: 12km (7.5 miles)
Fuselage diameter: 230mm (9in)	Speed: Mach 3.2
Wingspan: 914mm (3ft)	Powerplant: Linnet solid-fuel motor
Launch weight: 154kg (339.5lb)	Guidance system: Infrared, limited all-aspect
Warhead weight: 31kg (68.3lb)	

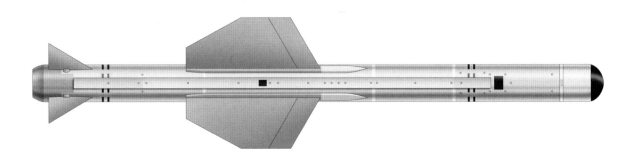

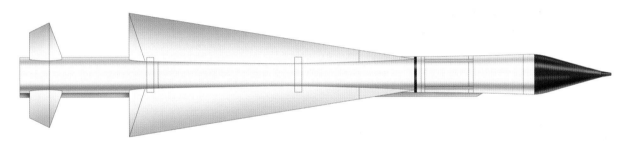

▲ R-4R (AA-5 'Ash')

Seen here in all-aspect SARH form, the R-4 was the primary armament of the world's largest interceptor, the Tu-128. In order to target both fast- and slow-moving bombers, the R-4R settings were selected prior to launch, being optimized for engagements at speeds of between 200 and 1600m/sec (656 and 5294ft/sec).

Specifications

Length overall: R-4T: 5200mm (17ft 1in); R-4R: 5450mm (17ft 11in)

Fuselage diameter: 310mm (12.2in)

Wingspan: 1300mm (51.8in)

Launch weight: T: 480kg (1058lb); R: 492.5kg (1086lb)

Warhead weight: 53kg (116.6lb)

Range: T: 2–15km (1.2–9.4 miles); R: 2–25km (1.2–15.5 miles)

Speed: Mach 1.6

Guidance system: T: infrared ; R semi-active radar

▲ Carrier strike

This French Navy F-7E(FN) Crusader fighter is armed with a single brightly coloured Matra R.530 AAM.

although the weapon was retired by the US Navy in 2004, it remains in use with the Islamic Republic of Iran Air Force.

Soviet missiles

In the Soviet Union, the first-generation K-5 series was followed by a number of more advanced medium- and long-range missiles, with the primitive and unreliable radio command guidance superseded by more advanced radar and IR homing.

The K-8 complex, which included the R-8 (AA-3 'Anab') missile, was developed for the Su-11 interceptor from the mid 1950s, and was fielded in SARH and IR-guided versions. The initial version R-8M missile entered production in 1961. The R-8M1 of 1963 was adapted for operations in conjunction with Su-15 (medium to high altitude) and Yak-28P (low to medium altitude) interceptors. An all-aspect capability was introduced with the R-98, again issued in both SARH and IR forms, and provided as primary armament for the Su-15 and its Oryol-D radar from 1967. When the Su-15 was further upgraded to produce the Su-15TM with Taifun radar, the armament was revised, leading to the definitive R-98M. The combination of the Su-15TM and R-98M gained notoriety when it was responsible for downing Korean Airlines Flight 007 over the Sea of Japan on 1 September 1983.

Part of the K-80 complex, the enormous R-4 (AA-5 'Ash') missile was only carried by the Soviet Air Defence Force's Tu-128 heavyweight interceptor, development of which began in the mid 1950s. Allied with the Tu-128's Smerch radar, the R-4 was available from 1963 with SARH or IR seeker heads and an improved version was issued in the late 1960s as the R-4M, compatible with the Smerch-M radar.

In order to arm the new, Mach 3-capable MiG-25 interceptor, in the early 1960s the Soviets developed the K-40 complex and the associated R-40 (AA-6 'Acrid') missile. The R-40 was available with an SARH or IR seeker head that were designed with a high degree of resistance to electronic countermeasures. When the MiG-25 was upgraded

as the MiG-25PD, the modernized aircraft was provided with updated weapons in the form of the R-40D series. In its IR-homing R-40TD form, the missile was also available as an option for the MiG-31, complementing that interceptor's primary armament of long-range R-33 missiles.

Missiles for the Mirage

In France, the competition to provide a new medium-range AAM was won by the R.530, which briefly received the AA.26 project designation and was initially planned to arm the Mirage III and Vautour, providing a true all-aspect and all-weather capability in concert with the Mirage's Cyrano radar. Development began in 1957 and the R.530 was selected in 1959, with a first live firing in 1960. The R.530 became the primary armament for the Mirage IIIC from 1962 and also equipped French Navy F-7E(FN) Crusaders. Although the initial requirement called for a SARH weapon, the R.530 was made available with an optional IR seeker head. As well as being widely exported, the R.530 was retained as the primary armament of the Mirage F.1C interceptor when this was first fielded, before giving way to the superior Super 530F in the early 1980s.

As a short-range complement to the R.530, Matra also developed the R.550 Magic as a private venture from 1969, with a first guided launch in 1972. Entering service in 1975 with the French Air Force and Navy, the missile used IR homing guidance and was widely exported to arm the Mirage family.

▼ **R-8MR (AA-3 'Anab')**

The basic R-8MR was intended for pursuit-mode intercepts (initially by the Su-11), in which the launch aircraft was required to be flying below and behind the target, typically a bomber. The missile's semi-active radar seeker required the target to be illuminated by the launch aircraft's radar from launch to detonation.

Specifications

Length overall: 4270mm (143ft)	Warhead weight: 40kg (88lb) blast
Fuselage diameter: 280mm (11in)	fragmentation
Wingspan: 1300mm (51.2in)	Range: 23km (14.4 miles)
Launch weight: 292kg (642lb)	Speed: Mach 2
	Guidance system: semi-active radar homing

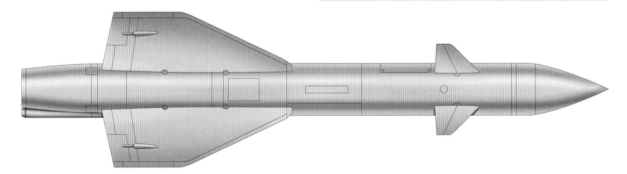

AAMs in Vietnam

Although US forces were hampered by strict rules of engagement, the air war over Southeast Asia served as a crucible in which to test AAMs and related combat tactics.

THE PERFORMANCE OF AAMs in Southeast Asia led to a re-evaluation of the effectiveness of such weapons. Single-shot kill probability for the SARH AIM-7 was 0.09, while the IR-guided AIM-9 recorded 0.18. Air combat tactics clearly needed to be revised in order to take into account the performance shortfall. In particular, AAMs proved to be of limited effectiveness when used in attacks on agile, fighter-sized targets flying at low level.

The first in-service AAM, the AIM-4 Falcon, was designed to tackle high-flying bomber targets, but saw combat service in Vietnam in its dogfight-optimized AIM-4D (previously GAR-2B) variant, carried by USAF F-4D Phantom IIs equipped for the purpose

▼ **Maintenance**
A US Navy aircrewman checks an AIM-9 Sidewinder missile is correctly fixed to an F-8 Crusader fighter onboard the USS *Bon Homme Richard* (CVA-31) during operations in the South China Sea, March 1967.

with LAU-42/A launchers. Ultimately, the combination of F-4D and AIM-4D accounted for four North Vietnamese Air Force (NVAF) MiG-17s and one MiG-21 destroyed. Without a proximity fuse, the AIM-4D missile required a direct hit in order to down a target, a restriction that made it poorly suited to fighter combat.

Perhaps the chief limitation experienced with the AIM-4D was its seeker head, the coolant for which was only sufficient for a limited period. As a result, the seeker cooling had to be initiated shortly before the missile was fired. The time to cool was invariably too great to engage a target in close-quarters combat. After a number of aborted launches the coolant reserve would be expended, and the missile could no longer be employed. Four-time MiG-killer Robin Olds, commander of the USAF's 8th Tactical Fighter Wing, ordered his Falcon-equipped F-4Ds to be re-wired for carriage of the Sidewinder.

More successful in combat over Vietnam was the AIM-7, employed by F-4s of the USAF, the US Navy and USMC. In theory, the Sparrow offered a useful standoff range, but in practice, the strict rules of engagement stipulated by Washington demanded that US fighters approach their targets in order to confirm a visual identification.

Sparrow shortfalls

With a minimum range of 1524m (5000ft), Sparrow targets were frequently too close, and when the launch parameters were satisfied, the Sparrow struggled to cope with low-flying or tightly manoeuvering targets. Inadequate training was another notable problem, as highlighted by the Ault Report that led to the establishment of the Navy Fighter Weapons School, or 'Top Gun'. When Captain Frank Ault led a fact-finding mission to help explain US Navy deficiencies in air combat, he found that, unlike the USAF, most US Navy F-4 pilots had never fired a missile under any conditions. In contrast, the USAF's 'Charging Sparrow' programme ensured that every Phantom crew sent to Southeast Asia had to perform an AIM-7 launch. There were notable successes for the Navy aviators, however. On 17 June 1965, two F-4Bs from the US Navy's VF-21

AA-2 KILLS IN THE VIETNAM WAR

Date	Launch aircraft	Victim	Date	Launch aircraft	Victim
4 March 1966	MiG-21	AQM-34	23 February 1968	MiG-21	F-4D
5 March 1966	MiG-21	AQM-34	7 May 1968	MiG-21	F-4B
7 July 1966	MiG-21	F-105D	16 June 1968	MiG-21	F-4J
11 July 1966	MiG-21	F-105D	August 1968	MiG-21	AQM-34
5 October 1966	MiG-21	F-4C	November 1969	MiG-21	AQM-34
9 October 1966	MiG-21	F-4B	December 1969	MiG-21	AQM-34
5 December 1966	MiG-21	F-105D	28 January 1970	MiG-21	HH-53B
14 December 1966	MiG-21	F-105D	27 April 1972	MiG-21	F-4B
28 April 1967	MiG-21	F-105D	10 May 1972	MiG-21	F-4J
30 April 1967	MiG-21	F-105D	10 May 1972	MiG-21	F-4B
30 April 1967	MiG-21	F-105D	10 May 1972	MiG-21	F-4B
30 April 1967	MiG-21	F-105D	11 May 1972	MiG-21	F-105G
23 August 1967	MiG-21	F-4D	11 May 1972	MiG-21	F-4D
23 August 1967	MiG-21	F-4D	23 May 1972	MiG-21	A-7B
16 September 1967	MiG-21	RF-101C	13 June 1972	MiG-21	F-4E
16 September 1967	MiG-21	RF-101C	21 June 1972	MiG-21	F-4E
7 October 1967	MiG-21	F-105F	24 June 1972	MiG-21	F-4E
9 October 1967	MiG-21	F-105D	24 June 1972	MiG-21	F-4D
8 November 1967	MiG-21	F-4D	27 June 1972	MiG-21	F-4E
18 November 1967	MiG-21	F-105F	27 June 1972	MiG-21	F-4E
18 November 1967	MiG-21	F-105D	27 June 1972	MiG-21	F-4E
20 November 1967	MiG-21	F-105D	5 July 1972	MiG-21	F-4E
16 December 1967	MiG-21	F-4D	5 July 1972	MiG-21	F-4E
17 December 1967	MiG-21	F-4C	8 July 1972	MiG-21	F-4E
17 December 1967	MiG-21	F-105D	24 July 1972	MiG-21	F-4E
3 January 1968	MiG-21	F-105D	29 July 1972	MiG-21	F-4E
14 January 1968	MiG-21	EB-66C	30 July 1972	MiG-21	F-4D
3 February 1968	MiG-21	F-102A	26 August 1972	MiG-21	F-4J
4 February 1968	MiG-21	F-105D			

▼ AIM-7E Sparrow

Originally developed as the AAM-N-6b, the AIM-7E was introduced into production in 1963 and was widely used in combat in Southeast Asia. The AIM-7E version benefited from a new Rocketdyne solid-fuel motor that permitted an increase in range and speed.

Specifications

Length overall: 3657mm (12ft)	Range: C/D: 32km (20 miles); E/E2: 45km
Fuselage diameter: 200mm (8in)	(28 miles)
Wingspan: 810mm (32in)	Speed: Mach 4
Launch weight: 230kg (510lb)	Powerplant: Rocketdyne rocket motor
Warhead weight: 30kg (65lb)	Guidance system: Semi-active radar

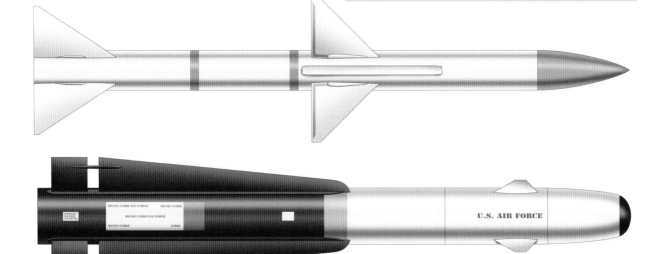

▲ AIM-4D Falcon

The AIM-4D was the 'tactical' version of the Falcon, intended for use in fighter-versus-fighter combat. The last of the Falcon line, it used an AIM-4C airframe combined with the IR seeker of the AIM-4G. In service from 1963, its performance in Vietnam was generally disappointing.

Specifications

Length overall: 1980mm (6ft 76in)	Range: 9.7km (6 miles)
Fuselage diameter: 163mm (6.4in)	Speed: Mach 3
Wingspan: 508mm (20in)	Powerplant: Thiokol M58 solid-fuel rocket
Launch weight: 61kg (135lb)	Guidance system: Rear-aspect IR
Warhead weight: 3.4kg (7.50lb)	

encountered four MiG-17s. Three of the MiGs were destroyed by AIM-7s, marking the first successful combat use of radar-homing AAMs.

In 1969 the improved AIM-7E-2 was introduced to combat, this being a considerably more rugged version offering improved dogfighting capabilities including a reduced minimum range, enhanced agility and a revised autopilot and fuse. Combined with Combat Tree identification friend or foe (IFF) interrogator and improved airborne early warning (AEW) coverage, the AIM-7E-2 scored well through 1972. In total, Sparrow missiles of various marks were credited with 61 kills during the course of the war.

Sidewinder ascendant

With 86 air-to-air kills credited, the Sidewinder was the most successful AAM in the Vietnam War, and saw action with the USAF, the US Navy and USMC. The top-achieving US fighter of the war in terms of aerial combat, the F-4 Phantom II, relied on variants of the Sidewinder for around 60 per cent of its total aerial victories. (USAF Phantom pilot Lieutenant

AIM-4 KILLS IN THE VIETNAM WAR

Date	Launch aircraft	Victim
26 October 1967	F-4D	MiG-17
17 December 1967	F-4D	MiG-17
3 January 1968	F-4D	MiG-17
18 January 1968	F-4D	MiG-17
5 February 1968	F-4D	MiG-21

AIM-7 KILLS IN THE VIETNAM WAR

Date	Launch aircraft	Victim	Date	Launch aircraft	Victim
17 June 1965	F-4B	MiG-17	16 June 1968	F-4B	MiG-21
17 June 1965	F-4B	MiG-17	21 February 1972	F-4D	MiG-21
17 June 1965	F-4B	MiG-17	1 March 1972	F-4D	MiG-21
6 October 1965	F-4B	MiG-17	30 March 1972	F-4D	MiG-21
14 June 1966	F-4B	An-2	16 April 1972	F-4D	MiG-21
14 June 1966	F-4B	An-2	16 April 1972	F-4D	MiG-21
5 November 1966	F-4C	MiG-21	16 April 1972	F-4D	MiG-21
20 December 1966	F-4B	An-2	8 May 1972	F-4D	MiG-19
20 December 1966	F-4B	An-2	8 May 1972	F-4D	MiG-21
2 January 1967	F-4C	MiG-21	10 May 1972	F-4D	J-6
2 January 1967	F-4C	MiG-21	10 May 1972	F-4D	J-6
2 January 1967	F-4C	MiG-21	11 May 1972	F-4D	MiG-21
2 January 1967	F-4C	MiG-21	12 May 1972	F-4D	J-6
6 January 1967	F-4C	MiG-21	23 May 1972	F-4E	MiG-19
6 January 1967	F-4C	MiG-21	31 May 1972	F-4D	MiG-21
23 April 1967	F-4C	MiG-21	8 July 1972	F-4E	MiG-21
26 April 1967	F-4C	MiG-21	8 July 1972	F-4E	MiG-21
13 May 1967	F-4C	MiG-17	29 July 1972	F-4D	MiG-21
14 May 1967	F-4C	MiG-17	29 July 1972	F-4E	MiG-21
20 May 1967	F-4C	MiG-21	10 August 1972	F-4J	MiG-21
20 May 1967	F-4C	MiG-17	12 August 1972	F-4E	MiG-21
5 June 1967	F-4C	MiG-17	15 August 1972	F-4E	MiG-21
26 October 1967	F-4D	MiG-21	19 August 1972	F-4E	MiG-21
26 October 1967	F-4D	MiG-17	28 August 1972	F-4D	MiG-21
26 October 1967	F-4B	MiG-21	2 September 1972	F-4E	J-6
30 October 1967	F-4B	MiG-17	5 October 1972	F-4E	MiG-21
6 February 1968	F-4D	MiG-21	13 October 1972	F-4D	MiG-21
12 February 1968	F-4D	MiG-21	18 December 1972	F-4E	MiG-21
14 February 1968	F-4D	MiG-17	28 December 1972	F-4D	MiG-21
9 May 1968	F-4B	MiG-21	7 January 1972	F-4D	MiG-21
9 May 1968	F-4B	MiG-21			

Colonel Robert Titus gained the distinction of scoring three MiG kills using three different weapons: the AIM-7, AIM-9 and cannon pod.) Of the total USAF Sidewinder victories, 28 were attained using the AIM-9B/E versions, with a kill probability of around 16 per cent. In contrast, the US Navy achieved most of its Sidewinder kills using the AIM-9D/G. In terms of kill ratio, the most successful Sidewinder model employed during the conflict was the AIM-9H, although only a limited number were used. The most successful US Navy fighter of the conflict was the F-8 Crusader, which recorded a total of 19 air-to-air kills, 14 using the AIM-9B/C.

The only AAM available to the North Vietnamese was the first-generation AA-2 'Atoll', which carried the Soviet designation R-3S. This was a weapon essentially comparable to the AIM-9B, and was therefore limited to tail-chase engagements. However, the pilots of the NVAF possessed an advantage in that all their MiG fighters were equipped with cannon as standard – a 'luxury' not afforded to many US Phantom crews.

AIM-9 KILLS IN THE VIETNAM WAR

Date	Launch aircraft	Victim	Date	Launch aircraft	Victim
10 July 1965	F-4C	MiG-17	10 July 1968	F-4J	MiG-21
10 July 1965	F-4C	MiG-17	29 July 1968	F-8E	MiG-17
23 April 1966	F-4C	MiG-17	1 August 1968	F-8H	MiG-21
23 April 1966	F-4C	MiG-17	19 December 1968	F-8C	MiG-21
26 April 1966	F-4C	MiG-21	28 March 1970	F-4J	MiG-21
26 April 1966	F-4C	MiG-17	28 March 1970	F-4J	MiG-17
30 April 1966	F-4C	MiG-17	19 January 1972	F-4J	MiG-21
12 May 1966	F-4C	MiG-17	6 March 1972	F-4B	MiG-17
12 June 1966	F-8E	MiG-17	6 May 1972	F-4B	MiG-17
21 June 1966	F-8E	MiG-17	6 May 1972	F-4J	MiG-21
13 July 1966	F-4B	MiG-17	6 May 1972	F-4J	MiG-21
14 July 1966	F-4C	MiG-21	8 May 1972	F-4J	MiG-17
14 July 1966	F-4C	MiG-21	10 May 1972	F-4J	MiG-21
16 September 1966	F-4C	MiG-17	10 May 1972	F-4J	MiG-17
9 October 1966	F-8E	MiG-21	10 May 1972	F-4J	MiG-17
5 November 1966	F-4C	MiG-21	10 May 1972	F-4J	MiG-17
2 January 1967	F-4C	MiG-21	10 May 1972	F-4J	MiG-17
2 January 1967	F-4C	MiG-21	10 May 1972	F-4J	MiG-17
2 January 1967	F-4C	MiG-21	10 May 1972	F-4J	MiG-17
24 April 1967	F-4B	MiG-17	10 May 1972	F-4B	MiG-17
24 April 1967	F-4B	MiG-17	18 May 1972	F-4B	MiG-17
1 May 1967	F-8E	MiG-17	18 May 1972	F-4B	MiG-19
4 May 1967	F-4C	MiG-21	18 May 1972	F-4B	MiG-19
13 May 1967	F-105D	MiG-17	23 May 1972	F-4B	MiG-17
13 May 1967	F-105D	MiG-17	23 May 1972	F-4B	MiG-17
13 May 1967	F-4C	MiG-17	31 May 1972	F-4E	MiG-21
19 May 1967	F-8E	MiG-17	11 June 1972	F-4B	MiG-17
19 May 1967	F-8E	MiG-17	11 June 1972	F-4B	MiG-17
19 May 1967	F-8C	MiG-17	21 June 1972	F-4J	MiG-21
19 May 1967	F-8C	MiG-17	21 June 1972	F-4E	MiG-21
20 May 1967	F-4C	MiG-21	8 July 1972	F-4E	MiG-21
20 May 1967	F-4C	MiG-17	18 July 1972	F-4E	MiG-21
20 May 1967	F-4C	MiG-17	9 September 1972	F-4D	MiG-19
20 May 1967	F-4C	MiG-17	9 September 1972	F-4D	MiG-19
22 May 1967	F-4C	MiG-21	11 September 1972	F-4J	MiG-21
3 June 1967	F-105D	MiG-17	12 September 1972	F-4E	MiG-21
5 June 1967	F-4C	MiG-17	12 September 1972	F-4D	MiG-21
21 July 1967	F-8C	MiG-17	16 September 1972	F-4E	MiG-21
10 August 1967	F-4B	MiG-21	15 October 1972	F-4E	MiG-21
10 August 1967	F-4B	MiG-21	15 October 1972	F-4D	MiG-21
21 September 1967	F-4B	MiG-17	22 December 1972	F-4E	MiG-21
14 December 1967	F-8E	MiG-17	28 December 1972	F-4J	MiG-21
26 June 1968	F-8H	MiG-21	12 January 1973	F-4B	MiG-17

AAMs in the Six-Day War

The first 'missile war' in the Middle East, the Six-Day War of 1967, gave Israel experience that led to the prioritization of IR-homing AAMs optimized for dogfighting, the first being the Shafrir.

THE FIRST INDIGENOUS Israeli AAM was the Shafrir I, which made its combat debut in the June 1967 Six-Day War. With the notable exception of the assisted destruction of an Iraqi Air Force Tu-16 bomber, downed on 6 June by the combination of a Mirage IIICJ and air defence artillery, the first iteration of the Shafrir did not score any further confirmed victories during the fighting. Improved performance would be recorded in the years following the Six-Day War, however, with Mirage IIICJs using Shafrir Is to account for five United Arab Republic Air Force (UARAF) and Egyptian MiG-21s in clashes between July 1967 and June 1969.

The other AAM used by Israeli fighters during the 1967 war was the French-built R.530, supplied as armament for the Mirage IIICJ. An example of this weapon scored an early kill against a UARAF MiG-19 in November 1966, taking down the fighter at a range of around 9km (5.6 miles), but the missile failed to register any further confirmed victories during the Six-Day War.

Egypt and Syria entered the June 1967 conflict having received R-3S missiles from the Soviet Union, in order to arm their MiG-21s. In the event, this weapon also proved to be less effective than anticipated. In particular, the R-3S was of limited value when attempting to tackle manoeuvering targets at low level. This problem was compounded by Israeli tactics that had been developed expressly to counter the MiG-21 after an example of the fighter was obtained from Iraq in 1966. As a result, the older MiG-21F-13 found favour among Arab pilots since it retained an internal cannon, considered a prerequisite of close-quarters aerial combat. However, 'missile-only' Egyptian Air Force (EAF) MiG-21PF pilots did use R-3S missiles to account for a pair of Israeli Defense Forces/Air Force (IDF/AF) Super Mystère B2s and a Mirage IIICJ during the fighting.

Captured missiles

Among the military hardware captured by the IDF were considerable quantities of R-3S AAMs found on Egyptian airfields that were overrun in the Sinai. With its own Shafrir failing to meet expectations, the IAF pressed the R-3S into service to arm its fighters, and a number were used in combat by Mirage IIICJ fighters. For all its limitations, the R-3S performed better than the Shafrir I, and an example of the missile claimed a kill (ironically against an Egyptian MiG) on 15 July 1967.

Specifications

Length overall: 2500mm (8ft 2.4in)	Range: 5km (3 miles)
Fuselage diameter: 140mm (5.5in)	Speed: Supersonic
Wingspan: 520mm (20.5in)	Powerplant: Solid-fuel rocket motor
Launch weight: 93kg (205lb)	Guidance system: Infrared
Warhead weight: 11kg (24.2lb)	

▲ **Shafrir I**

Produced by Rafael, the Shafrir (Dragonfly) short-range IR-guided missile was essentially an Israel development of the AIM-9B. The missile debuted in the 1967 Six-Day War, but was generally disliked by Israeli fighter pilots, who exhibited a preference for using cannon armament in close-quarters air combat.

AAMs in the War of Attrition

The Six-Day War had demonstrated the limitations of the first generation of AAMs, but in the intervening years Middle Eastern air forces began to re-equip with more advanced weapons.

IN THE AFTERMATH of the Six-Day War, the IDF/AF was still without an effective AAM, relying on the primitive Shafrir I and captured R-3S stocks. A clear priority was acquisition of a more capable AAM, which arrived in the form of the US-made AIM-9D Sidewinder, followed by the locally made Shafrir II. Introduction of these new weapons permitted targets to be engaged at increased ranges, but they remained generally restricted to tail-chase scenarios. More significant was the arrival in service of a beyond-visual-range (BVR) missile, in the form of the AIM-7E that equipped the IDF/AF F-4 fleet. In the event, the Sparrow, despite its advertised range of 15–20km (9.3–12.4 miles), would invariably be used at shorter ranges, partly on account of the missile's limited reliability. A more popular tactic was to fire the AIM-7 from shorter range into a formation of Arab aircraft, putting the opponent on the defensive.

The first AIM-9Ds became available to the IDF/AF in 1969, and around the same time the Shafrir II was refined and ready for service. The Shafrir II proved notably reliable, and emerged as the

▲ **Phantoms on patrol**
Israel began to receive the powerful F-4 Phantom II in 1969 and over the following two decades the type was widely used in combat. These F-4E Phantoms overflying Jerusalem belong to No. 119 'Bat' Squadron.

most successful missile of the War of Attrition fought between July 1967 and August 1970, and it again proved its lethality during the Yom Kippur War of 1973. Israel's first F-4Es were received in September 1969, together with AIM-7Es. The Israeli pilots experienced the same problems with the Sparrow as their US counterparts had over Vietnam: it was deficient against manoeuvring targets and at low altitude. Although the AIM-7 likely notched up only a single victory (against a Soviet-flown MiG-21MF) in the War of Attrition, the conflict became a test case for US tacticians, who closely oversaw the longer-ranged AIM-7 engagements.

Critical disadvantage

While the Israelis introduced advanced new AAMs, the Arab air forces at this time continued to rely on the R-3S. Based on their experience from the Six-Day War, IDF/AF pilots were well aware of the limitations of this missile's reliability, tracking and engagement envelope, and consequently developed tactics to exploit these factors, such as using the Mirage's power and agility to evade the missile.

With aerial battles typically flown at low level and at close quarters, EAF MiG-21PFs and MiG-21PFMs were critically disadvantaged, lacking internal cannon and carrying AAMs that could not be operated at low altitudes. In response, Arab pilots sought to pick out non-manoeuvring Israeli aircraft, which could be attacked from greater ranges from the rear aspect. This tactic bought some success, with 23 R-3S kills recorded by Egyptian and Syrian pilots during the war. The most important measure, however, was likely Egypt's introduction in 1970 of the improved MiG-21MF, which reinstated the MiG's internal gun with a 23mm cannon, and had four missiles, compared to two R-3S AAMs.

ISRAELI MISSILE KILLS 1966–73*

Date	Launch aircraft	Weapon	Victim	Operator
6 June 1967	Mirage IIICJ	Shafrir I	Tu-16	Iraq
15 July 1967	Mirage IIICJ	Shafrir I	MiG-21	UAR
15 July 1967	Mirage IIICJ	Shafrir I	MiG-21	UAR
15 July 1967	Mirage IIICJ	R-3S	MiG-17	UAR
29 May 1969	Mirage IIICJ	Shafrir I	MiG-21	Egypt
26 June 1969	Mirage IIICJ	Shafrir I	MiG-21	Egypt
26 June 1969	Mirage IIICJ	Shafrir I	MiG-21	Egypt
2 July 1969	Mirage IIICJ	Shafrir II	MiG-21	Egypt
2 July 1969	Mirage IIICJ	Shafrir II	MiG-21	Egypt
8 July 1969	Mirage IIICJ	Shafrir II	MiG-21	Syria
8 July 1969	Mirage IIICJ	Shafrir II	MiG-21	Syria
8 July 1969	Mirage IIICJ	Shafrir II	MiG-21	Syria
22 July 1969	Mirage IIICJ	Shafrir II	MiG-21	Egypt
8 February 1970	F-4E	AIM-9D	MiG-21	Egypt
8 February 1970	F-4E	AIM-9D	MiG-21	Egypt
25 March 1970	Mirage IIICJ	Shafrir II	MiG-21	Egypt
27 March 1970	Mirage IIICJ	AIM-9D	MiG-21	Egypt
10 July 1970	Mirage IIICJ	AIM-9D	MiG-21	Egypt
10 July 1970	Mirage IIICJ	AIM-9D	MiG-21	Egypt
27 July 1970	Mirage IIICJ	AIM-9D	MiG-17	Egypt
30 July 1970	Mirage IIICJ	Shafrir II	MiG-21MF	USSR
30 July 1970	F-4E	AIM-9D	MiG-21MF	USSR
30 July 1970	F-4E	AIM-7E	MiG-21MF	USSR
21 November 1972	F-4E	AIM-9D	MiG-21	Syria
8 January 1973	RF-4E	AIM-9D	MiG-21	Syria
8 January 1973	RF-4E	AIM-9D	MiG-21	Syria
13 September 1973	F-4E	AIM-9D	MiG-21	Syria
13 September 1973	Mirage IIICJ	AIM-9D	MiG-21	Syria
13 September 1973	Mirage IIICJ	AIM-9D	MiG-21	Syria

* This table only includes confirmed victories for which the weapon used can be positively identified. In total, confirmed Israeli victories for the period 1967 to 1973 amount to more than 200. Of these, a significant proportion are likely to have involved AAMs.

AAMs in the Yom Kippur War

By the outbreak of the Yom Kippur War in October 1973, both the Israeli and Arab air forces were well versed in missile combat, although the IDF/AF possessed a clear technical superiority.

FOR THE ISRAELI pilots involved in the Yom Kippur War, primary air-to-air armament was still based around the proven Shafrir II, as well as the US-supplied AIM-9D and AIM-7E, although the latter type failed to register any confirmed kills. By now the Nesher fighter (a variant of the Mirage 5 for Israeli service) was also available, and this, together with the Mirage III, could now carry either Sidewinder or Shafrir missiles underwing.

For the Arab forces, the situation was less favourable, with MiG-21s continuing to use the outdated and under-performing R-3S. Perhaps the only aspect in the Arabs' favour in terms of aerial armament was the availability of cannon as standard on the MiG-21MF variant. In the course of October 1973, Syrian Arab Air Force (SyAAF) MiG-21s of various types downed a confirmed total of 26 Israeli aircraft with R-3S AAMs, in addition to those destroyed using cannon, or manoeuvre kills. EAF MiG-21s meanwhile posted claims of at least 10 IDF/AF aircraft downed by R-3S missiles, in addition to kills by guns and other means.

Shafrir dominance

The successor to the universally disliked Shafrir I, the Shafrir II, came into its own during the Yom Kippur War, proving to be more reliable than the opposition's R-3S, and equipped with a larger warhead than the Sidewinder. According to Rafael, the manufacturer of the weapon, the Shafrir II had a 60 per cent kill ratio during combat encounters, including defective launches. While pilots of aircraft armed with the Shafrir I had continued to exercise their preference for using the onboard cannon, with the Shafrir II, the AAM finally became a weapon of choice.

Like the Sidewinder, the Shafrir II provided the pilot with an audio tone, as well as a visual indication, when the missile achieved a successful lock-on. While the AIM-9D sometimes only succeeded in damaging a MiG-21, the power of the Shafrir II's high-explosive/fragmentation warhead – carried within a body of increased diameter compared to the Sidewinder – could be enough to destroy the Soviet-built fighter totally. However, the IR seeker head remained relatively primitive, and could only be used to engage targets from the rear hemisphere.

As well as arming Mirage III and Nesher fighters, the Shafrir II was also provided for use by the Israeli-upgraded Super Mystère B2, known as the Sa'ar. Although optimized for air-to-ground missions, the Sa'ar received an extra weapons pylon under each wingroot for carrying a Shafrir II for self-defence.

In the closing stages of the war, the Shafrir II also recorded kills in combination with the two-seat Mirage IIIBJ combat trainer, when leading ace Giora Epstein downed two MiG-21s (with one more destroyed by 30mm/1.18in gunfire) during a single mission.

As far as the Sparrow was concerned, IDF/AF Phantom pilots now increasingly preferred to fly with their fuselage weapons bays carrying an electronic countermeasures (ECM) pod to provide defence against Arab ground-based air defences, and Sparrow bays were also adapted to accommodate Sidewinders.

▶ **Downed MiG**

An Egyptian MiG-17 is shot down during the 1973 war. The MiG was no match for the F-4 Phantom.

ISRAELI MISSILE KILLS IN THE YOM KIPPUR WAR*

Date	Launch aircraft	Weapon	Victim	Operator
6 October 1973	F-4E	AIM-9D	MiG-17	Egypt
6 October 1973	F-4E	AIM-9D	MiG-17	Egypt
6 October 1973	F-4E	AIM-9D	MiG-17	Egypt
6 October 1973	F-4E	AIM-9D	MiG-17	Egypt
6 October 1973	F-4E	AIM-9D	MiG-17	Egypt
6 October 1973	F-4E	AIM-9D	MiG-17	Egypt
6 October 1973	Mirage IIICJ	Shafrir II	Su-7	Egypt
6 October 1973	Mirage IIICJ	Shafrir II	Su-7	Egypt
6 October 1973	Nesher	Shafrir II	Su-7	Egypt
6 October 1973	Nesher	Shafrir II	MiG-17	Egypt
6 October 1973	F-4E	AIM-9D	Mi-8	Egypt
6 October 1973	F-4E	AIM-9D	Mi-8	Egypt
6 October 1973	F-4E	AIM-9D	Mi-8	Egypt
6 October 1973	F-4E	AIM-9D	Mi-8	Egypt
6 October 1973	F-4E	AIM-9D	Mi-8	Egypt
6 October 1973	F-4E	AIM-9D	Mi-8	Egypt
6 October 1973	F-4E	AIM-9D	Mi-8	Egypt
7 October 1973	Nesher	Shafrir II	MiG-21	Egypt
7 October 1973	Nesher	Shafrir II	MiG-21	Egypt
8 October 1973	Nesher	Shafrir II	Su-7	Egypt
8 October 1973	Nesher	AIM-9D	MiG-21	Syria
8 October 1973	Nesher	Shafrir II	Su-20	Egypt
8 October 1973	Mirage IIICJ	Shafrir II	Su-7	Egypt
8 October 1973	Mirage IIICJ	AIM-9D	Hunter	Iraq
12 October 1973	Nesher	Shafrir II	Su-7	Syria
12 October 1973	Nesher	Shafrir II	Su-7	Syria
13 October 1973	Nesher	Shafrir II	MiG-21	Iraq
14 October 1973	F-4E	AIM-9D	MiG-21	Egypt
18 October 1973	Nesher	Shafrir	Mirage 5	Egypt/Libya
19 October 1973	Nesher	AIM-9D	Su-7	Egypt
19 October 1973	Nesher	Shafrir II	Su-7	Egypt
20 October 1973	Nesher	Shafrir II	MiG-21	Egypt
20 October 1973	Nesher	Shafrir II	MiG-21	Egypt
21 October 1973	Nesher	Shafrir II	MiG-21	Egypt
21 October 1973	Nesher	Shafrir II	MiG-21	Egypt
22 October 1973	Nesher	Shafrir II	MiG-21	Syria
22 October 1973	Nesher	Shafrir II	MiG-21	Syria
24 October 1973	Mirage IIIBJ	AIM-9D	MiG-21	Egypt
24 October 1973	Mirage IIIBJ	AIM-9D	MiG-21	Egypt
24 October 1973	Mirage IIICJ	Shafrir II	MiG-21	Egypt

* This table only includes confirmed victories for which the weapon used can be positively identified. In total, confirmed Israeli victories during the Yom Kippur War amount to more than 180. Of these, a significant proportion are likely to have involved AAMs.

AAMs of the 1980s and 1990s

The AAM came of age during the early 1980s, with the combat debut of the first true all-aspect IR-guided weapons, and continued development of medium-range weapons in the East and West.

WHILE THE SOVIETS continued to introduce new AAMs as part of various weapons complexes, development of AAMs in the US continued on the basis of upgrading existing systems, with major breakthroughs including all-aspect engagement envelopes and lookdown/shootdown capability for medium-range weapons.

A new version of the Sparrow was introduced in 1982 as the AIM-7M, with an advanced seeker head providing a lookdown/shootdown capability. The key to the AIM-7M's expanded performance was its monopulse seeker, optimized for use at low level and in the face of ECM. The 'Mike' also introduced a digital computer, new warhead, an active fuse and an autopilot, the latter requiring the target to be 'painted' by the aircraft radar only for mid-course and terminal guidance.

The AIM-7P appeared in 1987 as an improved version of the AIM-7M, with updated electronics and computer, a new radar fuse and an autopilot uplink for mid-course guidance.

In 1969 the British took the AIM-7E, which they had acquired to arm the Phantom, and improved the missile to create the Skyflash. This used a new SARH monopulse seeker head with improved resistance to ECM, and it entered service in 1978, initially arming the RAF Phantom and later the Tornado F.Mk 3.

The Swedish Air Force adopted the Sky Flash as the Rb 71 for its JA 37 Viggen.

In the late 1970s, the Sidewinder remained numerically the most important Western AAM, and the next step in its development was a joint USAF/US Navy programme that introduced an all-aspect capability, in order to engage manoeuvering and high-speed targets. This was the AIM-9L, development of which was initiated in 1971. The AIM-9L entered production in 1978 and featured an all-new seeker head, plus improved warhead, better motor and laser proximity fuse. Sharing the performance and dimensions of the 'Lima', the AIM-9M differed in its use of a reduced-smoke motor and superior guidance system. Manufacture of the AIM-9M began in 1982, and the missile remains in front-line US service as the ultimate expression of the 'third-generation' Sidewinder.

Sidewinder for export

Offering slightly downgraded performance and lower acquisition cost than the AIM-9L/M, the AIM-9P was developed for the USAF but was primarily intended for export. Superficially similar to the AIM-9J/N, the AIM-9P has seen a number of added improvements, including a laser proximity fuse, reduced-smoke rocket motor and enhancements to

▲ **AIM-9P Sidewinder**
Although adopted by the USAF, the AIM-9P was developed as an export model, drawing heavily on the AIM-9J/N. The missile used a laser proximity fuse and later sub-variants incorporated some of the advanced technology from the AIM-9L/M.

Specifications	
Length overall: 3000mm (9ft 11in)	Range: 16km (10 miles)
Fuselage diameter: 127mm (5in)	Speed: Mach 2+
Wingspan: 640mm (25.2in)	Powerplant: Thiokol Hercules and Bermite MK 36
Launch weight: 80kg (178lb)	Mod 11; single-stage, solid-fuel rocket
Warhead weight: 9.9kg (22lb)	Guidance system: Passive infrared

▼ R-24R (AA-7 'Apex')

The aerodynamic configuration of the R-23/24 was inspired by the earlier R-4 missile. This is an example of the improved R-24R, optimized for carriage by the later versions of the MiG-23 fighter. Unlike the R-23, the mid-body wings on the R-24 featured forward sweep on the trailing edges, and rudders were simplified.

Specifications

Length overall: 4500mm (14ft 9in)	Warhead weight: 25kg (55lb)
Fuselage diameter: 223mm (8.8in)	Range: 35km (22 miles)
Wingspan: 1000mm (39.4in)	Speed: Mach 3
Launch weight: 222kg (489lb)	Guidance system: Semi-active radar

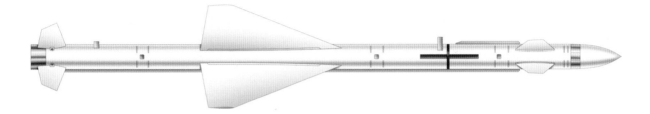

▼ R-60 (AA-8 'Aphid')

The diminutive R-60 was so light that it could also be carried by helicopters, and trials were made with the weapon on the Mi-24 assault helicopter. As well as arming tactical fighters, the R-60 was provided as complementary armament for attack aircraft, including the Su-24, and heavy interceptors like the MiG-25.

Specifications

Length overall: 2090mm (6ft 10in)	Range: 8km (5 miles)
Fuselage diameter: 120mm (4.8in)	Speed: Mach 2.7
Wingspan: 390mm (15.3in)	Powerplant: Solid-fuel rocket
Launch weight: 43.5kg (96lb)	Guidance system: Infrared
Warhead weight: 3kg (6.6lb)	

▼ Super 530D

The 'D' in its designation signifying 'Doppler', the Super 530D was intended to form the primary medium-range armament of the Mirage 2000, and it featured reduced-drag aerodynamics compared to the Super 530F that preceded it. The Super 530D was deployed to the Persian Gulf aboard French Air Force Mirage 2000Cs during Operation *Desert Storm*.

Specifications

Length overall: 3800mm (12ft 5in)	Range: 37km (23 miles)
Fuselage diameter: 263mm (10.4in)	Speed: Mach 4.5
Wingspan: 620mm (24.4in)	Powerplant: Dual-thrust solid-fuel motor
Launch weight: 270kg (595lb)	Guidance system: Semi-active radar
Warhead weight: 30kg (66lb)	

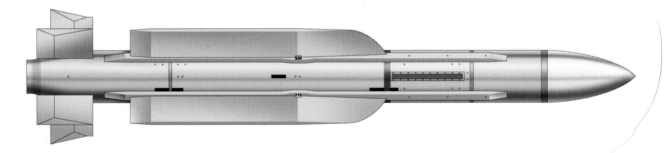

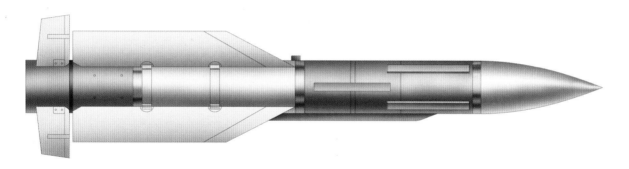

▲ R-33 (AA-9 'Amos')

The R-33 was developed specifically as armament for the MiG-31. Employing dual-mode guidance, the missile is initially flown under the control of its onboard autopilot, before switching to use its own semi-active radar homing seeker. The MiG-31 carries four such missiles semi-recessed under the fuselage.

Specifications

Length overall: 4150mm (13ft 7in)	Warhead weight: 47.5kg (104lb)
Fuselage diameter: 380mm (15in)	Range: 160km (99.4 miles)
Wingspan: 1160mm (45.6in)	Speed: Mach 4.5
Launch weight: 490kg (1080lb)	Guidance system: Inertial and semi-active radar

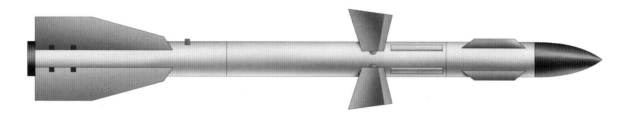

Specifications

Length overall: 4080mm (13ft 5in)	Range: Up to 80km (49.7 miles)
Fuselage diameter: 230mm (9.1in)	Speed: Mach 2.5–4.5
Wingspan: 772mm (30.4in)	Powerplant: Solid fuel rocket motor
Launch weight: 253kg (560lb)	Guidance system: Semi-active radar homing
Warhead weight: 39kg (86lb)	

▲ R-27R (AA-10 'Alamo')

The modular R-27 is constructed using five separate, interchangeable modules. The modules towards the tail of the missile house the warhead (Module 4) and the solid-fuel rocket motor (Module 5). In the extended-range versions, Module 5 contains a larger motor, leading to increased body length and diameter.

▼ R-73 (AA-11 'Archer')

The R-73 was one of the first super-agile short-range AAMs, and featured a then revolutionary combination of thrust-vectoring control and aerodynamic guidance systems. The R-73 remains the primary Russian dogfight missile, and a number of upgrades and further developments of the basic design have been schemed.

Specifications

Length overall: 2900mm (9ft 6in)	Range: (R-73E) 20km (12 miles); (R-73M1)
Fuselage diameter: 170mm (6.7in)	30km (19 miles); (R-73M2) 40km (25 miles)
Wingspan: 510mm (20in)	Speed: Mach 2.5
Launch weight: 105kg (231lb)	Powerplant: Solid-fuel rocket system
Warhead weight: 7.4kg (16.3lb)	Guidance system: All-aspect infrared

the guidance and control systems to permit a degree of all-aspect capability.

Broadly comparable to the Sparrow, the Soviet R-23 (AA-7 'Apex') was tailored for use by the MiG-23 fighter and its Sapfir-23 radar. Developed from the early 1960s by the same Bisnovat design bureau (later Vympel) responsible for the R-8 and R-98, the R-23 was similarly available with either IR-homing or SARH seeker heads, the MiG-23 typically carrying one example of each missile. Compared to its predecessors, the R-23 offered improved range and agility, as well an all-aspect capability. While the IR-guided R-23T was optimized for use in clear weather conditions against crossing targets or in the tail-chase mode, the radar-guided R-23R could be used in all weathers and offered a lookdown/shootdown capability. The basic R-23 entered service in 1970 and was followed by the improved R-24, again in IR and SARH variants. The R-24 was introduced in 1981 on the MiG-23ML, allied with the Sapfir-23ML radar. The latter allowed targets to be acquired at longer ranges, while the missile itself was more agile, thanks to its reduced weight, and received more sensitive seekers and an updated fuse.

In the same class as the R-23/24 is the R-27, designed from the outset to engage targets both at long range and in a dogfight. The R-27 was selected as primary armament for the MiG-29 and Su-27, providing a true lookdown/shootdown capability, all-aspect engagement envelope and high resistance to ECM. As well as being issued with optional IR or SARH seeker heads, the modular R-27 was also available in 'short-burn' and extended-range forms. The two different motors allow for engagements at

different ranges, and offer different thrust outputs, and long-range versions of the missile carry the suffix 'E' in their designation. The R-27T (or R-27ET) can receive target information from the fighter radar before launch, while the R-27R (or R-27ER) provides the option of being launched prior to target lock-on, thereafter receiving target data via mid-course guidance. Up to two missiles can be launched against two targets simultaneously.

Soviet short-range AAMs

In addition to the medium-range R-23/24 and R-27 families, the Soviet Union began to introduce new short-range missiles in order to supersede the ageing 'Atoll' series. The first of these was the R-60 (AA-8 'Aphid'), developed in the early 1970s and entering service towards the end of that decade as a complementary short-range weapon for interceptors and as a primary self-defence weapon for attack aircraft. The R-60 was an IR-homing dogfight weapon available with two different proximity fuses in order to defeat countermeasures. As a result, aircraft could carry a combination of optical-fuse and radar-fuse missiles to improve kill probability. An improved version of the 'Aphid' was developed as the R-60M, again with two fuse options, but with an improved seeker and a larger warhead.

Successor to the R-60 in the short-range category was the R-73 (AA-11 'Archer'), one of the most influential AAMs of all time. The appearance of this weapon came as a shock to the West, since for the first time it offered performance capabilities beyond those of comparable US missiles. Above all, the R-73 offered outstanding agility as a result of its

▼ **Skyflash**
The British developed the Skyflash as an improvement of the AIM-7E-2 Sparrow, combining the airframe, motor and warhead of the US original with a new monopulse seeker developed by Marconi. The seeker was considerably more resistant to jamming than the conically scanned seeker of the AIM-7F.

Specifications

Length overall: 3680mm (12ft 1in)	Range: 45km (28 miles)
Fuselage diameter: 203mm (8in)	Speed: Mach 4
Wingspan: 1020mm (40in)	Powerplant: Rocketdyne solid-fuel rocket motor
Launch weight: 193kg (425lb)	Guidance system: Marconi inverse monopulse
Warhead weight: 39.5kg (87lb)	semi-active radar

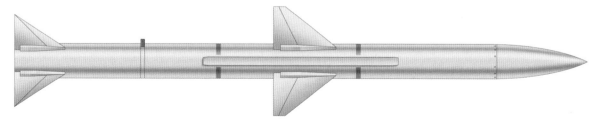

combination of aerodynamic and reaction controls, the latter taking the form of thrust-vectoring vanes to deflect the exhaust. High-G attacks could be launched by the pilot of a MiG-29 or Su-27 from any aspect, altitude or speed, including in conjunction with a helmet-mounted sight, allowing the use of 'point and shoot' tactics. An extended-range version of the R-73 was also developed as the R-73E.

Armament for the MiG-31 interceptor was based around a new very long-range missile, the R-33 (AA-

▲ Shooting range

A Soviet-built MiG-29 Fulcrum fighter flown by Major Peter Meisberger, from Germany's 73rd Fighter Wing, Laage Air Base, Germany, fires a radar-guided AA-10 short-burn AAM at a QF-4 'Rhino' full-scale aerial target.

9 'Amos'), optimized for use against low-flying targets including cruise missiles in an ECM environment. In order to destroy targets at great distances, the R-33 uses a combination of inertial guidance with mid-course correction together with SARH. When aspects of the MiG-31's weapons system were compromised in 1985, the Soviets developed the follow-on R-33S,

▼ Aspide

Developed by Selenia (later Alenia), the Aspide was another improvement of the basic AIM-7E Sparrow, and differed from the US weapon in its adoption of a monopulse seeker and a larger rocket motor. An active radar development known as Idra was planned, but abandoned in favour of a more modest upgrade.

Specifications

Length overall: 3650mm (3ft 8in)	Speed: Mach 4
Fuselage diameter: 203mm (8in)	Powerplant: One SNIA-Viscosa solid-fuel rocket
Wingspan: 1000mm (39.4in)	motor
Launch weight: 230kg (507lb)	Guidance system: Selenia monopulse
Warhead weight: 33kg (72.75lb)	semi-active radar
Range: 75km (46.6 miles)	

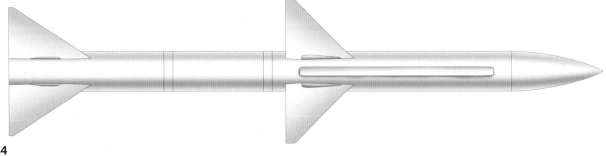

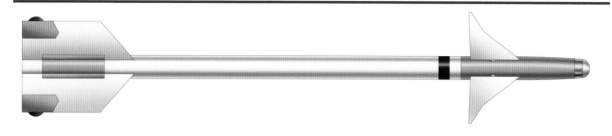

Specifications

Length overall: 2890mm (9ft 5.8in)	Range: 0.5–18km (0.3–11 miles)
Fuselage diameter: 127mm (5in)	Speed: Mach 2.5
Wingspan: 617mm (24.3in)	Powerplant: Solid-fuel rocket
Launch weight: 83kg (183lb)	Guidance system: Infrared homing, multi-
Warhead weight: 6kg (13.3lb)	element, dual band detector

▲ PL-5

Among China's first-generation AAMs was a simple reverse-engineered copy of the early Sidewinder, the PL-5, begun in 1966. This is broadly comparable to the AIM-9G and therefore lacks an all-aspect attack capability. An SARH PL-5A was tested but cancelled in the early 1980s, and thereafter development focused exclusively on the IR-homing version.

▲ PL-7

Externally similar to the Magic, the export-optimized PL-7 may be a reverse-engineered version of the French missile. Primary applications are the export versions of the J-7 fighter and Q-5 attack aircraft (F-7 and A-5), as the weapon is not in PLA service. The basic IR seeker head only allows tail-chase type engagements.

Specifications

Length overall: 2743mm (9ft)	Range: 7km (4.35 miles)
Fuselage diameter: 165mm (6.5in)	Speed: Mach 2.5
Wingspan: 508mm (20in)	Powerplant: Solid-fuel rocket motor
Launch weight: 89kg (196lb)	Guidance system: Infrared
Warhead weight: 12.5kg (27.6lb)	

for the updated MiG-31B and MiG-31BS. The primary difference of this weapon was its further increased resistance to ECM.

European AAMs

In France, the Matra 530 family continued to be developed, producing the Super 530F. A long-range weapon with SARH guidance, the Super 530F was designed for carriage by the Mirage F.1C interceptor and became operational in 1979. When the Mirage 2000C was introduced into service, a revised version of the missile was developed in order to complement that fighter's Doppler radar. As a result, the Super 530D (D for Doppler) that entered service in 1987 added a continuous-wave monopulse Doppler SARH seeker head, and was capable of snap-down engagement of low-flying targets as well as high-altitude attacks against targets flying at speeds of up to Mach 3. Other changes to the missile included

digital data processing and reduced drag. The Super 530 series was complemented by an updated version of the short-range R.550, known as the Magic 2. Entering development in the late 1970s, this weapon was first deployed in 1985 and differed from the original Magic 1 in its use of a more sensitive, all-aspect IR seeker, which can be slaved to the launching aircraft's radar for a target lock-on prior to launch. Another change was the addition of an all-sector proximity fuse that provides improved performance during head-on interceptions; the Magic 1 had been limited to tail-aspect engagements only on account of its limited IR-seeker performance.

The first Italian AAM to enter production was the Aspide, based on the design of the AIM-7E, and therefore comparable to the British Skyflash. A first feasibility study was initiated in 1969, with initial flight tests following in 1974. Unlike Skyflash, the Aspide was intended for both air- and surface-

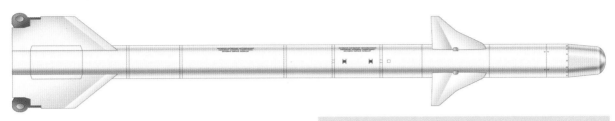

▲ PL-9

Another export-optimized Chinese missile, the PL-9 is very similar in appearance to the Python III, and was developed in parallel with the similar PL-8 for local use. The PL-9 has been exported to a number of customers of the F-7 series fighter, with the current model being the PL-9C with much improved range and agility.

Specifications

Length overall: 2900mm (9ft 6in)	Range: 22km (13.7 miles)
Fuselage diameter: 157mm (6.2in)	Speed: Mach 3+
Wingspan: 856mm (33.7in)	Powerplant: Solid-fuel rocket
Launch weight: 115kg (253.5lb)	Guidance system: Multi-element infrared
Warhead weight: 11.8kg (26.8lb)	

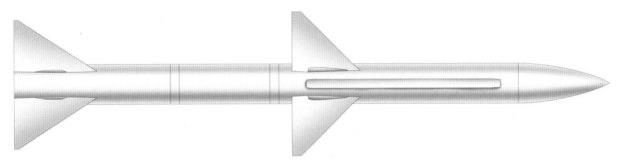

Specifications

Length overall: 3890mm (12ft 10in)	Range: 40–75km (25–46 miles)
Fuselage diameter: 208mm (8.19in)	Speed: Mach 4
Wingspan: 680mm (26.7in)	Powerplant: Solid fuel
Launch weight: 220kg (485lb)	Guidance system: Semi-active radar
Warhead weight: n/a	

▲ PL-11

Bearing a strong resemblance to the Sparrow, the PL-11 is China's first in-service medium-range AAM. Advanced developments include the PL-11A with extended range and a more powerful warhead. The PL-11A only requires target illumination by the launch aircraft in the terminal phase of the engagement. The PL-11B is a reported active radar-homing version of the PL-11A.

launched applications, and introduced continuous-wave monopulse guidance and a larger rocket motor. As an AAM, the Aspide 1 was restricted to the Italian Air Force's F-104S Starfighter interceptors. In the 1980s the missile was considerably upgraded as the Aspide 2, this adding a new active radar seeker. The weapon used strap-down inertial guidance for the mid-course phase of flight, with in-flight updates provided via datalink, but was eventually cancelled.

Chinese developments

Development of Chinese AAMs began with the PL-1, a copy of the Soviet K-5. This was followed by the PL-2, a licence-built copy of the tail-chase R-3S that entered service in 1967. Production began in 1970, and the PL-2 made its combat debut in 1966, when a PLA J-7 fighter shot down a USAF AQM-34 Firebee reconnaissance drone. An improved PL-2B,

with a new rocket motor, was introduced in 1975. Successor to the PL-2 was the PL-5, again based on R-3S technology, but superficially similar to the US-made AIM-9G. Development of the missile began in 1966, initially in both IR and SARH forms, but was not completed until the early 1980s, with the IR-homing PL-5B entering service in the late 1980s. Subsequent improvements have produced the PL-5C and the PL-5E with all-aspect capability and revised forward control surfaces.

The PL-7 was another short-range IR homing AAM, this time apparently inspired by the R.550 Magic. Produced exclusively for export, the PL-7 was test-launched in 1984 and production began in 1987. The PL-8 is China's licensed copy of the Israeli Python III, and entered PLA service in the early 1990s. Drawing on experience gained with the PL-8, China developed the PL-9 as a parallel programme

from 1986, this allying PL-5 and PL-7 airframe components with a new IR seeker informed by Python III technology. China's first successful medium-range AAM project is the PL-11, which uses seeker technology from the Italian Aspide, examples of which were delivered to China for trials use in the mid 1980s. Licensed production of the Aspide was curtailed in the wake of the Tiananmen Square massacre in 1989, but development of an indigenous missile continued, this using a monopulse SARH seeker head copied from that used in the Aspide. A first test launch was achieved in 1992 and the missile was issued to units of the PLA from the mid 1990s.

▲ **Test fire**
A USAF F-16 Fighting Falcon fires an AIM-9 missile off the coast of South Korea during a live-fire exercise. The F-16 is assigned to the 80th Fighter Squadron at Kunsan Air Base, South Korea.

Across the Taiwan Strait, Taiwan was also working on indigenous AAMs. The Tien Chien (Sky Sword) family comprises the Sky Sword I, an all-aspect IR-guided weapon based on the AIM-9, and first tested in 1986, and the Sky Sword II, a medium-range radar-guided weapon likely based on the AIM-7. Developed from the late 1980s, the Sky Sword II is primary armament for Taiwan's FC-K-1 fighter.

▲ **Sky Sword II**
Characterized by its clipped, small-span wings, the Sky Sword II arms Taiwan's fleet of indigenous FC-K-1 Ching-Kuo fighters, each of which can carry a pair of the missiles in parallel beneath the fuselage. The missile seeker head is a Motorola/Raytheon product that was originally developed for the AMRAAM.

Specifications

Length overall: 3600mm (11ft 9.6in)	Speed: n/a
Fuselage diameter: 203mm (8in)	Powerplant: Solid propellant
Launch weight: 190kg (419lb)	Guidance system: Mid-range inertial guidance,
Warhead weight: 30kg (66lb)	terminal radar guidance
Range: 60km (37.3 miles)	

AAMs in the 1982 Lebanon War

Wars in the Middle East and South Atlantic in 1982 saw the short-range IR-guided AAM come of age, and all-aspect AIM-9L and Python III missiles saw considerable success over Lebanon.

THE AIR WAR over Lebanon's Beka'a Valley in summer 1982 saw the deployment of several significant new weapons and tactics developed in light of experience from previous conflicts in the Middle East and elsewhere. They included, for example, the widespread combat use of unmanned aerial vehicles (UAVs). In the field of air-to-air combat, among the most important developments was the Israeli use of all-aspect AAMs, in the form of the AIM-9L and the indigenous Python III. Now operating advanced F-15 Eagles and F-16 Fighting Falcons, the IDF/AF possessed a clear technological advantage. On 9 June alone, these fighters posted initial claims for 29 SyAAF jets shot down, for no losses.

Following Israel's 'Peace for Galilee' invasion of Lebanon on 6 June, IDF/AF F-15s repeatedly clashed with SyAAF MiG-21s and MiG-23s, with results clearly in favour of the Israelis. Examples of the more capable MiG-23MF, armed with medium-range AAMs, were available to the Syrians, but they had little chance to make their presence felt, and although Syrian MiG-23MF pilots claimed three aerial victories in the course of the campaign, they also acknowledged three losses on their own side.

While in the years preceding the war, Israel had been provided with some of the most advanced US military technology, the Syrians and other Middle Eastern forces had been hampered by Moscow's unwillingness to deliver high-technology weaponry. SyAAF MiG-23MS fighters were still armed with the outdated 'Atoll' missile as their primary weapon, and while the MiG-21 fleet had gradually begun to receive more capable R-3R and R-13M missiles, for an extended period of time the Soviets would not supply the latest R-60 short-range AAMs.

Improved 'Atolls'

Representing improved versions of the primitive R-3S, the R-3R used SARH guidance, while the R-13M retained IR guidance. The R-3R was designed for use in conjunction with the RP-22 radar used in later versions of the MiG-21, and entered service in 1966. The R-13M used a liquid nitrogen-cooled IR seeker, radar fuse and more powerful warhead. Entering service in 1973, the missile was further refined as the R-13M1 of 1976, this having revised control surfaces. Neither weapon was a match for the Python III, however, which made its combat debut over the Beka'a Valley. This highly agile, all-aspect IR-guided

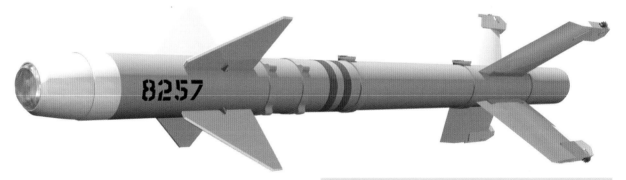

▲ **Python III**
The Python III (originally known as the Shafrir III) likely made its combat debut immediately prior to the 1982 invasion of Lebanon, having begun operational trials with the IDF/AF in 1981. Key elements of the design were a new all-aspect IR seeker with enhanced sensitivity and expanded look angle and improved resistance to enemy countermeasures.

Specifications

Length overall: 2950mm (9ft 8in)	Warhead weight: 11kg (24lb)
Fuselage diameter: 147mm (5.8in)	Range: 15km (9.3 miles)
Wingspan: 800mm (31.5in)	Speed: Mach 3.5
Launch weight: 120kg (264lb)	Guidance system: Infrared

▼ AIM-7F Sparrow

Throughout the second half of the 1970s, the primary production version of the Sparrow was the AIM-7F. This offered increased range through the use of a dual-thrust rocket motor with boost and sustain modes. For the first time, the guidance system was also optimized for use with modern pulse-Doppler radars, such as those used in the F-15 fighters of the IDF/AF over Lebanon.

Specifications

Length overall: 3700mm (12ft)	Speed: Mach 2.5
Fuselage diameter: 200mm (8in)	Powerplant: Hercules MK-58 solid-fuel rocket
Wingspan: 810mm (31.8in)	motor
Launch weight: 510kg (230lb)	Guidance system: Semi-active radar
Warhead weight: 40kg (88lb)	

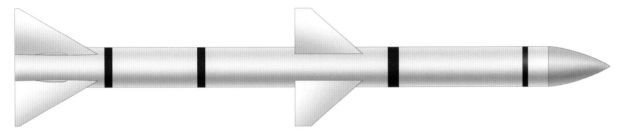

weapon was arguably the most capable short-range weapon then available, and was developed from 1978 with the aim of achieving far superior off-boresight capability, ECM resistance and improved seeker sensitivity. Operational trials began in 1981 and Israel claimed about 50 kills with the Python over Lebanon in 1982.

Israeli efforts to establish air superiority over the Beka'a Valley saw a major defence suppression operation launched on 9 June 1982. As well as destroying Syrian surface-to-air missile (SAM) sites (19 were claimed as destroyed on that day alone), the raids also succeeded in taking down much of the radar network in eastern Lebanon, upon which the SyAAF interceptors were dependent. At the same time, air defence radars in Syria were jammed by the Israelis, further diminishing the capabilities of the Syrian fighters. While the Syrian MiGs were denied

the protection of a SAM umbrella and communications with their ground-control intercept stations, IDF/AF F-15 and F-16 pilots benefited from the battlespace picture and targeting data provided by E-2C Hawkeye AEW aircraft. These could track up to 250 enemy aircraft simultaneously, and direct the interception of up to 30 targets.

On the Syrian side, despite claims of up to 19 Israeli aircraft destroyed over Lebanon between April 1981 and June 1982, only three kills can be verified according to Israeli data: a SyAAF MiG-23 accounted for an Israeli reconnaissance drone, and MiG-21s downed a Kfir and an F-4E. Syrian sources acknowledge losses of 85 aircraft between 6 and 11 June, the same sources claiming 21 Israeli aircraft shot down. To this day, Israel refuses to admit any losses in air combat, while posting claims of between 82 and 85 Syrian aircraft destroyed in the air.

ISRAELI MISSILE KILLS IN MAY–JUNE 1982*

Date	Launch aircraft	Weapon	Victim
25 May 1982	F-15	AIM-7F	MiG-21
25 May 1982	F-15	AIM-7F	MiG-21
26 May 1982	F-16	AIM-9L	MiG-21
26 May 1982	F-16	AIM-9L	MiG-21
26 May 1982	F-16	AIM-9L	MiG-21
6 June 1982	F-15	AIM-7F	MiG-23MS
7 June 1982	F-15	Python III	MiG-23
8 June 1982	F-15	AIM-7F	MiG-21
8 June 1982	F-15	Python III	MiG-21
8 June 1982	F-16	Python III	MiG-23BN

Date	Launch aircraft	Weapon	Victim
8 June 1982	F-16	Python III	MiG-23BN
8 June 1982	F-16	Python III	MiG-23BN
8 June 1982	F-15	AIM-9L	MiG-23BN
9 June 1982	F-15	AIM-9L	MiG-23MF
9 June 1982	F-15	Python III	MiG-21
9 June 1982	F-15	AIM-9L	MiG-21
9 June 1982	F-16	AIM-9L	MiG-21
9 June 1982	F-16	AIM-9L	MiG-21
9 June 1982	F-16	AIM-9L	MiG-21
9 June 1982	F-16	AIM-9L	MiG-21
9 June 1982	F-16	AIM-9L	MiG-21
9 June 1982	F-16	AIM-9L	MiG-21
9 June 1982	F-16	Python III	unknown MiG
9 June 1982	F-16	AIM-9L	unknown MiG
10 June 1982	F-15	AIM-7F	MiG-23
10 June 1982	F-15	AIM-7F	MiG-23
10 June 1982	F-15	AIM-9L	SA.342 Gazelle
10 June 1982	F-16	Python III	SA.342 Gazelle
10 June 1982	F-16	Python III	SA.342 Gazelle
10 June 1982	F-16	Python III	MiG-21
10 June 1982	F-16	Python III	MiG-21
10 June 1982	F-16	Python III	MiG-21
10 June 1982	F-16	Python III	MiG-21
10 June 1982	F-16	Python III	MiG-21
10 June 1982	F-16	Python III	MiG-21
10 June 1982	F-16	Python III	MiG-21
10 June 1982	F-16	AIM-9L	MiG-23MF
10 June 1982	F-4E	Python III	MiG-21
11 June 1982	F-15	Python III	MiG-21
11 June 1982	F-15	AIM-7F	MiG-23
11 June 1982	F-15	AIM-7F	MiG-23
11 June 1982	F-16	Python III	MiG-21
11 June 1982	F-16	Python III	MiG-21
11 June 1982	F-16	AIM-9L	MiG-23BN
11 June 1982	F-16	AIM-9L	MiG-23BN
11 June 1982	F-16	AIM-9L	MiG-23BN
11 June 1982	F-16	AIM-9L	MiG-23BN
11 June 1982	F-16	AIM-9L	SA.342 Gazelle
24 June 1982	F-16	Python III	MiG-23BN
24 June 1982	F-16	Python III	MiG-23BN

* This table only includes confirmed victories for which the weapon used can be positively identified. In total, confirmed Israeli victories for the Lebanon War of 1982 amount to over 90. Of these, a significant proportion are likely to have involved AAMs.

AAMs in the Falklands

The Falklands War saw the British Royal Navy achieve dominance in the air-to-air battles. The Sea Harrier emerged victorious, although much of its success was down to the AIM-9L missile.

PRIOR TO THE outbreak of conflict between Argentina and the UK over the Falkland Islands in April 1982, the primary short-range AAMs in service with the RAF and Fleet Air Arm (FAA) were the AIM-9D/G Sidewinder models, with limited all-aspect capability. With the early provision of the AIM-9L to the British, the FAA's Sea Harrier FRS.Mk 1 force of just 20 aircraft proved more than capable of achieving air superiority in the face of about 60 Argentine Mirage and Dagger fighters.

The AIM-9Ls were among a number of advanced missile systems rushed from the US to the British Task Force prior to the start of the Falklands campaign. So new was the AIM-9L that armourers worked round the clock to adapt the Sea Harriers to the new weapon while the Task Force sailed to the war zone, with fire-control software codes provided by secure satellite link from the UK. A few Sea Harrier pilots had the chance to make practice AIM-9L shots against flare targets during the journey south.

Sidewinder advantage

In the event, the Sea Harrier pilots engaged their Argentine targets almost exclusively from the rear hemisphere; however, their confidence in the AIM-9L and that weapon's reliability were clearly key factors in their success. Furthermore, since the Argentine pilots were aware that a Sidewinder might be fired at them from any aspect, they approached combat more cautiously. Sidewinders were also available for RAF Harrier GR.Mk 3s during the Falklands War. Although these aircraft were mainly reserved for offensive operations, at times they were armed with either AIM-9G or AIM-9L missiles.

While the Sea Harrier pilots enjoyed the high level of capability offered by the 'Nine Lima', their Argentine counterparts were hampered by the limited

FALKLANDS WAR MISSILE KILLS

Date	Launch aircraft	Weapon	Victim
1 May 1982	Sea Harrier	AIM-9L	Mirage IIIEA
1 May 1982	Sea Harrier	AIM-9L	Dagger
1 May 1982	Sea Harrier	AIM-9L	Canberra
21 May 1982	Sea Harrier	AIM-9L	A-4C
21 May 1982	Sea Harrier	AIM-9L	A-4C
21 May 1982	Sea Harrier	AIM-9L	Dagger
21 May 1982	Sea Harrier	AIM-9L	Dagger
21 May 1982	Sea Harrier	AIM-9L	Dagger
21 May 1982	Sea Harrier	AIM-9L	Dagger
21 May 1982	Sea Harrier	AIM-9L	A-4Q
23 May 1982	Sea Harrier	AIM-9L	Dagger
24 May 1982	Sea Harrier	AIM-9L	Dagger
24 May 1982	Sea Harrier	AIM-9L	Dagger
24 May 1982	Sea Harrier	AIM-9L	Dagger
1 June 1982	Sea Harrier	AIM-9L	C-130E
8 June 1982	Sea Harrier	AIM-9L	A-4B
8 June 1982	Sea Harrier	AIM-9L	A-4B
8 June 1982	Sea Harrier	AIM-9L	A-4B

performance of their available AAMs. The Mirage interceptor force carried the radar-guided R.530, a weapon that was singularly ill-suited to the type of aerial combat taking place over the South Atlantic. Indeed, it was proposed at one stage to use the R.530 in the anti-shipping role instead, to supplement the Exocet, although this policy was never instigated.

The Argentine Air Force began to receive R.550 Magic missiles in April 1982, and a number of Mirages were still only wired for the R.530. Whenever possible, the Magic-wired Mirages were used for combat missions, and only two sorties were conducted with aircraft armed only with the R.530, and only a single example of this missile was fired, without success. On more than one occasion, Mirages were in the position for a missile shot, but the radar failed to provide adequate detection for a lock-on. Argentine pilots were further hampered by the fact that they were operating at the edge of their radius of action, and over the Falklands they typically only had enough fuel for a single attack.

For the attack-optimized Dagger, the primary AAM was the Israeli-made Shafrir II, Argentina's first short-range AAM. This was judged inferior to the Magic. In one instance, a pilot managed to get

behind a Sea Harrier in the 6 o'clock position at a range of 2 miles, but a successful missile shot was prohibited due to the effects of the sun on the missile's seeker head. When configured for the air defence mission, the Dagger was armed with two Shafrir IIs and its pair of 30mm (1.18in) internal cannon. The only other missile available to the Argentines was the ageing AIM-9B.

The final tally

In the course of the air battles between 1 May and 8 June 1982, Sea Harriers destroyed a total of nine Daggers, eight A-4 Skyhawks, one Mirage III, one Canberra, one Pucará, one C-130 Hercules and two helicopters. Of these, 18 fell to AIM-9Ls (one Mirage frequently credited as a Sea Harrier/AIM-9L kill was only damaged by the missile, before being shot down in error by Argentine air defences on the Falkland Islands). A total of 27 of these missiles were launched during the campaign, 24 of these finding their targets, and the weapon has been described as the most effective of the entire war. In return for their claims, two Sea Harriers were lost to ground fire.

There were no other air-to-air kills achieved with missiles in the course of the conflict. Following the end of the war the RAF continued to re-equip with the AIM-9L, which went on to arm Phantom interceptors, as well as advancing the defensive capabilities of the Buccaneer, Tornado and Nimrod.

▼ **Sea Harrier**

A Sea Harrier from 800 Naval Air Squadron armed with AIM-9 Sidewinder missiles prepares to take off from HMS *Hermes*.

AAMs in India and Pakistan

On three occasions since it declared independence in 1947, Pakistan has gone to war with India, and aircraft from both nations have been involved in numerous other skirmishes.

THE FIRST AIR war between India and Pakistan to feature the combat use of AAMs was the 1965 conflict that broke out over the disputed region of Kashmir.

At this time, the only missile-armed fighters in the opposing inventories were the Indian Air Force's (IAF) MiG-21 and the Pakistan Air Force's (PAF) F-86 Sabre and F-104 Starfighter, armed with the R-3S and the AIM-9B Sidewinder, respectively. Early on in the fighting an IAF MiG-21 succeeded in damaging a Pakistani F-86 with a pair of R-3S missiles, but Indian fighters failed to score any confirmed missile kills during the war, and the bulk of air combats were disputed by cannon-armed IAF Gnat, Hunter and Mystère fighters. Indeed, the IAF's sole MiG-21 squadron at the time was in a depleted state and still in the process of attaining full operational capability, and its role was therefore restricted.

More successful in missile combat was the PAF Sabre fleet, around 30 of which were armed with Sidewinders, which accounted for three confirmed aerial victories. Meanwhile the Starfighter – the only radar-equipped fighter of the conflict – made one confirmed kill against an IAF Canberra.

By the time of the outbreak of the 1971 war, the IAF had undergone large-scale re-equipment with eight squadrons of missile-armed MiG-21s, while the PAF had introduced Chinese-supplied F-6 fighters equipped with AIM-9Bs, and French-built Mirage IIIs armed with R.530s and AIM-9Bs. In addition, the Sidewinder-armed F-86 and F-104 remained in service. Pakistan received additional F-104s from Jordan during the course of the fighting, but these new additions were not equipped with provision for carrying Sidewinders. From the fleet of around 50 Sabres, by 1971 24 F-86Fs were modified to launch the AIM-9B. Unfortunately for the PAF, only a relatively small number of AIM-9Bs had been supplied since 1964, and some of these were now approaching the end of their service life. Among the F-6 fleet, 18 aircraft had been adapted for carriage of the AIM-9B, with US assistance.

The Mirage III was the most potent fighter available to the PAF in 1971, and although the Cyrano Ibis radar and R.530 missiles proved lacking in terms of reliability, the French fighters succeeded in posting five confirmed victories against the Indian opposition.

Indian victories

The only confirmed IAF missile victories of the war were achieved by MiG-21FLs, which downed three F-104s and a single F-6. The MiG-21 and R-3S combination was not best suited to the air-superiority role assigned it during the war, and a hurried adaptation was made to add a 23mm (0.9in) cannon pack under the fuselage. Once again, the majority of Indian air-to-air kills were recorded by cannon-armed Gnat and Hunter fighters. In addition, there was at least one recorded instance of 'blue on blue', when an IAF MiG-21 downed another of its kind with an R-3S on 11 December.

The Soviet conflict in Afghanistan from December 1979 provided the PAF with further opportunities for aerial combat, as both Soviet and Democratic Republic of Afghanistan Air Force (DRAAF) aircraft

INDIAN MISSILE KILLS

Date	Launch aircraft	Weapon	Victim
6 December 1971	MiG-21FL	R-3S and cannon	F-6
17 December 1971	MiG-21FL	R-3S	F-104A
17 December 1971	MiG-21FL	R-3S	F-104A
17 December 1971	MiG-21FL	R-3S	F-104A
10 August 1999	MiG-21bis	R-60	Atlantique

▲ **IAF 'Flanker'**

An IAF Sukhoi Su-30 'Flanker' aircraft lands at Nellis Air Force Base, Nevada, 2008, during joint exercises with the USAF.

strayed across the border into Pakistan. A first clash between an F-6 and a DRAAF An-26 transport occurred as early as March 1980, while the years between 1986 and 1988 saw a relative flurry of incursions met with an armed response by the PAF. Confirmed missile kills recorded by PAF fighters during this conflict amounted to eight, all claimed by F-16s, while a further Su-22 fell to gunfire from the same type on 17 May 1986. On another occasion, a

pair of Soviet MiG-23MLDs were targeted by a PAF F-16. Although some Pakistani sources credited a double AIM-9L kill, one of the MiGs was damaged and the other escaped unharmed.

Subsequently, there have been sporadic clashes between the IAF and the Pakistan air arms, including the shooting down of a Pakistan Navy Atlantique maritime patrol aircraft in August 1999 by a MiG-21bis armed with an R-60 (some sources state the weapon used was an R.550 Magic missile). More recently, an Indian Searcher I UAV was shot down at night near Lahore by a PAF F-16, at a time of escalating Indo-Pakistan tensions in 2002.

PAKISTANI MISSILE KILL CLAIMS (CONFIRMED VICTORIES IN BOLD)

6 September 1965	F-104A	AIM-9B	Mystère IVA	India
7 September 1965	F-86E	AIM-9B	Hunter	India
7 September 1965	F-86E	AIM-9B	Hunter	India
7 September 1965	**F-86E**	**AIM-9B**	**Mystère IVA**	**India**
10 September 1965	F-86E	AIM-9B	Gnat	India
10 September 1965	F-86E	AIM-9B	Gnat	India
13 September 1965	**F-86E**	**AIM-9B**	**Gnat**	**India**

Date	Launch aircraft	Weapon	Victim	Operator
14 September 1965	F-104A	AIM-9B	Canberra	India
14 September 1965	F-86F	AIM-9B	Canberra	India
16 September 1965	**F-86E**	**AIM-9B**	**Hunter**	**India**
18 September 1965	F-86E	AIM-9B	Gnat	India
18 September 1965	F-86E	AIM-9B	C-119K	India
22 September 1965	**F-104A**	**AIM-9B**	**Canberra**	**India**
4 December 1971	F-104A	AIM-9B	Gnat	India
4 December 1971	F-104A	AIM-9B	Gnat	India
4 December 1971	**F-6**	**AIM-9B**	**Su-7**	**India**
4 December 1971	**Mirage IIIEP**	**AIM-9B**	**Hunter**	**India**
4 December 1971	**Mirage IIIEP**	**R.530 and AIM-9B**	**Canberra**	**India**
5 December 1971	Mirage IIIEP	AIM-9B	Hunter	India
5 December 1971	**Mirage IIIEP**	**AIM-9B**	**Hunter**	**India**
5 December 1971	**Mirage IIIEP**	**AIM-9B**	**Hunter**	**India**
5 December 1971	Mirage IIIEP	AIM-9B	Hunter	India
6 December 1971	**Mirage IIIEP**	**AIM-9B**	**Su-7**	**India**
6 December 1971	Mirage IIIEP	R.530	Su-7	India
7 December 1971	F-6	AIM-9B	Su-7	India
7 December 1971	F-104A	AIM-9B	Canberra	India
10 December 1971	**F-104A**	**AIM-9B**	**Alizé**	**India**
11 December 1971	**Sabre Mk 6**	**AIM-9B**	**Su-7**	**India**
11 December 1971	Mirage IIIEP	R.530	Canberra	India
14 December 1971	F-6	AIM-9B	MiG-21	India
17 December 1971	Mirage IIIEP	R.530	Canberra	India
16 April 1986	Mirage IIIEP	AIM-9P	MiG-21	Afghanistan
10 May 1986	Mirage IIIEP	AIM-9P	MiG-21	Afghanistan
17 May 1986	**F-16A**	**AIM-9P**	**Su-22**	**Afghanistan**
30 March 1987	**F-16A**	**AIM-9P**	**An-26**	**Afghanistan**
16 April 1987	**F-16A**	**AIM-9P**	**Su-22**	**Afghanistan**
16 April 1987	F-16A	AIM-9P	Su-22	Afghanistan
April 1987	F-16A	AIM-9	An-26	Afghanistan?
April 1987	F-16A	AIM-9	An-26	Afghanistan?
April 1987	F-16A	AIM-9	Mi-8	Afghanistan?
April 1987	F-16A	AIM-9	Mi-8	Afghanistan?
April 1987	F-16A	AIM-9	Mi-8	Afghanistan?
April 1987	F-16A	AIM-9	Mi-8	Afghanistan?
August 1987	F-16A	AIM-9	An-26	Afghanistan
17 May 1988	**F-16A**	**AIM-9L**	**Su-22**	**Afghanistan**
17 May 1988	**F-16A**	**AIM-9L**	**Su-22**	**Afghanistan**
4 August 1988	**F-16A**	**AIM-9L**	**Su-25**	**USSR**
3 November 1988	**F-16A**	**AIM-9L**	**Su-22**	**Afghanistan**
21 November 1988	**F-16A**	**AIM-9L**	**An-26**	**Afghanistan**
8 June 2002	**F-16B**	**AIM-9L**	**Searcher I UAV**	**India**

AAMs in the Iran–Iraq War

In contrast to other air wars in the Middle East, the Iran–Iraq War saw both sides equipped with some of the most advanced Eastern and Western fighter aircraft – and their related weaponry.

THE MOST EXTENSIVE – and, from a technological viewpoint, arguably the most sophisticated – air-to-air combats of the missile era occurred during the protracted Iran–Iraq War (1980–88). Significantly, the Iran–Iraq War was the first in which both sides made extensive use of medium- and long-range AAMs, including the very-long-range AIM-54A Phoenix and the Soviet-made R-40. In terms of aerial combat, the conflict's significance as a testing ground for modern warfare was also demonstrated by the significant use made of electronic countermeasures.

The most capable fighter asset of the Islamic Republic of Iran Air Force (IRIAF) was the F-14A, with its powerful armoury of AIM-54A, AIM-7E and AIM-9P missiles. In numerical terms, the backbone of the IRIAF combat fleet was provided by the F-4D/E aircraft, armed with AIM-7Es and AIM-9Ps for air-to-air combat. These heavyweights were supported by the F-5E, primarily used for ground attack, but also able to carry AIM-9J/P missiles for self-defence. While the IRIAF relied on fighters and AAMs that had been delivered to the then Imperial

Iranian Air Force (IIAF) by the US prior to the Revolution, the Iraqi Air Force (IrAF) began the war with a combat fleet dominated by Soviet equipment.

MiG mainstay

The MiG-21, with around 100 examples in service, was the cornerstone of the IrAF air defence. Available missiles comprised the R-3S (as originally supplied with the first-generation MiG-21F-13, MiG-21FL and MiG-21PFM types now retired from first-line service), R-13M1 (supplied to arm the MiG-21MF) and R-60 (delivered with the MiG-21bis variant). Interestingly, Iraq also wired its MiG-21s for the carriage of the French-made R.550 Magic 1, the first of which were delivered in 1980. The R-3 and R-13 proved unreliable in service, and Iraq made attempts to acquire Sidewinders, eventually obtaining 200 AIM-9Bs from Jordan in 1983. According to Iraqi sources, these missiles were integrated with the MiG-21, and the combination succeeded in downing five Iranian aircraft and helicopters. Despite its flaws, Iranian pilots were impressed by its agility. In a

IRAQI KILLS IN THE IRAN–IRAQ WAR*

Date	Launch aircraft	Weapon	Victim	Operator
23 September 1980	MiG-21MF	R-13	F-5E	Iran
23 September 1980	MiG-21MF	R-13	F-5E	Iran
25 September 1980?	MiG-21MF	R-13	RF-4E	Iran
9 October 1980	MiG-21MF	R.550	F-4D	Iran
12 October 1980	MiG-21MF	R-13	F-5E	Iran
12 October 1980	MiG-21MF	R-13	AB.214C	Iran
12 October 1980	MiG-21MF	R-13	AB.214C	Iran
15 October 1980	MiG-23MS	R-13	F-4E	Iran
15 October 1980	MiG-23MS	R-13	F-4E	Iran
15 October 1980	MiG-21MF	R-13	F-4E	Iran
19 October 1980	MiG-21MF	R-13	F-4E	Iran
20 October 1980	MiG-21MF	R-13	F-5E	Iran
20 October 1980	MiG-21MF	R-13	F-5E	Iran
23 October 1980	MiG-21MF	R-13	F-5E	Iran
23 October 1980	MiG-21MF	R-13	F-5E	Iran

Date	Launch aircraft	Weapon	Victim	Operator
November 1980	MiG-21MF	R-13	F-5E	Iran
14 November 1980	MiG-23MS	R-13	F-5E	Iran
22 November 1980	MiG-23MS	R-13	F-4D	Iran
26 November 1980	MiG-21MF	R-13	F-5E	Iran
28 November 1980	MiG-23MS	R-13	F-4E	Iran
16 October 1980	MiG-23MS	R-13	F-4E	Iran
16 December 1980	MiG-21	R-13	F-5E	Iran
18 January 1981	MiG-21	R-13	F-4E	Iran
April 1981	MiG-21MF	R.550 Magic	MiG-21R	Syria
3 May 1981	MiG-25PD	R-60	Gulfstream III	Algeria
May 1981	MiG-21MF	R.550 Magic	F-4E	Iran
May 1981	MiG-21MF	R.550 Magic	F-4E	Iran
May 1981	MiG-21MF	R.550 Magic	F-5E	Iran
May 1981	MiG-21MF	R.550 Magic	F-5E	Iran
May 1981	MiG-21MF	R.550 Magic	AH-1J	Iran
7 May 1981	MiG-21MF	R.550 Magic	F-4E	Iran
8 May 1981	MiG-21MF	R.550 Magic	F-5E	Iran
27 January 1982	Mirage F.1EQ	Super 530F	RF-4E	Iran
26 February 1982	Mirage F.1EQ	Super 530F	F-5E	Iran
6 July 1982	Mirage F.1EQ	R.550 Magic	F-4E	Iran
December 1982	MiG-23MF	R-23	F-5E	Iran
27 January 1983	Mirage F.1EQ	Super 530F	RF-4E	Iran
August/September 1983	Mirage F.1EQ	Super 530F	F-4E	Iran
January 1983	Mirage F.1EQ	Super 530F	F-100	Turkey
January 1983	Mirage F.1EQ	Super 530F	F-100	Turkey
1984	Mirage F.1EQ	Super 530F	F-5E	Iran
1984	Mirage F.1EQ	Super 530F	EC-130	Iran
11 August 1984	MiG-23ML	R-60	F-14A	Iran
29 December 1984	Mirage F.1EQ	Super 530F	F-4E	Iran
February/March 1985	Mirage F.1EQ	Super 530F	F-4E	Iran
21 March 1985	MiG-25PD	R-40	F-4D	Iran
5 June 1985	MiG-25PD	R-40	F-4E	Iran
13 February 1986	MiG-23ML	R-24	F-5E	Iran
15 February 1986	Mirage F.1EQ	R.550 Magic	F-4E	Iran
23 February 1986	MiG-25PD	R-40	EC-130E	Iran
10 June 1986	MiG-25PD	R-40	RF-4E	Iran
2 October 1986	MiG-25PD	R-40	MiG-21RF	Syria
27 March 1987	Mirage F.1EQ-4	R.550 Magic	F-4E	Iran
19 July 1988	Mirage F.1EQ-6	Super 530D	F-14A	Iran
19 July 1988	Mirage F.1EQ-6	Super 530D	F-14A	Iran
19 July 1988	Mirage F.1EQ-6	Super 530D	F-4E	Iran

* This table only includes kills where a positive identification of the missile used is available, and those which involved the use of dedicated AAMs.

IRANIAN KILLS IN THE IRAN-IRAQ WAR*

Date	Launch aircraft	Weapon	Victim	Operator
14 September 1980	F-14A	AIM-54A	Su-20M	Iraq
17 September 1980	F-14A	AIM-54A	MiG-21MF	Iraq
23 September 1980	F-14A	AIM-54A	MiG-21RF	Iraq
23 September 1980	F-14A	AIM-7E	MiG-23	Iraq
23 September 1980	F-14A	AIM-7E	MiG-23MS	Iraq
23 September 1980	F-5E	AIM-9J	Su-20	Iraq
23 September 1980	F-14A	AIM-9P	MiG-21MF	Iraq
24 September 1980	F-14A	AIM-7E	MiG-21MF	Iraq
24 September 1980	F-14A	AIM-9P	MiG-21MF	Iraq
24 September 1980	F-14A	AIM-54A	MiG-21MF	Iraq
25 September 1980	F-4E	AIM-9P	An-26	Iraq
25 September 1980	F-4E	AIM-9P	MiG-21MF	Iraq
25 September 1980	F-14A	AIM-54A	MiG-21MF	Iraq
25 September 1980	F-14A	AIM-9P	MiG-21MF	Iraq
25 September 1980	F-4E	AIM-9P	MiG-23MS	Iraq
25 September 1980	F-14A	AIM-7E	MiG-23BN	Iraq
25 September 1980	F-4E	AIM-9P	MiG-23BN	Iraq
25 September 1980	F-4E	AIM-9P	MiG-21MF	Iraq
27 September 1980	F-4E	AIM-9P	MiG-23BN	Iraq
27 September 1980	F-4E	AIM-9P	MiG-23BN	Iraq
28 September 1980	F-4E	AIM-7E	MiG-23BN	Iraq
28 September 1980	F-4E	AIM-7E	MiG-23BN	Iraq
28 September 1980	F-4E	AIM-7E	MiG-23BN	Iraq
28 September 1980	F-4E	AIM-7E	MiG-23BN	Iraq
2 October 1980	F-14A	AIM-9P	MiG-23MS	Iraq
3 October 1980	F-4D	AIM-9P	MiG-21MF	Iraq
3 October 1980	F-4D	AIM-9P	MiG-21MF	Iraq
8 October 1980	F-5E	AIM-9J	Su-20	Iraq
8 October 1980	F-5E	AIM-9J	Su-20	Iraq
12 October 1980	F-14A	AIM-9P	Su-20	Iraq
13 October 1980	F-4E	AIM-9P	MiG-23BN	Iraq
18 October 1980	F-14A	AIM-9P	MiG-23BN	Iraq
18 October 1980	F-14A	AIM-9P	MiG-23BN	Iraq
20 October 1980	F-14A	AIM-7E	MiG-21MF	Iraq
22 October 1980	F-14A	AIM-9P	MiG-21MF	Iraq
25 October 1980	F-14A	AIM-9P	Su-20	Iraq
26 October 1980	F-14A	AIM-9P	MiG-21MF	Iraq
26 October 1980	F-14A	AIM-9P	MiG-21MF	Iraq
29 October 1980	F-14A	AIM-54A	MiG-23MLA	Iraq
29 October 1980	F-14A	AIM-54A	MiG-23MLA	Iraq
29 October 1980	F-14A	AIM-9P	MiG-23MLA	Iraq
29 October 1980	F-14A	AIM-9P	MiG-23MLA	Iraq
29 October 1980	F-14A	AIM-54A	Tu-22B	Iraq

Date	Launch aircraft	Weapon	Victim	Operator
10 November 1980	F-14A	AIM-7E	MiG-23BN	Iraq
21 November 1980	F-14A	AIM-7E	MiG-21	Iraq
27 November 1980	F-14A	AIM-54A	MiG-21MF	Iraq
2 December 1980	F-14A	AIM-54A	MiG-21MF	Iraq
7 December 1980	F-4E	AIM-7E	MiG-23BN	Iraq
19 December 1980	F-4E	AIM-9P	Su-20	Iraq
19 December 1980	F-4E	AIM-9P	Su-20	Iraq
19 December 1980	F-4E	AIM-9P	Su-20	Iraq
22 December 1980	F-14A	AIM-54A	MiG-21 or Su-20	Iraq
22 December 1980	F-14A	AIM-54A	MiG-21 or Su-20	Iraq
7 January 1981	F-14A	AIM-54A	MiG-23BN	Iraq
7 January 1981	F-14A	AIM-54A	MiG-23BN	Iraq
7 January 1981	F-14A	AIM-54A	MiG-23BN	Iraq
14 January 1981	F-5E	AIM-9P	Mi-25	Iraq
21 January 1981	F-4E	AIM-9P	MiG-23BN	Iraq
21 January 1981	F-4E	AIM-9P	MiG-23BN	Iraq
29 January 1981	F-14A	AIM-54A	Su-22M-3K	Iraq
21 April 1981	F-14A	AIM-9P	MiG-23BN	Iraq
26 April 1981	F-4E	AIM-9P	MiG-21MF	Iraq
26 April 1981	F-4E	AIM-9P	MiG-23BN	Iraq
15 May 1981	F-14A	AIM-9P	MiG-21MF	Iraq
15 May 1981	F-4E	AIM-9P	MiG-21MF	Iraq
1 September 1981	F-4D	AIM-7E	MiG-23MF	Iraq
22 September 1981	F-4E	AIM-9P	MiG-21MF	Iraq
22 October 1981	F-14A	AIM-54A	Mirage F.1EQ	Iraq
22 October 1981	F-14A	AIM-54A	Mirage F.1EQ	Iraq
22 October 1981	F-14A	AIM-54A	Mirage F.1EQ	Iraq
22 October 1981	F-14A	AIM-54A	MiG-21MF	Iraq
11 December 1981	F-14A	AIM-54A	Mirage F.1EQ	Iraq
11 December 1981	F-14A	AIM-54A	MiG-21	Iraq
1982	F-4	AIM-7E	Mirage F.1EQ	Iraq
1982	F-4	AIM-7E	Mirage F.1EQ	Iraq
19 March 1982	F-4E	AIM-9P	MiG-21MF	Iraq
4 April 1982	F-4E	AIM-9P	MiG-21MF	Iraq
22 April 1982	F-4E	AIM-9P	An-26	Iraq
1982	F-14A	AIM-54A	MiG-25RB	Iraq
16 July 1982	F-4E	AIM-9P	MiG-21MF	Iraq
21 July 1982	F-14A	AIM-54A	2 x MiG-23MF	Iraq
21 July 1982	F-14A	AIM-54A	MiG-23MF	Iraq
28 August 1982	F-4E	AIM-9P	An-26TV	Iraq
15 September 1982	F-4E	AIM-9P	MiG-21MF	Iraq
16 September 1982	F-14A	AIM-54A	MiG-25RB	Iraq
10 October 1982	F-14A	AIM-54A	MiG-23BN	Iraq

Date	Launch aircraft	Weapon	Victim	Operator
10 October 1982	F-14A	AIM-54A	MiG-23BN	Iraq
7 November 1982	F-14A	AIM-7E	Su-22M-3K	Iraq
20 November 1982	F-4E	AIM-9P	MiG-23BN	Iraq
20 November 1982	F-5E	AIM-9P	Mi-8	Iraq
20 November 1982	F-5E	AIM-9P	MiG-21MF	Iraq
21 November 1982	F-14A	AIM-54A	MiG-23MF	Iraq
21 November 1982	F-14A	AIM-54A	MiG-23MF	Iraq
21 November 1982	F-14A	AIM-7E	MiG-21MF	Iraq
21 November 1982	F-4E	AIM-9P	Su-22M-3K	Iraq
1 December 1982	F-14A	AIM-54A	MiG-25RB	Iraq
4 December 1982	F-14A	AIM-54A	MiG-25PD	Iraq
4 May 1983	F-4E	AIM-9P	Su-22M-3K	Iraq
6 August 1983	F-14A and F-5E	AIM-54A and AIM-9J	MiG-25RB	Iraq
September 1983	F-14A	AIM-54A	Su-22M	Iraq
September 1983	F-14A	AIM-54A	Su-22M	Iraq
October 1983	F-14A	AIM-54A	Su-22M	Iraq
25 February 1984	F-14A	AIM-54A	MiG-21bis	Iraq
25 February 1984	F-14A	AIM-54A	unknown jet	Iraq
25 February 1984	F-14A	AIM-54A	unknown jet	Iraq
25 February 1984	F-14A	AIM-9P	MiG-21bis	Iraq
1 March 1984	F-14A	AIM-54A	Su-22M-3K	Iraq
25 March 1984	F-14A	AIM-54A	Tu-22B	Iraq
2 April 1984	F-4E	AIM-7E	Super Etendard	Iraq
6 April 1984	F-14A	AIM-54A	Tu-22B	Iraq
6 April 1984	F-14A	AIM-54A	Tu-22B	Iraq
26 July 1984	F-14A	AIM-54A	Super Etendard	Iraq
14 January 1985	F-4E	AIM-9P	MiG-23BN	Iraq
9 March 1985	F-4E	AIM-9P	unknown MiG	Iraq
11 March 1985	F-4E	AIM-9P	MiG-23BN	Iraq
15 March 1985	F-4E	AIM-9P	MiG-23BN	Iraq
March 1985	F-14A	AIM-54A	MiG-27	USSR?
March 1985	F-14A	AIM-54A	MiG-27	USSR?
March 1985	F-4E	AIM-9P	MiG-27	USSR
26 March 1985	F-14A	AIM-54A	Mirage F.1EQ	Iraq
19 April 1985	F-4E	AIM-9P	MiG-21MF	Iraq
11 May 1985	F-4E	AIM-7E	Su-22	Iraq
15 May 1985	F-4E	AIM-9P	Su-22	Iraq
15 February 1986	F-14A	AIM-54A	MiG-25RB	Iraq
14 March 1986	F-14A	AIM-9P	Mirage 5SDE	Egypt
April 1986	F-5E	AIM-9P	Su-20	Iraq
18 June 1986	F-4D	AIM-7E	Su-22M	Iraq
12 July 1986	F-14A	AIM-7E	MiG-23ML	Iraq
7 October 1986	F-14A	AIM-54A	Mirage F.1EQ-5	Iraq
14 October 1986	F-14A	AIM-54A	MiG-23ML	Iraq

Date	Launch aircraft	Weapon	Victim	Operator
15 November 1986	F-4E	AIM-9P	MiG-23BN	Iraq
1986	F-14A	AIM-54A	MiG-25BM	USSR
18 February 1987	F-14A	AIM-7E	Mirage F.1EQ	Iraq
18 February 1987	F-14A	AIM-9P	Mirage F.1EQ	Iraq
18 February 1987	F-14A	AIM-54A	Mirage F.1EQ	Iraq
24 June 1987	F-14A	AIM-54A	SA.321GV Super Frelon	Iraq
11 November 1987	F-14A	AIM-54A	MiG-25BM	USSR
15 November 1987	F-14A	AIM-7E	Mirage F.1EQ-5	Iraq
17 November 1987	F-4E	AIM-9P	Su-22M-4K	Iraq
22 November 1987	F-4E	AIM-9P	MiG-23BN	Iraq
25 November 1987	F-5E	AIM-9P	Su-22M-4K	Iraq
February 1988	F-14A	AIM-9P	Mirage F.1EQ-5	Iraq
February 1988	F-14A	AIM-9P	Mirage F.1EQ-5	Iraq
9 February 1988	F-14A	AIM-7E	Mirage F.1EQ-5	Iraq
9 February 1988	F-14A	AIM-9P	Mirage F.1EQ-5	Iraq
9 February 1988	F-14A	AIM-9P	Mirage F.1EQ-5	Iraq
15 February 1988	F-14A	AIM-54A	Mirage F.1EQ-5	Iraq
16 February 1988	F-14A	AIM-9P	Mirage F.1EQ-4	Iraq
16 February 1988	F-14A	AIM-9P	Mirage F.1EQ-4	Iraq
25 February 1988	F-14A	AIM-54A	B-6D	Iraq
25 February 1988	F-14A	AIM-54A	C-601 (missile)	Iraq
6 March 1988	F-4E?	AIM-7E	Mirage F.1EQ	Iraq
19 March 1988	F-14A	AIM-54A	Tu-22B	Iraq
19 March 1988	F-14A	AIM-54A	MiG-25RBS	Iraq
19 March 1988	F-4E	AIM-7E	Tu-22B	Iraq
20 March 1988	F-14A	AIM-54A	MiG-25RB	Iraq
22 March 1988	F-14A	AIM-54A	MiG-25RB	Iraq
24 March 1988	F-14A	AIM-54A	Mirage F.1EQ	Iraq
15 May 1988	F-14A	AIM-9P	Mirage F.1EQ	Iraq
14 June 1988	F-4E	AIM-9P	MiG-23MF	Iraq
14 June 1988	F-14A	AIM-9P	Mirage F.1EQ	Iraq

* This table only includes kills where a positive identification of the missile used is available, and those which involved the use of dedicated air-to-air missiles.

dogfight, however, Iraqi pilots preferred to use the 23mm (0.9in) cannon rather than unreliable missiles.

Also in use were MiG-23s of various marks, and Su-20/22 attack aircraft. First-generation MiG-23MS could carry R-3S and R-13M1 missiles, while the more capable MiG-23MF/ML added the medium-range R-23R/24R and the R-60 to its armoury. The Su-22M-3K and M-4K could carry R-60s for self-defence, although these were rarely used. The MiG-23 was the most modern combat type in service early in the war, although it was not to meet the Iraqi pilots' expectations, and its armament was also found wanting. Prior to the Iraqi invasion of Iran on 22 September 1980, however, Baghdad had placed orders with Moscow for more sophisticated combat equipment, including MiG-25s and Mi-25 helicopter gunships. In its interceptor variant, the former could be armed with R-40R and R-40RD/TD and R-60 missiles. Equally significantly, Iraq had also placed major orders with France, and was in line to receive advanced Western equipment in the form of Mirage F.1 fighters and combat helicopters.

Early in the war, the superiority of the IRIAF was clear, with Iranian incursions into Iraq in autumn 1980 resulting in IrAF fighters suffering heavy losses. Such attrition was repeated when the IrAF attempted to launch raids against Iranian targets.

Mirage in combat

The IrAF introduced the Mirage F.1EQ series into service in 1981 and the aircraft won an enviable reputation in the interception role, armed with Super 530F and Magic 1 AAMs. More surprisingly, the IrAF also received examples of the advanced Super 530D later in the conflict, primarily for evaluation.

In 1986 the IRIAF upped its integration of SAMs and interceptors, with the F-14 proving particularly effective in destroying IrAF aircraft lured into 'kill boxes'. Such was the respect of Iraqi pilots for the F-14 that around 60 per cent of engagements against the type ended in a retreat by the IrAF asset, without a shot being fired.

By the mid 1980s, it was clear to the IRIAF that they lacked the resources to win a war of attrition, while the Iraqis were now well aware of their technical inferiority. To address the latter, Iraq began to introduce more advanced aircraft and weapons of Soviet and French origin.

The war was now headed for stalemate, however, particularly with US involvement in the shape of Operation *Praying Mantis*, which hit the Iranian Navy particularly hard.

Specifications

Length overall: 3540mm (11ft 7in)	Range: 25km (15.5 miles)
Fuselage diameter: 263mm (10.4in)	Speed: Mach 4.5
Wingspan: 880mm (34.6in)	Powerplant: Solid propellant
Launch weight: 245kg (540lb)	Guidance system: Semi-active radar
Warhead weight: 30kg (66lb)	

▼ Super 530F

A further development of the R.530, the Super 530F introduced a differential altitude capability that was optimized for the Cyrano IV radar of the Mirage F.1C interceptor. It was also retained by the initial Mirage 2000C variants with the interim RDM radar. In Iraqi service, the Super 530F was allied with the Mirage F.1EQ, one example of which was credited with 14 victories against the IRIAF.

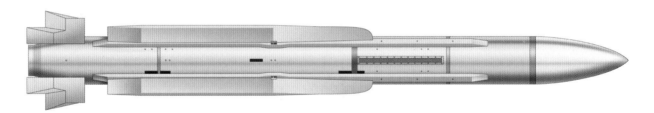

▼ AIM-54A Phoenix

In Iranian hands, the combination of F-14 Tomcat and AIM-54 Phoenix enjoyed its greatest combat success during the war with Iraq. On one notable occasion in January 1981, an IRIAF F-14 fired a single Phoenix against a formation of four Iraqi Air Force MiG-23BNs. In the process of destroying the lead MiG, the missile detonation damaged another two MiGs, causing them both to crash.

Specifications

Length overall: 4000mm (13ft)	Range: 184km (115 miles)
Fuselage diameter: 380mm (15in)	Speed: Mach 5
Wingspan: 910mm (3ft)	Powerplant: Solid propellant rocket motor
Launch weight: 450–470kg (1000–1040lb)	Guidance system: Semi-active and active radar
Warhead weight: 61kg (135lb)	homing

AAMs in sub-Saharan Africa

The numerous conflicts that have afflicted post-war Africa have seen intermittent use of AAMs, with South Africa being the most experienced operator – and developer – on the continent.

OSTRACIZED FROM the international community from the 1960s, South Africa developed its own AAMs for the confrontations around its borders. The Kukri was developed as a successor to the AIM-9B, and was based on the Magic.

The initial V3A that entered production in 1973 was succeeded by the V3B in 1981, which featured a more sensitive IR seeker and could be used in conjunction with a helmet-mounted sight. Kukri-armed Mirage fighters took on Angolan and Cuban-flown missile-armed MiG-21s and

MiG-23s during the Bush War in the 1980s. V3Bs claimed one confirmed kill, plus three MiG-23s damaged.

East African Wars

In more recent years, the conflict between Eritrea and Ethiopia has seen considerable use of modern Soviet-made AAMs. The Badme War saw clashes between MiG-29s and Su-27s, with Ethiopian Su-27s in particular achieving a number of successful missile engagements at beyond visual range.

▼ R-27R (AA-10 'Alamo')

The R-27 became the standard medium-range AAM for Soviet-designed fighters in the 1980s and went on to record its most significant combat success in Africa, in the hands of the Eritrean and Ethiopian air forces. The weapon is used by both the MiG-29 and Su-27, although only the latter carries the extended-range versions.

Specifications

Length overall: 4080mm (13ft 4.6in)

Fuselage diameter: 230mm (9.1in)

Wingspan: 772mm (30.4in)

Launch weight: 253kg (560lb)

Warhead weight: 39kg (86lb)

Range: Up to 80km (49.7 miles)

Speed: Mach 2.5–4.5

Powerplant: Solid-fuel rocket motor

Guidance system: Semi-active radar

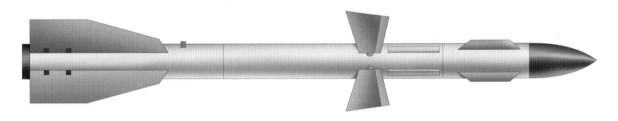

SUB-SAHARAN AFRICAN MISSILE KILLS

Date	Operator	Launch aircraft	Weapon	Victim	Operator
26 July 1977	Ethiopia	F-5A	AIM-9B	MiG-21MF	Somalia
28 July 1977	Ethiopia	F-5A	AIM-9B	MiG-21	Somalia
5 December 1985	South Africa	Mirage F.1CZ	V3B Kukri	An-26	Angola
3 April 1986	Angola	MiG-23ML	R-23	L-100 Hercules	South Africa
25 February 1999	Eritrea	MiG-29	R-27R	MiG-23BN	Ethiopia
25 February 1999	Ethiopia	Su-27	R-27R	MiG-29	Eritrea
25 February 1999	Ethiopia	Su-27	R-73	MiG-29	Eritrea
26 February 1999	Eritrea	MiG-29	R-73	MiG-21	Ethiopia
26 February 1999	Eritrea	MiG-29	R-73	MiG-21	Ethiopia
18 March 1999	Ethiopia	Su-27	R-27R	MiG-29	Eritrea
18 March 1999	Ethiopia	Su-27	R-27R	MiG-29	Eritrea
18 May 2000	Ethiopia	Su-27	R-73	MiG-29	Eritrea

AAMs in Latin America

Guided missiles came relatively late to the air arms of Latin America, but since their introduction, AAMs have played a crucial role in a number of aerial engagements.

WITH THE EXCEPTION of a handful of close calls achieved by Argentine pilots in the Falklands, the first concerted use of AAMs in Latin American air combat occurred during the Venezuelan coup attempt of 1992. A single F-16A downed a pair of OV-10E Broncos, while another scored a Tucano kill with 20mm (0.79in) gunfire; other accounts note a total of two gun kills by Venezuelan F-16s. In the course of the air battles, the two F-16s involved were flown by pilots who remained loyal to the government, while the OV-10E and Tucano were in the hands of rebel pilots. The action was sufficient to quash the airborne component of the coup. Establishing air supremacy over Caracas, the F-16s also succeeded in turning away a rebel-flown Mirage.

Air war over Alta-Cenepa

The culmination of a long-term border dispute between Ecuador and Peru – the Alta-Cenepa

conflict of February 1995 – saw Ecuadorian Mirage F.1JAs and Kfir C2 fighters score three aerial kills against Peruvian Air Force Su-22 and A-37B attack aircraft that had been conducting air strikes over Ecuadorian border posts. Until 10 February, Peruvian Air Force A-37Bs, Canberras, Mirage 5Ps and Su-22s had flown their missions unmolested by the Ecuadorian Air Force. On this day, however, the incoming raiders were detected by the Ecuadorian air defence system and two Mirage F.1s were scrambled. They detected two Su-22s, initially using their radar, and later establishing visual contact. The lead Mirage pilot and his wingman each used two Magics to dispatch the Sukhoi pair. At the same time, Ecuadorian Kfirs were on patrol in the area, and although one A-37B managed to make its escape at low level, the other jet was struck in the centre section by a Shafrir II launched from the lead Kfir.

▼ R.550 Magic 2

With the Mirage family of fighters a popular choice among Latin American operators, the R.550 Magic has seen combat use in the region. Although it arrived too late in Argentine service to see action in the Falklands campaign, the Magic is credited with two aerial victories by Ecuadorian Mirages F.1s.

Specifications

Length overall: 2720mm (8ft 11in)	Range: 15km (9.3 miles)
Fuselage diameter: 157mm (6.18in)	Speed: Mach 3
Wingspan: 660mm (26in)	Powerplant: Solid
Launch weight: 89kg (196lb)	Guidance system: Infrared
Warhead weight: 13kg (28.67lb)	

LATIN AMERICAN MISSILE KILLS*

Date	Operator	Launch aircraft	Weapon	Victim	Operator
27 November 1992	Venezuela	F-16A	AIM-9P	OV-10	Venezuela
27 November 1992	Venezuela	F-16A	AIM-9P	OV-10	Venezuela
10 February 1995	Ecuador	Mirage F.1JA	R.550 Magic 2	Su-22	Peru
10 February 1995	Ecuador	Mirage F.1JA	R.550 Magic 2	Su-22	Peru
10 February 1995	Ecuador	Kfir C2	Shafrir II	A-37B	Peru

* Victories listed are for aerial combat only, and kills against drug-smuggling and other civilian types are not included.

Modern AAMs

Although the end of the Cold War generally slowed AAM development, by the 1990s a new generation of multi-purpose missiles were coming on line, combining agility with endurance.

UNDER A JOINT agreement signed in 1980, the US, UK, France and West Germany began work to replace the ageing AIM-7 and AIM-9 with new classes of AAM. The US was to be responsible for the entrant in the medium-range category, the AIM-120 Advanced Medium-Range Air-to-Air Missile (AMRAAM). In contrast to the SARH AIM-7, the AMRAAM adopted a fire-and-forget guidance system. Prior to launch, the missile's inertial autopilot receives data from the launch aircraft. The missile can receive mid-course updates during flight for longer-range engagements, and once in the vicinity of the target the AMRAAM switches over to its own active radar seeker for terminal-phase autonomous homing.

The AMRAAM development contract was awarded to Hughes in 1981 and a first test launch followed in 1984. The first production AIM-120A was delivered in 1988.

Successive models of the AMRAAM comprise the AIM-120B with an updated guidance system and the AIM-120C with clipped control surfaces to allow internal carriage in the F-22 and F-35. The AIM-120C also introduces a further updated guidance system and an improved warhead. Sub-variants include the AIM-120C-5 with enlarged motor and enhanced ECCM, and the AIM-120C-6, with improved target detection capabilities. The AIM-120C-7 with further enhanced ECCM, updated seeker and increased range, was developed as a successor to the US Navy's AIM-54 Phoenix. The latest AIM-120D adds a two-way datalink, Global Positioning Satellite (GPS) navigation, increased range, and enhanced off-boresight performance.

The US military had once intended to acquire the European AIM-132 Advanced Short-Range Air-to-Air Missile (ASRAAM) as the successor to the

Specifications

Length overall: 3000mm (9ft 10in)	Warhead weight: 9.4kg (20.8lb)
Fuselage diameter: 127mm (5in)	Range: More than 40km (25 miles)
Wingspan: 353mm (13.9in)	Powerplant: Hercules/Bermite MK 36
Launch weight: 85kg (118lb)	Guidance system: Imaging infrared

▼ AIM-9X Sidewinder

As well as being compatible with previous AIM-9 interfaces, the AIM-9X can be carried internally in the F-22 and F-35 and is also compatible with the Joint Helmet-Mounted Cueing System (JHMCS) for target acquisition. A high level of agility is assured through the use of jet-vane steering in the propulsion section.

▼ AIM-132 ASRAAM

Primary short-range armament for RAF Typhoon fighters, the ASRAAM can be used in high off-boresight engagements, allowing the pilot to fire 'over-the-shoulder' using the lock-on after launch (LOAL) mode. For such engagements, the ASRAAM would be used in conjunction with a helmet-mounted display. The first export customer for the ASRAAM was Australia, for its F/A-18 Hornets.

Specifications

Length overall: 2900mm (9ft 6in)	Range: 300m–18km (984ft– 11.2 miles)
Fuselage diameter: 166mm (6.5in)	Speed: Mach 3+
Wingspan: 450mm (17.7in)	Powerplant: Solid rocket motor
Launch weight: 88kg (194lb)	Guidance system: Imaging infrared
Warhead weight: 10kg (22lb)	

▼ R-77 (AA-12 'Adder')

Russia has proposed several derivatives of its fire-and-forget R-77, including a next-generation, ramjet-powered model with much increased range. Illustrated is the basic R-77, characterized by its novel lattice-type rudders.

Specifications

Length overall: 3600mm (11ft 1in)	Range: 40–80km (24.8–49.7 miles)
Fuselage diameter: 200mm (7.87in)	Speed: Mach 4.5
Wingspan: 350mm (13.8in)	Powerplant: Solid fuel rocket motor
Launch weight: 175kg (386lb)	Guidance system: Inertial with mid-course
Warhead weight: 22kg (48.5lb)	update and terminal active radar

▼ Meteor

The Meteor represents the first of a new generation of AAMs powered by a rocket/ramjet motor, ensuring that the missile retains sufficient energy to engage manoeuvering targets even at ranges in excess of 100km (62 miles).

Specifications

Length overall: 3650mm (12ft)	Speed: More than Mach 4
Fuselage diameter: 178mm (7in)	Powerplant: Throttleable ducted rocket
Wingspan: n/a	Guidance system: Inertial mid-course with
Launch weight: 185kg (407lb)	datalinked updates, active radar
Range: More than 100km (62 miles)	

▼ Load-out

USAF Major Phillip Campbell, an F-15 Eagle instructor pilot, fires a radar-guided, air-to-air AIM-7 Sparrow at an aerial target drone during a weapons evaluation mission. The major is assigned to the 95th Fighter Squadron at Tyndall Air Force Base, Florida.

ubiquitous AIM-9, before the decision was taken in 1991 to develop a modernized Sidewinder, known as AIM-9X. A demonstration programme began in 1994, with Hughes (later Raytheon) awarded the development contract in 1996. The first test firings followed in 1998, and the initial examples of the AIM-9X were delivered to the USAF and US Navy in 2002. The AIM-9X allies the motor and warhead of the AIM-9M with an all-new airframe featuring low-drag control surfaces. A new imaging infrared (IIR) seeker is used, and manoeuvrability is enhanced through the use of jet-vane deflection.

Europe's short-range AAMs

Although the US opted to develop its own Sidewinder successor, Europe continued with ASRAAM, developed from 1980, initially as a joint British/German/Norwegian project. In the event, the German team withdrew in 1989 to pursue the rival

IRIS-T, and BAe Dynamics (now part of MBDA Missile Systems) was eventually left to complete development on its own. In 1991 the UK Ministry of Defence (MOD) announced a requirement for a new dogfight missile, and in 1992 awarded the contract to BAe. After the first firing trials in 1994, the ASRAAM was delivered to the RAF in 1998, with operational capability following in 2002. The ASRAAM uses a combination of low-drag control surfaces and a powerful motor to ensure agility. The IIR seeker is designed to operate at long ranges, and provides a high off-boresight capability. The ASRAAM can also be used in the lock-on after launch (LOAL) mode.

The UK tailored ASRAAM to meet the requirements of high speed and long range, while Germany – influenced by the Soviet R-73 acquired from the former East German Air Force – now demanded a missile that prioritised agility. As a result, Germany left the ASRAAM programme and began to develop an alternative Sidewinder successor using thrust-vectoring control. This new weapon emerged as the IRIS-T (Infra-Red Imaging System Tail/Thrust Vector-Controlled), now run as a joint programme involving Germany, Greece, Italy, Norway, Spain and Sweden. Key features of the weapon include an IIR seeker with LOAL option, and the manufacturer also claims a unique anti-missile capability.

Europe is also home to two BVR missile projects, the French Mica and the Meteor. The Meteor is under development for use by six European nations (the UK, France, Germany, Italy, Spain and Sweden)

Specifications

Length overall: 3100mm (10ft 2in)	Range: 60km (37.3 miles)
Fuselage diameter: 160mm (6.3in)	Speed: Mach 4
Wingspan: 560mm (22in)	Powerplant: SNPE solid-fuel rocket
Launch weight: 112kg (247lb)	Guidance system: Infrared
Warhead weight: 12kg (26.5lb)	

▼ MICA IR

The MICA IR uses a passive imaging IR seeker head optimized for shorter-range engagements. One of two interoperable versions, the MICA IR can be fired in either lock-on after launch (LOAL) or lock-on before launch (LOBL) mode.

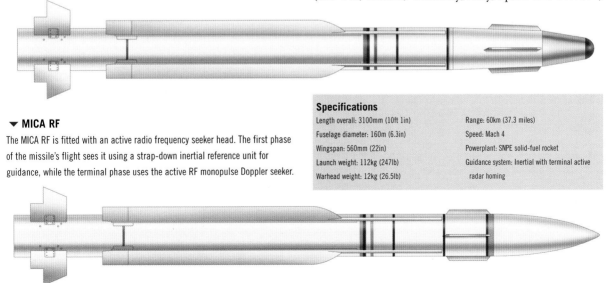

▼ MICA RF

The MICA RF is fitted with an active radio frequency seeker head. The first phase of the missile's flight sees it using a strap-down inertial reference unit for guidance, while the terminal phase uses the active RF monopulse Doppler seeker.

Specifications

Length overall: 3100mm (10ft 1in)	Range: 60km (37.3 miles)
Fuselage diameter: 160m (6.3in)	Speed: Mach 4
Wingspan: 560mm (22in)	Powerplant: SNPE solid-fuel rocket
Launch weight: 112kg (247lb)	Guidance system: Inertial with terminal active
Warhead weight: 12kg (26.5lb)	radar homing

▲ IRIS-T

The IRIS-T entered service with the six European partner nations in late 2005, and export customers include Austria (for the EF2000), South Africa (Gripen) and Saudi Arabia (Typhoon). The leader of the industrial consortium responsible for the missile is Diehl BGT of Germany, which formerly licence-built the Sidewinder.

Specifications

Length overall: 2936mm (9ft 7.6in)	Range: Around 25km (15.5 miles)
Fuselage diameter: 127mm (5in)	Speed: Mach 3
Wingspan: 447mm (17.6in)	Powerplant: Solid-fuel rocket
Launch weight: 87.4kg (192.6lb)	Guidance system: Infrared
Warhead weight: n/a	

and is primarily intended for carriage by the Eurofighter Typhoon, Gripen and Rafale. The Meteor uses an active radar seeker and has ramjet propulsion to ensure long standoff range with a high kill probability. Meteor contract signature was recorded in 2002 and the first guided test launches were achieved in 2008.

BVR capabilities

As well as Meteor, MBDA is now responsible for the Matra-developed MICA, which is replacing both the Super 530 and Magic as a dual-role missile for the Rafale and the latest versions of the Mirage 2000. Therefore, the weapon can span both short- and medium-range BVR scenarios. Unusually for a Western missile, the MICA is also available with two interoperable seeker head options: active radio frequency seeker or passive IIR.

The latest production Russian AAM is also a BVR weapon, the R-77 (AA-12 'Adder'), developed to arm updated versions of the MiG-29 and Su-27, among others. It uses active radar homing and also offers a high level of agility, using unusual lattice-type tailfins.

In Israel, development of the Python has continued, resulting in the Python IV and V. Despite its name, the Python IV has little in common with its predecessor, and was developed in response to the appearance of the R-73, stressing a high level of agility for short-range engagements. The Python IV entered IDF/AF service in 1993 and export operators include Ecuador. A lightweight weapon, the Python IV uses a a complex array of 18 different control fins and strakes in place of thrust-vectoring, and is fitted with an all-aspect IR seeker. The follow-on Python V is externally similar, but adds an electro-optical IIR seeker. Related to the Python IV is the Derby, which introduces BVR capability through its use of an active radar seeker, which is combined with a lock-on before launch (LOBL) mode for close-in dogfights. The Derby has been exported to a number of operators, including Brazil, where it arms the upgraded F-5BR fighter.

South Africa's recent history of AAM development has produced the Darter family. The first of these was the short-range, IR-homing V3C Darter of 1990, intended as an improved, all-aspect version of the

Specifications

Length overall: 3.62m (11ft 11in)	Warhead weight: n/a
Fuselage diameter: 160mm (6.3in)	Range: More than 60km (37 miles)
Wingspan:	Powerplant: Solid-fuel rocket
Launch weight: 118kg (260lb)	Guidance system: Active radar

▼ R-Darter

Now retired from South African service, the R-Darter is very similar in outward appearance to the Israeli Derby. The weapon was apparently only ever cleared for use on the South African Air Force's Cheetah C/D fighter, and after entering service in around 1995 was retired together with the Cheetah in 2008.

Specifications

Length: 2800mm (9ft 2in)	Warhead weight: 12kg (26.4lb)
Fuselage diameter: 150mm (5.9in)	Range: 6km (4 miles)
Wingspan: 660mm (26in)	Powerplant: Solid-fuel rocket
Launch weight: 89kg (196lb)	Guidance: Infrared

▲ **Weapons loader**

USAF groundcrew unload an AMRAAM from an F-22A Raptor following a mission.

▼ **MAA-1 Piranha**

Development of Brazil's first indigenous AAM began in 1976, in order to replace the AIM-9B. Classified until 1981, the programme stalled in the mid 1980s before recovering in the 1990s. The weapon is now due to be replaced by the A-Darter.

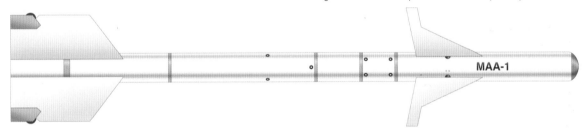

▼ **Astra**

Subject to protracted development, the Astra is India's contender in the BVR missile field. Once development is complete, it is expected to enter service on the Su-30MKI and Tejas. The Astra was revealed in 1998 and uses a terminal active radar seeker plus internal guidance system with mid-course updates.

Specifications

Length overall: 3570mm (11ft 8.5in)	Range: 80–100km (49.7–62.1 miles)
Fuselage diameter: 168mm (6.6in)	Speed: Mach 4+
Wingspan: 254mm (10in)	Powerplant: Solid-fuel rocket
Launch weight: 154kg (339.5lb)	Guidance system: Inertial, mid-course update
Warhead weight: 15kg (33lb)	and terminal active radar

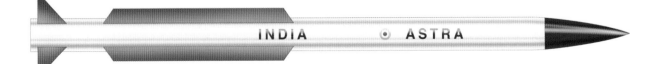

V3B Kukri. The V3C was soon superseded by the larger U-Darter, with short-/medium-range capability. The U-Darter was in service with the Cheetah fighter until its retirement in 2008. The V4 or R-Darter is an active radar-guided, all-aspect BVR missile that entered South African service in the mid 1990s, and was also retired together with the Cheetah. Although the missile is very similar in appearance to the Israeli Derby, South African engineers deny any Israeli involvement in its design. Development is now focused on the A-Darter, since 2006 a joint South African–Brazilian programme to

▲ PL-12

In PLA service the fire-and-forget PL-12 has been integrated on the indigenous J-8F and J-10 fighters, as well as the J-11B, a licence-built Su-27. Details of the all-important missile seeker are scarce, but it has been reported to be a locally produced active seeker, perhaps developed with either Russian or Israeli assistance.

Specifications

Length overall: 3930mm (12ft 11in)	Range: 90km (56 miles)
Fuselage diameter: 203mm (8in)	Speed: Mach 4
Wingspan: 670mm (26.4in)	Powerplant: Solid fuel dual-thrust rocket motor
Launch weight: 199kg (434lb)	Guidance system: Inertial with terminal active radar

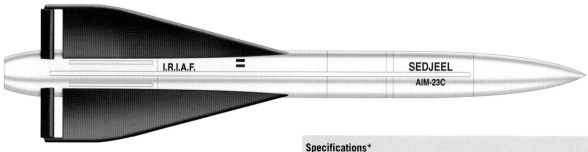

▲ AIM-23C Sedjil

An indigenous Iranian development intended to arm the F-14A, the Sedjil is an air-launched version of the MIM-23 HAWK SAM. Integration on the F-14A appears to have begun during the Iran–Iraq War, but ran into problems. Today, only a handful of Tomcats are likely adapted to carry the Sedjil.

Specifications*

Length overall: 5.08m (16ft 8in)	Range: 40km (25 miles)
Fuselage diameter: 37cm (14.5in)	Speed: Mach 2.5
Wingspan: 1190mm (46.9in)	Powerplant: Aerojet M112 dual-thrust solid-fueled rocket
Launch weight: 635kg (1400lb)	
Warhead weight: 74kg (163lb) blast-fragmentation	*Data is for the MIM-23B, from which AIM-23C is derived

Specifications

Length overall: 3620mm (11ft 10.5in)	Warhead weight: 23kg (50.7lb)
Fuselage diameter: 160mm (6.3in)	Range: 50km (31 miles)
Wingspan: 640mm (25in)	Speed: Mach 4
Launch weight: 118kg (260lb)	Powerplant: n/a
	Guidance system: Active radar

▲ Derby

A radar-guided weapon intended for use from close range to BVR, the Derby offers an active radar seeker, lookdown/shootdown capability and a LOBL mode for close-quarters dogfights. Operators include Brazil and Chile, both of which have integrated the missile into upgraded F-5E/F fighters.

produce a new IR-guided short-range AAM. Offering high levels of agility through thrust-vectoring, the missile has an IIR seeker and is planned to be integrated on South African Gripens by 2015, as well as being offered for export. Initial test firings were conducted in 2010. Brazil, meanwhile, also has

experience in short-range AAMs, having fielded and developed the Piranha. China has also made significant progress in AAM development, with the latest PL-12 being a fire-and-forget BVR weapon in the AMRAAM class. Development began in 1997 and the PL-12 began its test campaign in 2005.

Specifications

Length overall: 3000mm (9ft 10in)	Warhead weight: 11kg (24lb)
Fuselage diameter: 160mm (6.3in)	Range: 15km (9.3 miles)
Wingspan: 500mm (19.7in)	Speed: Mach 3.5 or better
Launch weight: 120kg (264lb)	Guidance system: Infrared

▼ Python IV

Developed partly in response to the Soviet R-73, the Python IV represents a significant improvement over the Python III, and includes a host of advanced features, including an all-aspect gimballed seeker that is suitable for extreme off-boresight acquisition and tracking angles, and advanced aerodynamics.

▼ AAM-4 (Type 99)

The latest Japanese products in the AAM field are the Mitsubishi AAM-3 (Type 90) and AAM-4 (illustrated), the former an agile dogfight missile developed from the mid 1980s, and the latter a radar-guided BVR weapon with active radar homing that is replacing the Sparrow in Japan Air Self-Defense Force (JASDF) service since 1999. A follow-on, highly advanced dogfight missile is the AAM-5 (Type 04).

Specifications

Length overall: 3667mm (12ft)	Range: 100km (62 miles)
Fuselage diameter: 203mm (8in)	Speed: Mach 4–5
Wingspan: 800mm (31.5in)	Powerplant: n/a
Launch weight: 222kg (489lb)	Guidance system: Data link + active radar

Specifications

Length overall: 1900mm (6ft 2in)	Range: 6km (3.7 miles)
Fuselage diameter: 90mm (3.5in)	Speed: Mach 2
Launch weight: 20kg (44lb)	Powerplant: Solid fuel rocket motor
Warhead weight: 3kg (6.61lb)	Guidance system: Infrared

▼ TY-90

In the past the French-designed Mistral and the US Stinger surface-launched missiles have been adapted for air launch, as has the Soviet-designed Igla series, but China's TY-90 is presently unique in that it was designed from the outset as an air-to-air weapon for helicopter use. The IR-homing missile is optimized for use against enemy helicopters at low level.

AAMs in combat from 1990

Successive air campaigns fought by Coalition forces over Iraq and the former Yugoslavia have provided an opportunity to test in combat some of the latest generation of AAMs.

THE COALITION AIR forces entered Operation *Desert Storm* in 1991 relying primarily on the proven AIM-7 and AIM-9 families of AAMs for air combat taskings, and despite the presence of British and French AAMs in theatre, only the Sparrow and Sidewinder were successfully deployed in combat.

All examples of the Sparrow used in combat by US aircraft appear to have been of the much-improved AIM-7M variant. In total, 26 Iraqi aircraft fell victim to Sparrows, with 71 AIM-7s being fired to achieve a success rate of 37 per cent. Taking into account examples of the missile that actually failed to be released, were jettisoned, or were lost aboard aircraft that were themselves shot down, a total of 88 Sparrows were expended during the war.

Meanwhile, the Sidewinder scored ten aerial victories in the course of *Desert Storm* in 1991, all but two of these being attributed to the AIM-9M model. The exceptions concerned the two kills scored by the Royal Saudi Air Force (RSAF), whose F-15Cs continued to deploy the previous-generation AIM-9P. The success rate of the Sidewinder must be seen against the fact that a total of 86 such weapons were expended during the course of the war.

Iraqi experiences

The Coalition air forces did not have it all their own way over Iraq, however. Despite their impressive final kill tally, a significant number of missiles failed to make their target, while the IrAF scored at least one confirmed victory (a MiG-25PDS and R-40 claiming a US Navy F/A-18C) and likely more. Persistent reports suggest that IrAF MiG-25s also succeeded in downing a USAF F-15C with an R-40R on 30 January 1991. With the local air defence system downed by Coalition air strikes, Iraqi MiG-21s saw only limited use, with two examples shot down during the type's only operational sortie of the campaign. MiG-23s fared better, firing missiles (inconclusively) against USAF F-111Fs on the first night of the war.

More unusual Coalition kills of the war involved the use of guided and unguided air-to-ground weapons to destroy Iraqi aircraft. Instances included: the destruction of a MiG-25 rolling on its runway by an RAF Tornado armed with JP233 weapons dispensers; destruction of an SA.321H helicopter by an AGM-62 Walleye launched from either a US Navy A-6 or F/A-18; and the use of a GBU-10 guided bomb launched from a USAF F-15E to destroy a Hughes 500 helicopter while it was in the hover.

It seems certain that at least a few AIM-120As were rushed to the region during the conflict, but this weapon was not utilized in combat (although some accounts do suggest non-official use of the AIM-120 during the war). For its first official combat use, the AMRAAM would have to wait until 27 December

▶ **Weapons load**
A 33rd Tactical Fighter Wing F-15C Eagle aircraft pulls into a climb, showing its two AIM-9 Sidewinder missiles on each wing and four AIM-120 advanced medium-range air-to-air missiles (AMRAAMs) on its fuselage weapons stations.

▲ **AIM-9M Sidewinder**

The AIM-9M was the standard dogfight AAM for US fighters in *Desert Storm*. However, with so many engagements conducted in BVR scenarios, the number of Sidewinder kills was restricted. Over the former Yugoslavia, the AIM-9M notched up another two close-range kills against Serbian-flown J-21 Jastreb jets.

Specifications	
Length overall: 2900mm (9ft 6in)	Range: 16km (10 miles)
Fuselage diameter: 127mm (5in)	Speed: Supersonic
Wingspan: 635mm (25in)	Powerplant: Thiokol Hercules and Bermite MK 36
Launch weight: 86kg (190lb)	Mod 11; single-stage, solid-fuel rocket motor
Warhead weight: 11.3kg (25lb)	Guidance system: Passive infrared

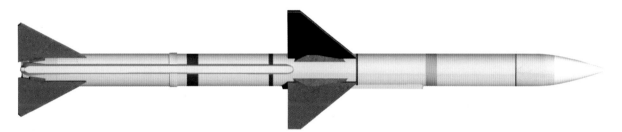

▲ **AIM-7M Sparrow**

The combat performance of the later-model Sparrows was far superior to the early generation. The 'Mike' was a much-improved model, and the first to feature a monopulse seeker to allow a true lookdown/shootdown capability. The AIM-7M also expanded its low-altitude capability and had enhanced ECCM characteristics.

Specifications	
Length overall: 3700mm (12ft 1.7in)	Range: 55km (34.2 miles)
Fuselage diameter: 200mm (7.87in)	Speed: Mach 3.58
Wingspan: 1000mm (39in)	Powerplant: Solid-propellant rocket fuel motor
Launch weight: 227kg (500lb)	Guidance system: Pulse-Doppler radar
Warhead weight: 40kg (88lb)	

1992, when an F-16C and AIM-120A downed an IrAF MiG-25 over Iraq during Operation *Southern Watch*. This victory also marked the first kill by the F-16 in USAF hands. From the end of *Desert Storm* until the invasion of Iraq in 2003, Coalition fighters were responsible for policing the Iraqi 'no-fly zone'. According to US accounts, the first three AMRAAM launches under combat conditions during this period resulted in two kills, both achieved by F-16s against Iraqi aircraft. The second victim was an IrAF MiG-23 downed on 17 January 1993, although Iraqi sources dispute both claims.

The game of cat and mouse over Iraq continued, and during Operation *Desert Fox* in 1998 Coalition warplanes were again in action against the IrAF. US Navy F-14s are known to have launched AIM-54Cs against IrAF MiG-23MLs. Although both missiles missed their targets, one of the MiGs ran out of fuel and crashed on landing. In January 1999, F-14s again clashed with MiG-23s, with at least one more AIM-

54C being fired, again missing its target. As well as having experienced combat against the AIM-54 since the days of the Iran–Iraq War, the MiG-23s used French- and Soviet/Russian-supplied ECM equipment to evade a number of AMRAAM shots.

The air wars over the former Yugoslavia saw more extensive combat use of the AMRAAM, with kills recorded during Operation *Deny Flight* in 1995 and Operation *Allied Force* in 1999. *Deny Flight* involved a 'no-fly zone' policing effort over Bosnia. When a group of eight Yugoslav aircraft violated the zone on 28 February 1994, USAF F-16Cs were quick to respond. The Serbian pilots refused to turn around, and so the USAF jets accounted for four J-21 Jastrebs. The first three kills were recorded by a pair of F-16Cs, and the final J-21 was claimed by another pair of F-16Cs.

During *Allied Force*, F-16s operated by the USAF and Royal Netherlands Air Force (RNAF) launched

at least three AMRAAMs, claiming two MiG-29s destroyed. USAF F-15Cs also made their mark, downing four more MiG-29s in the same campaign. All six of the air-to-air kills scored during *Allied Force* involved BVR engagements, conducted under close guidance from local Airborne Warning And Control System (AWACS) platforms.

The increasing importance of UAVs in air combat has resulted in several nations registering UAV kills with AAMs. During the run-up to the 2003 invasion

DESERT STORM MISSILE KILLS

Date	Operator	Launch aircraft	Weapon	Victim	Operator
17 January 1991	Iraq	MiG-25PDS	R-40	F/A-18C	US Navy
17 January 1991	USAF	F-15C	AIM-7M	MiG-29	Iraq
17 January 1991	USAF	F-15C	AIM-7M	Mirage F.1EQ	Iraq
17 January 1991	USAF	F-15C	AIM-7M	Mirage F.1EQ	Iraq
17 January 1991	USAF	F-15C	AIM-7M	Mirage F.1BQ	Iraq
17 January 1991	US Navy	F/A-18C	AIM-7M	MiG-21bis	Iraq
17 January 1991	US Navy	F/A-18C	AIM-9M	MiG-21bis	Iraq
17 January 1991	USAF	F-15C	AIM-7M	MiG-29	Iraq
17 January 1991	USAF	F-15C	AIM-7M	MiG-29	Iraq
19 January 1991	USAF	F-15C	AIM-7M	MiG-25PD	Iraq
19 January 1991	USAF	F-15C	AIM-7M	MiG-25PD	Iraq
19 January 1991	USAF	F-15C	AIM-7M	MiG-29	Iraq
19 January 1991	USAF	F-15C	AIM-7M	Mirage F.1EQ	Iraq
19 January 1991	USAF	F-15C	AIM-7M	Mirage F.1EQ	Iraq
24 January 1991	Saudi Arabia	F-15C	AIM-9P	Mirage F.1EQ	Iraq
24 January 1991	Saudi Arabia	F-15C	AIM-9P	Mirage F.1EQ	Iraq
26 January 1991	USAF	F-15C	AIM-7M	MiG-23MF	Iraq
26 January 1991	USAF	F-15C	AIM-7M	MiG-23MF	Iraq
26 January 1991	USAF	F-15C	AIM-7M	MiG-23MF	Iraq
27 January 1991	USAF	F-15C	AIM-9M	MiG-23MF	Iraq
27 January 1991	USAF	F-15C	AIM-9M	MiG-23MF	Iraq
27 January 1991	USAF	F-15C	AIM-7M	MiG-23MF	Iraq
27 January 1991	USAF	F-15C	AIM-7M	Mirage F.1EQ	Iraq
29 January 1991	USAF	F-15C	AIM-7M	MiG-23	Iraq
29 January 1991	USAF	F-15C	AIM-7M	MiG-23	Iraq
2 February 1991	USAF	F-15C	AIM-7M and cannon	Il-76	Iraq
6 February 1991	USAF	F-15C	AIM-9M	MiG-21bis	Iraq
6 February 1991	USAF	F-15C	AIM-9M	MiG-21bis	Iraq
6 February 1991	USAF	F-15C	AIM-9M	Su-25K	Iraq
6 February 1991	USAF	F-15C	AIM-9M	Su-25K	Iraq
6 February 1991	US Navy	F-14A	AIM-9M	Mi-17	Iraq
6 February 1991	USAF	F-15C	AIM-7M	Su-22M-3K	Iraq
7 February 1991	USAF	F-15C	AIM-7M	Su-22M-3K	Iraq
7 February 1991	USAF	F-15C	AIM-7M	Su-22M-3K	Iraq
7 February 1991	USAF	F-15C	AIM-7M	Mi-24	Iraq
11 February 1991	USAF	F-15C	AIM-7M	SA.330 Puma/Mi-8	Iraq
11 February 1991	USAF	F-15C	AIM-7M	Mi-8	Iraq

MISSILE KILLS OVER THE FORMER YUGOSLAVIA

Date	Operator	Launch aircraft	Weapon	Victim	Operator
28 February 1994	USAF	F-16C	AIM-120A	J-21	Serbia
28 February 1994	USAF	F-16C	AIM-120A	J-21	Serbia
28 February 1994	USAF	F-16C	AIM-9M	J-21	Serbia
28 February 1994	USAF	F-16C	AIM-9M	J-21	Serbia
24 March 1999	Netherlands	F-16A-MLU	AIM-120A	MiG-29	Serbia
24 March 1999	USAF	F-15C	AIM-120C	MiG-29	Serbia
24 March 1999	USAF	F-15C	AIM-120C	MiG-29	Serbia
26 March 1999	USAF	F-15C	AIM-120C	MiG-29	Serbia
26 March 1999	USAF	F-15C	AIM-120C	MiG-29	Serbia
4 May 1999	USAF	F-16C	AIM-120C	MiG-29	Serbia

of Iraq, the IrAF made concerted efforts to down US-operated UAVs. In December 2002, an IrAF MiG-25 destroyed a USAF-operated RQ-1A Predator UAV with a guided missile. In the Middle East, the first reported combat use of the Python V AAM came when an IDF/AF F-16 downed a UAV operated by Hezbollah during the 2006 Lebanon War. The Python V had entered service the previous year, following a secretive development programme that began around 1999.

Israel and Syria

Regular clashes between Syrian and Israeli fighters have also led to AAM kills in recent years. Notably, on 14 September 2001 a pair of Israeli F-15Cs used an AIM-9M and a Python IV to down a pair of SyAAF MiG-29s sent to intercept them. Indeed, these were not the first MiG-29 kills recorded by the IDF/AF, with another pair of the Soviet-built fighters taken out by F-15Cs on 2 June 1989. In turn, a Syrian MiG-23 accounted for an Israeli UAV in April 2002, hunting and destroying the drone with an

AAM after it had crossed the Syrian border from Jordanian airspace.

Frequent skirmishes between Greek and Turkish warplanes over the Aegean Sea have almost certainly led to further AAM kills. Among the most publicized incidents is the shooting down of a Turkish Air Force (TuAF) F-16D by an Hellenic Air Force (HAF) Mirage 2000EG in October 1996, the Greek pilot having fired a Magic 2 AAM. Other Greek and Turkish fighters have been lost during hard manoeuvering in the course of mock dogfights following interceptions.

The wars that have afflicted the former USSR since its dissolution have also seen their fair share of combat use of AAMs, although many details remain unconfirmed. During the First Chechen War, a Russian Su-27 used an R-73 to down a Chechen-operated L-39 on 4 September 1994. A further Russian air-to-air kill was reportedly recorded by a Su-27 during the South Ossetia War, the victim in this instance being a Georgian-flown Su-25 brought down over Tskhinval on 9 August 2008.

▼ AIM-120C AMRAAM

The AMRAAM arrived just too late for active participation in Operation *Desert Storm*, becoming operational in September 1991. Key features of the missile include a fragmentation warhead and combined proximity and impact fuses. This is the clipped-wing AIM-120C version, which can be carried internally.

Specifications

Length overall: 3700mm (12ft)	Speed: Mach 4
Fuselage diameter: 180mm (7in)	Powerplant: High-performance directed rocket
Wingspan: 530mm (20.7in)	motor
Launch weight: 152kg (335lb)	Guidance system: Inertial navigation system
Warhead weight: 23kg (50lb)	(INS), active radar
Range: 48km (30 miles)	

Chapter 2

Air-to-Surface Missiles

The first effective guided air-to-surface missiles (ASMs) were deployed by the German *Luftwaffe* in World War II. Already at this early stage, the development of such weapons followed two very different paths: longer-ranged, heavyweight cruise missiles designed to destroy strategic targets, and shorter-ranged missiles intended to destroy important tactical objectives such as bridges and warships. Immediately after the war, the superpowers concentrated their efforts on fielding nuclear-armed cruise missiles, before the 1960s saw the emergence of the first generation of practical tactical air-to-ground missiles (AGMs), including those dedicated to the destruction of enemy air defence systems.

◀ **Tankbuster**

An A-10 Thunderbolt II breaks over the Pacific Alaska Range Complex, April 2007, during live-fire training. This ground-attack aircraft is from the 355th Fighter Squadron from Eielson Air Force Base, Alaska. The 355th Fighter Squadron is tasked with providing mission-ready A-10s and a search-and-rescue capability, to be deployed in Alaska and sites worldwide.

Early Cold War strategic ASMs

At the end of the war, a number of German V-1 flying bombs fell into Soviet and US hands, and inspired both nations to develop nuclear-armed air-launched cruise missiles (ALCMs).

THE GERMAN-DEVELOPED V-1 flying bomb was technologically crude, but it demonstrated significant potential, and on both sides of the Iron Curtain it served as a conceptual predecessor for what would later become known as cruise missiles. After developing a range of reverse-engineered V-1 copies, the Soviets abandoned these efforts in favour of a new missile inspired by the design of the MiG-15 jet fighter and developed from 1947. This was the KS-1 Komet, which received the NATO/Air Standardization Coordinating Committee (ASCC) reporting name AS-1 'Kennel'. It was primarily developed for anti-shipping use, although it also had potential for use against strategic land targets. The missile was based on a scaled-down MiG-15 with a reduced-power turbojet engine, and was intended for carriage by the Tu-4 bomber, a version of the B-29 Superfortress. Later, the KS-1 would arm missile-carrier versions of the Tu-16 jet bomber.

The KS-1 required the launch aircraft to illuminate the target for the duration of the flight. In order to prove the guidance system, a manned version of the KS-1 was developed and tested from 1951, paving the way for the missile to enter service in 1953. The missile was also exported (with the Tu-16) to Egypt and Indonesia. Versions of the Komet

missile for foreign service were only equipped for deploying conventional warheads, while the Soviet-operated KS-1 could also mount a nuclear warhead.

While the KS-1 had been inspired by the aerodynamics of the MiG-15, the subsequent Kh-20 (AS-3 'Kangaroo') employed the basic configuration of the MiG-21 supersonic jet fighter (in fact it was based on the experimental I-7, a progenitor of the MiG-21). Compared to its predecessor, the Kh-20 was optimized for use against land targets, chiefly political and industrial centres and major military installations. Allied with the Tu-95K bomber, the Kh-20 was turbojet-powered and used an inertial guidance system that received mid-course updates from the launch aircraft. Armed with a megaton-class nuclear warhead, the Kh-20 entered Soviet service in 1959.

While the KS-1 and Kh-20 had been developed by Mikoyan-Gurevich, responsibility for a new family of ALCMs fell on the Bereznyak design bureau (later Raduga). The KSR-2 (AS-5 'Kelt') missile was powered by a liquid-fuel rocket motor and was a dual-role anti-shipping and land-attack weapon. It entered service with the Tu-16 in 1962 and was also exported (in conventionally armed form) to Egypt, which employed the weapon in

▼ KS-1 Komet (AS-1 'Kennel')

The first ALCM to enter service in the USSR, the Mikoyan-Gurevich developed KS-1 was also adapted for use by naval and land forces. The FKR-1 was issued as a battlefield cruise missile, the S-2 was used by coastal defence forces, and the KSS was employed by surface warships of the Soviet fleet.

Specifications

Length overall: 8290mm (27ft 2.4in)	Range: 80km (50 miles)
Fuselage diameter: 1150m (45.3in)	Speed: 1060km/h (659mph)
Wingspan: 4720mm (185.8in)	Powerplant: Klimov RD-500K turbojet
Launch weight: 2735kg (6030lb)	Guidance system: Semi-active radar with
Warhead weight: 800kg (1764lb)	passive terminal homing

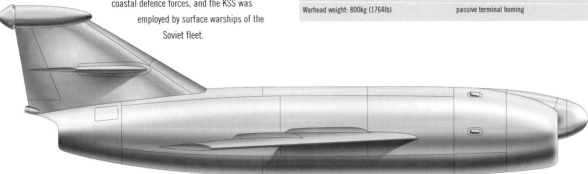

the 1973 Yom Kippur War. The KSR-11 used the same airframe as the KSR-2 – and retained the same ASCC reporting name – but was adapted as an anti-radar weapon, again with conventional-only payload.

Hound Dog for the B-52

The Americans and the British both had high hopes of introducing a new class of weapon, the air-launched ballistic missile (ALBM). This was first developed as the GAM-87 Skybolt, a joint US–British project to arm USAF B-52s and RAF Vulcan bombers (at one stage, plans were also made to equip RAF Victors, and even VC10 airliners, with the Skybolt). Yet Skybolt was cancelled in 1962, falling foul of budgetary and political problems. Instead, within Strategic Air Command (SAC), the

GAM-77 (redesignated AGM-28 under the Tri-Service Aircraft Designation System introduced in 1962) Hound Dog was the only available long-range air-launched strategic missile for much of the Cold War. Serving from 1961 until 1976 – when it was finally replaced by the new AGM-69 Short-Range Attack Missile (SRAM) – it was the first such weapon to attain operational capability in the United States. Armed with a one megaton nuclear warhead, the turbojet-powered Hound Dog used an inertial guidance system that received updates from the launch aircraft immediately prior to launch, and was provided with ECM to defeat Soviet air defences. The AGM-28 armed SAC's B-52G/H fleet, with just under 600 missiles in service by the early 1960s.

In the UK, the air-launched standoff bomb (the term 'cruise missile' was only adopted subsequently)

▼ AGM-28 Hound Dog

A notable feature of the Hound Dog was its ability to provide additional thrust for the B-52 launch aircraft. Linked to the fuel supply system of the Stratofortress, the missile's J52 engine could be powered up to aid a rapid take-off by the bomber. Each B-52G/H could carry two such missiles, one under each wing.

Specifications

Length overall: 12.95m (42ft 6in)	Range: 1263km (785 miles)
Fuselage diameter: n/a	Speed: Mach 2.1
Height: 2800mm (110in)	Powerplant: Pratt & Whitney J52-P-3 Turbojet
Wingspan: 3700mm (145.6in)	Guidance system: Inertial Navigation System
Launch weight: 4603kg (10,147lb)	with star-tracker correction
Warhead weight: 790kg (1742lb)	

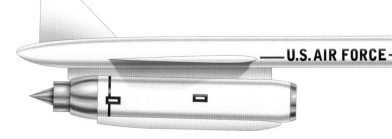

▼ Kh-20 (AS-3 'Kangaroo')

Carried exclusively by the Tu-95K 'Bear-B' bomber, the enormous Kh-20 remained in service until the late 1970s, when it was superseded by a new generation of cruise missiles. For guidance it used a preprogrammed autopilot for launch and climb, an autopilot with command guidance for mid-course flight, and a preprogrammed dive to target.

Specifications

Length overall: 14.9m (49ft)	Range: 650km (404 miles)
Fuselage diameter: 1900mm (74.8in)	Speed: 2280km/h (1417mph)
Wingspan: 9200mm (362in)	Powerplant: Tumansky R-11 twin spool turbojet
Launch weight: 11,000kg (24,251lb)	with afterburner
Warhead weight: 2300kg (5071lb)	Guidance system: Beam riding

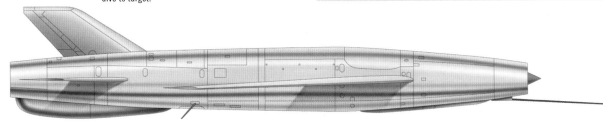

▲ **Storage**
Avro Blue Steel standoff nuclear weapons stand in rows in a hangar somewhere in the United Kingdom, 1973.

was conceived as a means of improving the efficiency and survivability of the Vulcan and Victor bombers of the RAF's V-Force. The Blue Steel used a liquid-fuel rocket motor to achieve supersonic performance and a single example could be carried in a semi-recessed installation on adapted versions of the Vulcan B.Mk 2 and Victor B.Mk 2. A relatively short-ranged weapon, the Blue Steel was intended to obviate the need for the launch aircraft to approach heavily defended targets, and it was declared operational with the Vulcans of the RAF's No. 617 Squadron in 1962. With the cancellation of the Skybolt, the Blue Steel remained the primary weapon of the V-Force until it lost its strategic tasking in 1969, handing over responsibility to the Royal Navy's submarine-launched Polaris missile.

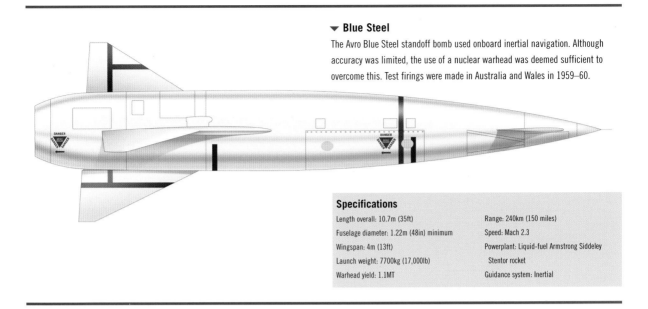

▼ Blue Steel

The Avro Blue Steel standoff bomb used onboard inertial navigation. Although accuracy was limited, the use of a nuclear warhead was deemed sufficient to overcome this. Test firings were made in Australia and Wales in 1959–60.

Specifications

Length overall: 10.7m (35ft)	Range: 240km (150 miles)
Fuselage diameter: 1.22m (48in) minimum	Speed: Mach 2.3
Wingspan: 4m (13ft)	Powerplant: Liquid-fuel Armstrong Siddeley
Launch weight: 7700kg (17,000lb)	Stentor rocket
Warhead yield: 1.1MT	Guidance system: Inertial

Late Cold War strategic ASMs

Continuing improvements in SAMs and fighter defences led to the requirement for a new generation of more capable air-launched strategic missiles from the late 1960s.

WITH THE RETIREMENT of the Blue Steel in 1969, it was left to the Americans and Soviets to develop a new class of more capable ALCMs, while France also introduced its first such weapon in the mid 1980s.

In the US, the AGM-69 SRAM emerged as the successor to the Hound Dog. Conceptually very different to its predecessor, the SRAM was small enough to be carried internally by the B-52 or the FB-111 and used a ballistic-type trajectory and a two-stage solid-fuel rocket motor. Up to 20 examples could be carried by the B-52G/H, both internally (eight) and on underwing pylons (12), while the FB-111A could carry six.

Developed from 1964, the SRAM became operational in 1972 and was intended to be used against fixed targets including air defence sites on the route to the primary target(s). The SRAM was retired from service in 1990 after some 1500 had been built.

In the Soviet Union, development of liquid-fuelled cruise missiles continued at the Raduga bureau, beginning with the Kh-22 (AS-4 'Kitchen') that was designed in parallel with the Tu-22 strike aircraft. Development of the Kh-22 began in 1958 and from the outset the weapon was to be used for land or maritime attack, with either an active radar seeker for operations against single targets, or an inertial dead-reckoning system for attacking large-area targets. The warhead was either nuclear or conventional high-explosive/armour-piercing.

The Kh-22 became a long-lived and critically important weapon, entering service on the Tu-22 (which carried one such missile) in 1967. From 1975 an improved Kh-22M began to arm the Tu-95K-22 (two missiles) and Tu-22M (up to three missiles). Upgraded a number of times, the Kh-22 was ultimately fielded with a third guidance option, when a passive radar seeker was added for use in the anti-radar mission.

Similar in concept to the Kh-22 was the KSR-5 (AS-6 'Kingfish'), which armed missile-carrier versions of the Tu-16 from 1974. Primarily utilized for anti-shipping strikes, the missile could also be applied against large land targets. In common with its forebear, the KSR-2, the basic active radar homing KSR-5 was also adapted for the anti-radar mission, resulting in the KSR-5P version of 1979, with a new, passive seeker.

Cold War cruise

In the early 1980s, the first of a new generation of cruise missiles became available, and both the US and USSR deployed such weapons as a relatively inexpensive way of maximizing the offensive value and survivability of their respective bomber fleets. Eventually, both the US and USSR opted for similar solutions, fielding long-range, turbofan-powered missiles designed to fly at low level to evade increasingly sophisticated enemy air defences. These weapons were relatively small, permitting multiple carriage internally, as well as on external hardpoints.

Development of the AGM-86 ALCM for the B-52G/H began in 1968, although a development contract was not issued until 1974. The initial AGM-86A introduced Terrain Contour Matching (TERCOM) inertial navigation to achieve a high level of accuracy, but did not make it into service. After a fly-off competitor against the AGM-109, an air-launched version of the surface-launched Tomahawk cruise missile, the longer-range AGM-

86B version was declared the winner, and entered production and service in 1981. The B-52H can carry 20 ALCMs: eight internally and 12 on two underwing pylons.

The Soviet Kh-55 (AS-15 'Kent') was developed to arm the new Tu-95MS and Tu-160 strategic bombers and entered service in 1983. The Tu-95MS can carry six such weapons internally and up to 10 more on external hardpoints, while the Tu-160 can carry 12 in two internal bays. Like the ALCM, the Kh-55 is a subsonic weapon initially fielded with a thermonuclear warhead. In contrast to the ALCM, the extended-range version, unofficially known as the Kh-55SM, makes use of conformal fuel tanks.

In order to replace its fleet of Mirage IVA strategic bombers armed with free-fall nuclear bombs, France developed an its own ALCM, the ASMP. The missile entered service on the 18 upgraded Mirage IVPs in 1986 before equipping this aircraft's successor in the nuclear strike role, the Mirage 2000N, and the French Navy's Super Etendard.

▼ AGM-69A SRAM

Boeing's SRAM was carried operationally by the B-52G/H and FB-111A. There were plans for it to be introduced on both the B-1A and later the B-1B. These were dropped in turn (the B-1A being cancelled) and the weapon was finally removed from the inventory following the end of the Cold War.

Specifications

Length overall: 4830mm (15ft 10.2in) (with tail fairing)	Range: 169km (105 miles)
	Speed: Mach 3.5
Fuselage diameter: 450mm (17.5in)	Powerplant: Lockheed SR75-LP-1 two-stage
Wingspan: 760mm (30in)	solid-fuel rocket motor
Launch weight: 1010kg (2230lb)	Guidance system: General Precision/Kearfott KT-
Warhead weight: n/a	76 inertial and Stewart-Warner radar altimeter

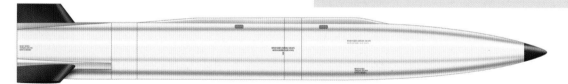

▼ Kh-55 (AS-15 'Kent')

Seen here with its pop-out wings and turbofan engine deployed for flight, the Kh-55 is a fully autonomous terrain-following weapon. After a rapid development, the missile began operational trials in advance of the USAF's equivalent ALCM.

Specifications

Length overall: 2300mm (7ft 6.6in)	Range: 15km (9.3 miles)
Fuselage diameter: 180mm (7.06in)	Speed: 1000km/h (62mph)
Wingspan: 580mm (22.8in)	Powerplant: Smokeless nitramite solid propellant
Launch weight: 100kg (220.5lb)	rocket motor
Warhead weight: 30kg (66lb)	Guidance system: Radio commands

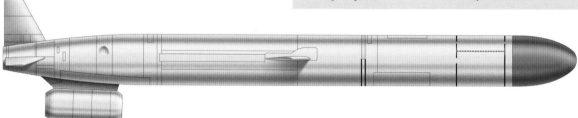

▼ ASMP

Powered by a liquid-fuel ramjet and a solid-fuel rocket booster, the supersonic ASMP was developed by Aérospatiale from 1978. An inertial platform provides terrain-following flight to the target. Live test launches began in 1983.

Specifications

Length overall: 5.38m (17ft 8in)	Range: 80–300km (50–62 miles)
Fuselage diameter: 300mm (11.8in)	Speed: Mach 2 to Mach 3
Wingspan: n/a	Powerplant: Liquid fuelled ramjet
Launch weight: 860kg (1896lb)	Guidance system: Infrared
Warhead weight: 150–300KT	

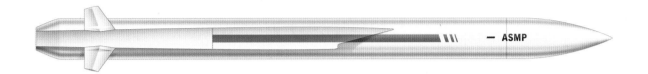

— ASMP

Modern strategic ASMs

Following the end of the Cold War, the importance of the nuclear mission was diminished, and several ALCMs began to be adapted to carry conventional warheads.

THE FIRST OF the Cold War-era cruise missiles to 'go conventional' in the USAF inventory was the ALCM. From 1986 examples of the AGM-86B began to be modified to AGM-86C standard, also known as the Conventional ALCM (CALCM). This replaces the nuclear payload with a 909kg (2000lb) blast-fragmentation warhead, and also introduces GPS guidance. For use against hardened targets, an AGM-86D CALCM was first tested in 2001, this carrying a penetrating warhead.

While the B-52H's ALCM was adapted for the conventional mission, the stealthy AGM-129 Advanced Cruise Missile (ACM), carried by the same aircraft, was an exclusively nuclear-armed weapon. Development of this missile began in 1982, with production deliveries commencing in 1990. Carrying

the same thermonuclear warhead as the AGM-86B, the ACM featured forward-swept wings and tailfins, and TERCOM guidance. Before the ACM was decommissioned from 2007, the B-52H could carry 20 such weapons, eight of them internally.

Russia followed the US lead in developing conventional versions of its main ALCM, with the Kh-555 modification of the Kh-55. As well as a new warhead, the Kh-555 adds electro-optical terminal guidance to provide the required accuracy. Previously, and apparently also inspired by US developments, the USSR fielded the Kh-15 (AS-16 'Kickback') as an SRAM to arm the Tu-160 and Tu-22M-3. Also using a ballistic profile, the Kh-15 began operational trials in 1988 and is available in two guidance versions: inertial navigation for use against area targets (with a

▼ AGM-129 ACM

Once envisaged as a successor to the AGM-86, the ACM was cut short in production at 460 units. The AGM-129 was carried only by the B-52H, but began to be decommissioned in 2007 under the Moscow Treaty guidelines. The ACM was selected for retirement over the more prolific ALCM primarily on cost grounds. Key features of the missile were its concealed engine intake and forward-swept wings.

Specifications

Length overall: 6350m (20ft 10in)	Speed: 800km/h (500mph)
Fuselage diameter: 705mm (27.8in)	Powerplant: Williams Intenational F112-WR-100
Wingspan: 3100mm (122in)	Turbofan
Launch weight: 1334kg (3500lb)	Guidance system: Inertial guidance system
Range: 3704km (2000 nautical miles)	enhanced with Lidar TERCOM

nuclear warhead), and passive radar homing for use against radar installations. The latter model was reportedly abandoned as a result of political machinations. An anti-ship version, the Kh-15S, has a conventional warhead and an active radar seeker, but this may not have entered service.

The Kh-101 designation refers to an all-new Russian cruise missile, a long-range, subsonic weapon that features a low-observable design and is intended to replace the Kh-55/555. The Kh-101 was first observed in 2008, during trials aboard a Tu-95MS bomber equipped for external carriage of eight of the missiles. The dimensions of the Kh-101 probably preclude internal carriage in the Tu-95MS. It was reported in mid 2008 that as many as eight Tu-95MS aircraft had been upgraded for deploying the Kh-101. The missile's guidance system adds electro-optical correction, and there may also be a GPS receiver for improved accuracy. The Kh-102 is reportedly a nuclear-armed version utilizing the same airframe and powerplant.

France's successor to the ASMP is the ASMP-A, the revised designation signifying Air-Sol Moyenne

Portée Amélioré, or Air-to-Surface Medium Range – Improved. The weapon entered service with the Mirage 2000N in 2009 and was declared operational with the French Air Force Rafale in 2010.

In China, missile-carrying H-6 bombers were for long reliant upon adaptations of the vintage YJ-6 anti-ship missiles for their long-range needs. More recently, development has focused on a considerably modernised development of the YJ-6, the YJ-63, an air-launched land-attack cruise missile (LACM) for use by the H-6H bomber.

In service since around 2005, the YJ-63 has a turbojet powerplant and inertial guidance with satellite input and mid-course updates provided by the launch aircraft. Terminal guidance is apparently achieved using passive homing, or via radio command. An all-new LACM is represented by the DH-10, which may be based on technology from the Russian Kh-55, acquired from Ukraine. The DH-10 is in service as a ground-launched cruise missile with the PLA but may also provide the basis for an air-launched missile that has been noted on the modernised H-6K bomber.

▼ Kh-15 (AS-16 'Kickback')

The Kh-15 is carried by the Tu-160 (24 weapons in two internal bays) and the Tu-22M-3 (six internal and four external). Like the SRAM, the Kh-15 uses a ballistic flight profile, accelerating to maximum speed and entering the stratosphere before assuming the correct trajectory and diving upon the target.

Specifications

Length overall: 4780m (15ft 8.2in)	Range: 300km (160 nautical miles)
Fuselage diameter: 455mm (17.9in)	Speed: Up to Mach 5
Wingspan: 920mm (362in)	Powerplant: n/a
Launch weight: 1200kg (2650lb)	Guidance system: Inertial, active radar or anti-radiation
Warhead weight: 150kg (331lb)	

Specifications

Length overall: 5380mm (17ft 8in)	Range: n/a
Fuselage diameter: 300mm (11.8in)	Speed: Mach 2 – Mach 3
Wingspan: n/a	Powerplant: Liquid-fuelled ramjet
Launch weight: 860kg (1896lb)	Guidance system: Infrared
Warhead weight: n/a	

▼ ASMP-A

France's new-generation air-launched nuclear missile is the ASMP-A, tailored for carriage by the Air Force and Navy Standard F3 Rafale fighter. By 2011 the ASMP-A will have replaced the ASMP in French service. Improvements have been made to the missile's range, trajectory options and penetration capability.

▲ YJ-63

A further development of the YJ-6, the YJ-63 is a land-attack cruise missile that provides the armament for the H-6H bomber, each of which can carry two examples underwing. The alternative designation KD-63 is also applied to the weapon. Unlike the YJ-6, the YJ-63 has a cruciform tail unit.

Specifications

Length overall: n/a	Range: 200km (108 nautical miles)
Fuselage diameter: n/a	Speed: Subsonic
Wingspan: n/a	Powerplant: Turbojet
Launch weight: n/a	Guidance system: Inertial + satellite mid-course
Warhead weight: 500kg (1102lb)	correction + terminal

Cold War tactical ASMs

It took some years for the guided ASM to be successfully adapted for launch by tactical aircraft, with early efforts in this direction frequently hampered by primitive guidance.

THE FIRST OF the guided ASMs to enter service in the US was the Bullpup, which became operational with the FJ-4 Fury fighter-bombers of the US Navy, when they embarked aboard USS *Lexington* with these weapons in 1959. Employing command guidance typical of such first-generation ASMs, the Bullpup was steered to its target by the pilot or another crew member, the cockpit of the aircraft being outfitted with a joystick and control box. Bullpup development began in 1953 on the request of the US Navy, with Martin winning the contract in 1954. Initially designated ASM-N-7, the missile was first test-launched in 1955. The ASM-N-7 was powered by a solid-fuel rocket motor. An improved ASM-N-7a Bullpup A appeared in 1960, with a liquid-fuel rocket motor.

Larger warhead

With the original missile proving less destructive than anticipated, the ASM-N-7b Bullpup B of 1964 introduced a 454kg (1000lb) warhead and was powered by an increased-thrust motor.

As they had with the Sidewinder, the USAF also adopted the Bullpup (as the GAM-83), at the same time requesting the option of a nuclear warhead. The GAM-83A was equivalent to the Navy's ASM-N-7a Bullpup A, while the GAM-83B was the nuclear version, with an optional kiloton-yield warhead. In

1963, the Bullpup family received new designations in the AGM-12 series. The AGM-12 remained in US service in decreasing numbers into the early 1980s.

Anti-radar Shrike

First of the dedicated anti-radar missiles (ARMs) to enter service in the US was the AGM-45 Shrike. Heralding a new type of air-launched guided missile, the ARM was intended either to destroy enemy ground-based air defence radars, or force them to be shut down, thereby reducing the threat to conventional attack aircraft. The Shrike gained fame as the initial armament of the F-105F/G 'Wild Weasel' defence-suppression aircraft used in combat in Vietnam. Another notable use of the AGM-45 was in two of the 'Black Buck' raids carried out by RAF Vulcans against Port Stanley in the Falklands in 1982, while the Shrike also proved central to the success of the Israeli invasion of Lebanon in the same year. Development of the Shrike (then known as the ASM-N-10) began on the request of the US Navy in 1958, with production from 1963. The Shrike used the AAM-N-6 Sparrow AAM airframe and ultimately could be configured with 13 different seeker heads to target different threat systems. This actually reflected a key drawback of the weapon: the seeker was fixed to a specific frequency, requiring a new seeker head to be employed against each threat type. Furthermore, if

▲ **Mission check**

While the pilot of the A-4 Skyhawk attack aircraft waits, an AGM-62 Walleye missile is checked prior to flying a mission over Vietnam, July 1967.

the targeted radar were to shut down, the Shrike would lose its lock entirely. Since the seeker had a fixed field of view, the missile also had to be launched in the direction of the target.

Service entry for the Shrike occurred in 1965, initially with the US Navy. After numerous sub-variants of the AGM-45A, the AGM-45B was issued in the early 1970s, bringing improvements to the motor and warhead and increasing range and destructive power. Of the 18,500 Shrikes produced, most were delivered to the USAF.

The TV-guided AGM-62 Walleye was in fact an unpowered weapon, and therefore strictly falls into the category of guided bombs. However, it was assigned a missile designation when development began at the US Naval Weapons Center in 1963.

Entering service in 1967, the Walleye used a fire-and-forget mode of guidance, with a TV camera in the nose transmitting imagery back to the cockpit. The pilot selected a target on the screen, gained a lock-on, and the weapon could be released. Thereafter, the weapon would then be guided to the target using the target's contrast pattern, with the pilot only providing course corrections if the Walleye strayed off course. Before long, the Walleye was reclassified as a Guided Weapon, rather than a missile, and subsequent models included the Walleye ER (Extended Range). The next major version was the Mk 5 Walleye II with a more powerful warhead and revised fins. Combat-tested in 1973, the Walleye II was accepted by the Navy in 1974. The Mk 6 was similar to the Walleye II, but carried a low-yield nuclear warhead.

The AGM-65 Maverick, however, was the first US AGM with true fire-and-forget guidance and tactical application. Powered by a dual-thrust solid-fuel rocket motor and schemed as a successor to the

Bullpup, the Maverick began life as a USAF programme in 1965, the first version to enter service being the electro-optically guided AGM-65A, in 1972. With a TV picture transmitted from the missile to a screen in the cockpit, the pilot moved a cursor on the display to select a target, as pioneered in the Walleye. Once locked-on, the missile could be fired and would home in on the target autonomously, using contrast matching. The improved AGM-65B was intended to overcome the problem of limited TV magnification experienced with the first model, and tests began in 1975. The 'Bravo' used scene-magnification to double the size of the TV image and increase clarity. As a result, the pilot could lock-on and fire the missile more quickly, and could make use of greater slant ranges and attack smaller and more distant targets.

The AGM-65C was developed for the USMC, and introduced a change to semi-active laser guidance. However, this version was cancelled in favour of the AGM-65E, which was issued in 1985. It added a penetrating blast-fragmentation warhead of increased weight, with three selectable fusing options, and used a reduced-smoke motor. The AGM-65E is guided to its target by a laser designator, either airborne or ground-based.

Another form of guidance was introduced in 1977, with the AGM-65D equipped with an IIR seeker. The AGM-65D was designed to meet a USAF requirement and allowed targets to be acquired at almost twice the previous range. The missile could be launched at night and in adverse weather, and was intended for use with the Low Altitude Navigation and Targeting Infrared for Night (LANTIRN)

Bullpup ASM designations

Original designation	Post-June 1963 designation
ASM-N-7	AGM-12A
GAM-83	AGM-12A
ASM-N-7a	AGM-12B
GAM-83A	AGM-12B
ASM-N-7b	AGM-12C
GAM-83B	AGM-12D
TGAM-83	ATM-12

targeting system, with the first missiles deployed in 1983. The similar AGM-65F was tailored for the US Navy, and combined the AGM-65D's IIR seeker with the warhead and motor of the AGM-65E. The weapon was primarily focused on the anti-shipping role, with a guidance system for this purpose.

In order to address many of the shortcomings of the Shrike ARM, development of the AGM-78 began in 1966, this time using the RIM-66 Standard naval air-defence missile as its basis. Compared to the Shrike, the Standard had a much increased lock-on capability and could be launched from greater range. In order to hurry the new weapon into service from 1968, the Shrike's seeker was retained for the initial AGM-78A model. The AGM-78B of 1969 added a badly needed gimbaled seeker and a memory circuit that enabled a target to be prosecuted even if the hostile radar was shut down. The reduced-cost AGM-78C was developed for the USAF, while the final AGM-78D added further increased seeker capabilities. Production ended in 1976, by which time over 3000 Standard ARMs had been built.

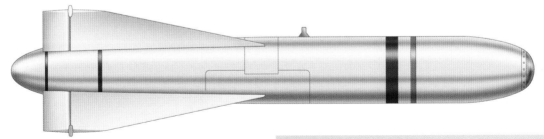

▲ **AGM-62 Walleye I**
Although unpowered, the Walleye was initially classified as a guided missile by the US Navy. The LOBL guidance system of the weapon was accurate as long as the target provided sufficient contrast against the surroundings. The Walleye II introduced a warhead that was more than twice as heavy.

Specifications

Length overall: 3475mm (11ft 3in)

Fuselage diameter: 320mm (12.6in)

Wingspan: 1143mm (45in)

Launch weight: 998kg (1100lb)

Warhead weight: 748kg (825lbs) HE

Range: 26km (16 miles)

Speed: n/a

Powerplant: Ram air turbine (RAT)

Guidance system: Closed-circuit television system

By the early 1990s, the ageing Shrike and Standard had been entirely replaced in US service by a much more capable weapon, the AGM-88 High-speed Anti-Radiation Missile (HARM). In development at the Naval Weapons Center from 1969, the missile stressed high speed to enable the target to be engaged before the operator had the opportunity to shut down the radar. After a first flight in 1975 the initial production AGM-88A was delivered from 1983 and the first combat usage was recorded during US raids on Libya in 1986.

Powered by a dual-thrust solid-fuel rocket motor, the AGM-88A has a blast-fragmentation warhead and a seeker that can be programmed before flight to meet likely threats. The launch options comprise pre-briefed 'blind' launch towards a known target, with autonomous terminal homing; target of opportunity, using the missile seeker to detect a target; and self-protection, in which the coordinates are handed over to the missile seeker by the launch aircraft's radar warning receiver.

Soviet efforts

In the USSR, efforts to create a tactical ASM began with the Kh-66, which was based on an AAM, the RS-2US. The original control system was retained, while the motor came from the R-8 AAM. Design work began in 1966 and the missile was fielded the same year on the MiG-21. Always considered an interim weapon, the Kh-66 was succeeded by the Kh-23 (AS-7 'Kerry'), outwardly similar, but with radio command guidance rather than beam-riding guidance. The Kh-23 armed the MiG-23 series from the early 1970s. In order to rectify the shortcomings of the Kh-23's command guidance, the weapon was refined to produce the Kh-25 (AS-10 'Karen') with laser guidance and a more powerful warhead. The Kh-25 was tested from 1973 and primarily armed the

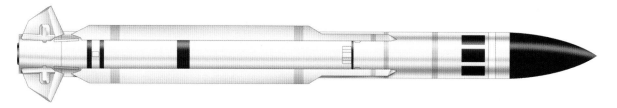

▲ **AGM-78 Standard**

The Standard anti-radar missile (ARM) utilized the airframe of the RIM-66 Standard naval SAM, the initial version emerging as a combination of the RIM-66A with the anti-radar seeker of the AGM-45A Shrike. Powered by a dual-thrust solid rocket, the missile was armed with a blast-fragmentation warhead. In Vietnam 'Wild Weasels' often carried a combination of Standard and Shrike.

Specifications

Length overall: 4600mm (15ft)	Range: 90km (56 miles)
Fuselage diameter: 343mm (13.5in)	Speed: Mach 2
Finspan: 1000mm (39.4in)	Powerplant: Aerojet Mk 27, Mod 4 solid rocket
Launch weight: 610–820kg (1350–1800lb)	motor
Warhead weight: 100kg (220lb)	Guidance system: n/a

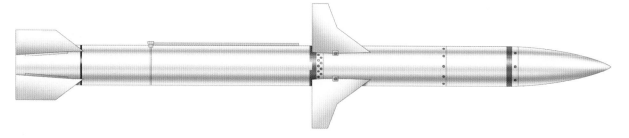

Specifications

Length overall: 4100m (13ft)	Range: 106km (65.9 miles)
Fuselage diameter: 254mm (10in)	Speed: 2280km/h (1420mph)
Wingspan: 1100mm (43.3in)	Powerplant: Thiokol SR113-TC-1 dual-thrust
Launch weight: 355kg (780lb)	rocket engine
Warhead weight: 66kg (150lb)	Guidance system: Active radar homing

▲ **AGM-88A HARM**

Designed to overcome the deficiencies of the Shrike and Standard ARMs, the technologically ambitious HARM suffered a protracted development. Although development began in 1974, with a first flight in 1975, it was 1985 before the initial AGM-88A was declared fully operational, at first with the US Navy.

▼ AGM-122 Sidearm

The AGM-122 was a novel 1980s concept for re-using unwanted AIM-9C AAMs, to create a low-cost air-to-ground ARM that was light enough to arm helicopters. Around 1000 AIM-9Cs were modified with broader-band passive seekers and new proximity fuses. Primary launch platform was the US Marine Corps A-1W.

Specifications

Length overall: 2870mm (9ft 5in)

Fuselage diameter: 127mm (5in)

Wingspan: 630mm (24.8in)

Launch weight: 88.5kg (195lb)

Warhead weight: 11.3kg (25lb)

Range: 16.5km (10 miles)

Speed: Mach 2.3

Powerplant: Hercules Mk 36 Mod 11 solid fuel

Guidance system: Narrow-band passive radar seeker

▼ AGM-123 Skipper II

Unique to the US Navy, the AGM-123 Skipper II was essentially a rocket-boosted laser-guided bomb, comprising a solid-propellant motor added to a 454kg (1000lb) GBU-16 Paveway II. The missile climbed after launch to maximize range.

Specifications

Length overall: 4300mm (14ft 1in)

Fuselage diameter: 500mm (19.6in)

Wingspan: 1600mm (63in)

Launch weight: 582kg (1283lb)

Warhead weight: 450kg (1000lb)

Range: 25km (15.5 miles)

Speed: 1100km/h (680mph)

Powerplant: Aerojet MK 78 dual-thrusted solid-fuel rocket

Guidance system: n/a

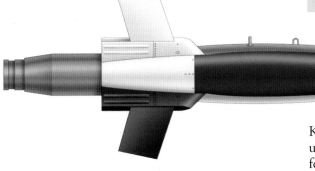

Su-17. The Kh-27PS was developed as a passive radar homing, extended-range ARM version for the MiG-27, before it was decided in the early 1980s to revamp the entire family as the Kh-25M series, which would be made available with a range of seeker head options that could be allied with a modular missile body. The new Kh-25M was based on the airframe of the Kh-27PS and could be fitted with the same passive radar seeker (Kh-25MP), a laser seeker (Kh-25ML), TV guidance (Kh-25MT), or radio command guidance (Kh-25MR). ASCC reporting names were AS-10 'Karen' for the TV-guided version, and AS-12 'Kegler' for the Kh-25MP ARM.

The Kh-28 (AS-9 'Kyle') was another tactical ARM, based on a scaled-down Kh-22. Powered by a liquid-fuel rocket motor, the Kh-28 had a passive radar seeker and autopilot, the latter receiving target data from the launch aircraft. The successor to the Kh-28 was the Kh-58 (AS-11 'Kilter') that could be used against radars of various wavebands, and which featured a solid-fuel rocket motor.

In France, tactical ASM development began with the Nord AS.20 (previously Nord 5110), which used radio command guidance and was essentially an ASM adaptation of the air-to-air AA.20. France's first in-service ASM also saw use in Italy and West Germany. Looking like a scaled-up AS.20, the Aérospatiale AS.30 (formerly Nord 5401) began life in 1958 and entered service in 1963–64. It was a much-improved missile that initially retained radio command guidance before semi-automatic guidance was introduced in 1984. This used an IR sensor to monitor a flare on the missile's rear, the pilot only having to keep the target in the crosshairs. Ultimately the most important version was the AS.30L introduced into service in 1983, with laser guidance, allied to an Automatic Tracking and Laser Integration System (ATLIS) targeting pod. Laser guidance improved the accuracy to within 1m (3ft). Main launch platforms were the Jaguar and Mirage F.1.

The Anglo-French AS.37 Martel was developed in the early 1960s by Matra and Hawker Siddeley. It was supplied with a British-developed TV seeker or a passive anti-radar seeker configured to home on a particular wavelength before launch, or scan pre-set frequencies in flight. First fired in guided form in 1965, the Martel was also deployed in an updated anti-radar version, known as Armat. This latter was available for export to non-NATO members, and was cleared for use by the Mirage F.1 and Mirage 2000.

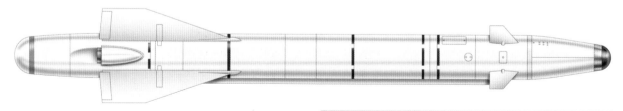

▲ Kh-25ML (AS-10 'Karen')

The Kh-25M was adopted for service in 1981 as a successor to the Kh-23 and was available with no fewer than five alternative seeker heads, offering different guidance modes according to the type of target and weather conditions. The Kh-25ML inherited the laser seeker head that was fitted to the previous Kh-25.

Specifications

Length overall: 3705mm (12ft 2in)	Range: 10km (6.2 miles)
Fuselage diameter: 27.5cm (10.8in)	Speed: 1370–2410km/h (850–1500mph)
Wingspan: 755mm (29.7in)	Powerplant: n/a
Launch weight: 299kg (659lb)	Guidance system: Various
Warhead weight: 86kg (190lb)	

Specifications

Length overall: 3525mm (11ft 7in)	Range: 2–10km (1.2–6.2 miles)
Fuselage diameter: 275mm (10.8in)	Speed: 2160–2700km/h (1340–1680mph)
Wingspan: 785mm (30.9in)	Powerplant: Solid-fuel rocket
Launch weight: 287kg (633lb)	Guidance system: Radio command
Warhead weight: 111kg (245lb)	

▲ Kh-23 (AS-7 'Kerry')

The Kh-23 entered flight test in 1968 and became the first Soviet tactical ASM to be produced in significant quantities. The major drawback of the Kh-23 was its primitive radio command guidance system, which required the pilot to guide the missile to its target using a joystick mounted in the cockpit. The pilot could track the course of the missile using a flare mounted on the tail of the weapon.

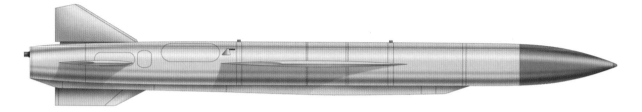

▲ Kh-28 (AS-9 'Kyle')

The Kh-28 ARM entered service in the mid 1970s and was carried by Su-17M fighter-bombers (with Metel detection/guidance pod) and early Su-24s (with the Filin provided as a detection/guidance pod or later carried internally).

Specifications

Length overall: 5970mm (19ft 7in)	Range: 110km (68.4 miles)
Fuselage diameter: 43cm (16.9in)	Speed: Mach 3
Wingspan: 1930mm (76in)	Powerplant: Two-stage liquid-fuel rocket
Launch weight: 720kg (1590lb)	Guidance system: Inertial with passive radar
Warhead weight: 160kg (353lb)	seeker

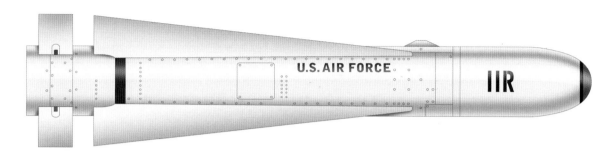

▲ AGM-65G Maverick

An improved IIR version of the Maverick for USAF service, the AGM-65G is optimized for attacking hardened tactical targets and is therefore equipped with the heavier warhead found in the AGM-65E/F. The first were delivered in 1989 and are now being updated with the charge coupled device (CCD) seeker.

Specifications

Length overall: 2490mm (8ft 2in)	Range: 28km (17.4 miles)
Fuselage diameter: 300mm (12in)	Speed: Mach 0.93
Wingspan: 710mm (28in)	Powerplant: Solid propellant rocket motor
Launch weight: 211–300kg (466–670lb)	Guidance system: Electro-optical in most models
Warhead weight: 57kg (125lb)	(some use IR imaging or laser guidance)

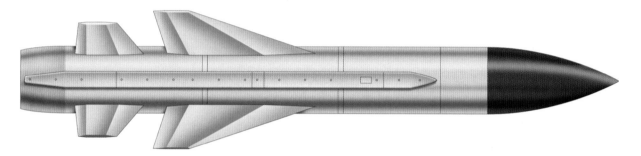

Specifications

Length overall: 4800mm (15ft 9in)	Range: 160km (99.4 miles)
Fuselage diameter: 380mm (15in)	Speed: Mach 3.6
Wingspan: 1170mm (46in)	Powerplant: Solid rocket
Launch weight: 650kg (1430lb)	Guidance system: Inertial with passive radar
Warhead weight: 149kg (328lb)	seeker

▲ Kh-58 (AS-11 'Kilter')

The Kh-58 ARM is associated with the MiG-25BM dedicated defence-suppression aircraft, as well as the Su-17M and Su-24M families. The missile receives target data from Viyuga or Fantasmagoriya radar detection/guidance equipment carried either internally or in podded form by the launch aircraft.

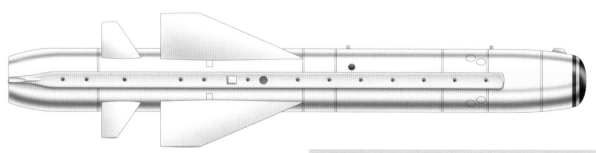

▲ AJ.168 Martel

The TV-guided version of the Martel was developed by Hawker Siddeley, with a Marconi seeker and datalink. The missile carried a TV camera that relayed imagery back to the operator through a datalink pod mounted on the aircraft.

Specifications

Length overall: 4180mm (13ft 8.4in)	Range: 60km (37.3 miles)
Fuselage diameter: 400mm (15.7in)	Speed: Mach 0.9+
Wingspan: 1200mm (47.2in)	Powerplant: Two-stage solid propellant rocket
Launch weight: 550kg (1212.5lb)	motors
Warhead weight: 150kg (330lb)	Guidance system: Passive radar homing

ASMs in Vietnam

The air war in Southeast Asia proved to be a stern test for the first generation of ASMs, but was notable for spurring the development and deployment of the first dedicated ARMs.

THE BULLPUP MISSILE saw its combat debut in Vietnam, where it was carried by aircraft such as the USAF's F-105 Thunderchief and US Navy A-4 Skyhawk. Pilots of the latter developed tactics whereby a target would be subject to the combined force of the Bullpup missile and strafing from the A-4's 20mm (0.79in) cannon. The missile, however, generally proved disappointing on account of its line-of-sight guidance, which demanded that the pilot guide the missile until it hit the target, tracking visually via a pair of flares located in the missile's tail. Another problem of the Bullpup, at least in its initial form, was its 113kg (250lb) warhead, which was typically insufficient to destroy the high-priority targets, such as bridges, against which it was assigned. During attacks on the Thanh Hoa bridge in 1965, F-105s deployed Bullpups in a vain attempt to destroy this vital target, the missiles reportedly bouncing off the bridge. Eventually, the missiles were traded for 'dumb' bombs. The Bullpup B followed, with a 454kg (1000lb) warhead. A variant of the Bullpup specifically developed for use in Southeast Asia was the AGM-12E. This was armed with a cluster bomb warhead for use against air defence installations.

First successful combat use of the AGM-62 Walleye TV-guided bomb was recorded in 1967, when the missile was launched by a US Navy A-4 against a military barracks at Sam Son. The Walleye went on to see considerable use during the conflict, with 920 examples being used in the course of 1972's Linebacker II offensive alone.

Bridge-busting

Typical targets were large buildings and bridges. Against the latter, the Walleye proved successful in knocking out wooden bridges, but was less effective against concrete or metal structures. In order to increase destructive power, the Walleye II was produced through modification, adding a more potent warhead. In order to attack targets at ranges beyond the view of the launch aircraft's pilot, the Extended Range Data Link (ERDL) version of the Walleye II was developed in 1972. A two-way datalink allowed the pilot to launch the Walleye out of visual range and then observe the relayed TV imagery until the target was sighted. In this way, the targeting could also be 'handed over' to a second aircraft. Three ERDL Walleye IIs were tested in combat in Vietnam in that year, all achieving direct hits against targets that were out of the pilot's range of vision, with a wingman gaining the lock-on and guiding the weapon. Entering service in 1972, the AGM-65 Maverick arrived just in time to see combat at the end of the Vietnam War, with at least 30 examples being expended in the course of that year.

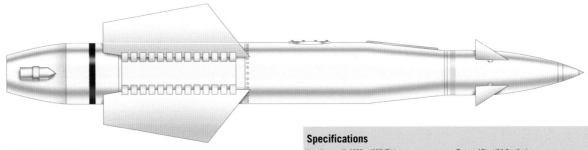

▲ **AGM-12C Bullpup**
Identified through its larger body, the AGM-12C (previously ASM-N-7b) introduced a more powerful 454kg (1000lb) warhead combined with larger control surfaces and a more powerful motor for extended range and greater destructive power. Trials began in 1962, and the weapon became operational in 1964.

Specifications

Length overall: 4100m (13ft 7in)	Range: 19km (11.8 miles)
Fuselage diameter: 460mm (18in)	Speed: Mach 1.8
Wingspan: 1200m (48in)	Powerplant: 140kN (30,000lb thrust) rocket
Launch weight: 810kg (1785lb)	Guidance system: Line-of-sight radio command
Warhead weight: 110–440kg (250–970lb)	

Flying the hazardous defence-suppression missions in Vietnam were the specialist 'Wild Weasel' aircraft, with their own array of dedicated anti-radar weapons, jamming pods, the Radar Homing and Warning System (RHAWS) and a missile-launch warning receiver. These aircraft were used for the 'Iron Hand' missions that sought to wage war on North Vietnam's anti-aircraft defences. The first of the 'Wild Weasel' family was the F-100F, four of which arrived in Southeast Asia in 1965, equipped with radar warning receivers and panoramic receivers. At the outset, the F-100F used its onboard equipment to pinpoint SAM sites for attack by F-105Ds, but within six months the F-100F was toting the Shrike ARM. The subsequent F-105F was initially armed with the Shrike, and some of these aircraft later added the AGM-78 Standard to their armoury. The 'Wild Weasel' F-105s first saw combat in 1966 and remained in action until the end of the war in 1973. From 1975 the improved F-105G model became available, with similar armament, albeit with AGM-78 compatibility from the outset.

The Standard had been introduced into Southeast Asia in 1967, when the first US Navy A-6As equipped with receiver sets and RHAWS arrived. The USAF was quick to follow, and six F-105Fs were modified in theatre, to be joined by four more that were sent from the US specifically for the Standard deployment. The US Navy's VA-75 aboard USS *Kitty Hawk* flew the first combat mission in March 1968, with an initial USAF mission in May, when F-105Fs attacked Fan Song missile guidance radars with eight Standards, five of which hit their targets.

▲ **Underwing Bullpup**
This 1969 photograph from Point Mugu, California, shows an A-4 Skyhawk armed with an AGM-12B Bullpup missile.

In the case of the F-105G aircraft, the baseline Standard ARM was the improved AGM-78B, with a new broadband seeker. This meant the missile could be employed against search radars and GCI stations, as well as SAM sites. Targets could be attacked from all aspects, and from outside SAM range. For the Navy, a dedicated defence-suppression asset was fielded as the A-6B, this also being equipped with the Standard ARM.

Other 'Wild Weasel' missions were flown by small numbers of F-4Cs armed with Shrike missiles and outfitted with RHAWS. The F-4C arrived in theatre in 1969 and was widely employed during 1972's *Linebacker* campaign. 'Iron Hand' missions were also conducted by the Navy, operating A-4s armed with AGM-45s, these aircraft being adapted to carry RHAWS under the nose.

▼ **AGM-45A Shrike**
The AGM-45A as used in Vietnam was powered by a solid-fuel rocket motor and could carry various different warheads, all of the blast-fragmentation type, with a dual-mode (proximity and impact) fuse. The AGM-45B added a dual-thrust motor.

Specifications

Length overall: 3050mm (10ft)	Range: 16–46km (10–28.8 miles)
Fuselage diameter: 203mm (8in)	Speed: Mach 2
Wingspan: 914mm (36in)	Powerplant: Rocketdyne Mk 39 or Aerojet Mk 53
Launch weight: 177kg (390lb)	polybutadiene solid-fuel rocket
Warhead weight: 67.5kg (149lb) or 66.6kg (147lb)	Guidance system: Passive radar homing

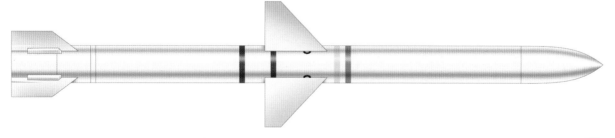

ASMs in the Middle East

In successive wars from 1973, Israel made pioneering use of ARMs and defence-suppression tactics, while the Iran–Iraq War saw a wide range of Eastern and Western ASMs put to use.

AMONG THE FIRST Israeli air-to-surface guided weapons were examples of the AGM-65 Maverick delivered by the US during the course of the 1973 Yom Kippur War, together with AGM-62 Walleye and Homing Bomb System (HOBOS) guided bombs. The Israelis credited the Maverick with 87 hits during the conflict, but a drawback was the limited magnification offered by the TV camera in the nose, which forced pilots to approach within close range of the target. The IDF/AF also put the AGM-45 Shrike ARM to use in the 1973 war, the weapons being launched against Syrian missile batteries by F-4Es. Losses to Arab air defences remained high, however.

A key to the success of the Israeli campaign in Lebanon in 1982 was the destruction of Syrian air defence sites, conducted primarily by IDF/AF F-4Es armed with AGM-45 and AGM-78 ARMs. Standoff protection was provided by modified Boeing 707s equipped to jam radars and transmit spoof signals. Further hampering the work of the Syrian SAM operators were UAVs, which were sent towards the SAM sites to prompt the tracking radars to be activated. The first wave of IDF/AF attacks saw missile launches from a range of around 35km (22 miles), out of range of hostile fire. These waves employed both types of ARM as well as AGM-65s

with TV guidance. The initial targets for the first wave were the key command-and-control centres and GCI stations. These strikes were followed by attacks on the SAM sites themselves, effectively knocking down the door to allow the next wake of attackers to get in closer. Compared to the AGM-45, the larger warhead of the AGM-78 meant it was more destructive, while its dual-thrust motor gave a useful advance in range over the Shrike.

Without their command-and-control assets, the SAM sites could be attacked from close range using 'dumb' bombs and cluster weapons, frequently dropped by Kfirs and A-4s. Within 10 minutes of the first wave of strike aircraft arriving, 10 of the 19 SAM sites were out of action. The end result, according to Israeli sources, was the destruction of no less than 17 out of 19 sites.

Persian Gulf

The Iran–Iraq War was contested between two nations equipped with some of the most advanced airborne weaponry then available, from both East and West. The Iranians did not receive the AGM-45 that they hoped to employ in the anti-radar role, and it was left to the AGM-65A (carried by the F-4E fleet) to serve as the primary ASM. The IRIAF's experience with the AGM-65 in the maritime

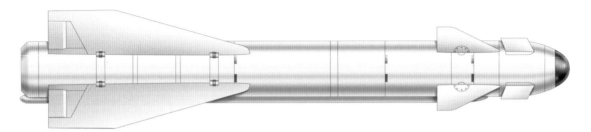

▲ **Kh-29T (AS-14 'Kedge')**

The Kh-29, seen here in its TV-guided form, was a potent weapon in the hands of the IrAF during the Iran–Iraq War. The weapon was compatible with the Su-22M-4K, one of the most versatile attack aircraft available to the Iranians. The Kh-29T was intended to work in conjunction with a laser rangefinder/marked target seeker carried internally by the launch aircraft.

Specifications

Length overall: 3875mm (12ft 8in)	Warhead weight: 317kg (699lb)
Fuselage diameter: 380mm (1ft 3in)	Range: 10–12km (6.2–7.5 miles)
Wingspan: 1100mm (43.3in)	Speed: 1470km/h (910mph)
Launch weight: Laser-guided 657kg (1448lb);	Powerplant: Solid rocket
TV-guided 680kg (1499lb)	Guidance system: Semi-active laser or TV

environment was so successful that it persuaded the US Navy to develop a 'navalized' Maverick, as the Iranian Phantoms almost single-handedly laid waste to the Iraqi Navy in late 1980.

On the Iraqi side, early deliveries of the primitive Kh-66 had been succeeded by the Kh-23 and then a range of altogether more formidable weapons, including the Kh-25 series, the Kh-28 ARM and the Kh-29. Indeed, the Iraqis only attempted to use the Kh-23 once in combat, when it was launched against a bridge – without success – from a Su-22 in 1982. The AS.30 and AS.30L were provided for the Mirage

F.1 fleet, together with the Martel and Armat (known in Iraqi service as the BAZAR). Generally, the AS.30L was preferred over the similar Kh-29L, on account of its ease of operation, but a solution for using the more powerful Soviet weapon was later found. Towards the end of the conflict, Mirages equipped with ATLIS targeting pods designated targets for Kh-29Ls launched by Su-22M-4Ks. Mirage F.1s also saw notable success in the anti-ship role, armed with the AS.30L, sinking a number of tankers, and the weapon proved a valuable adjunct to the Exocet, a dedicated anti-ship missile.

Modern tactical ASMs

Thanks to advanced guidance methods, the latest tactical AGMs possess greater accuracy than their predecessors and many are capable of hitting targets at standoff range.

THE MAVERICK REMAINS one of the most important ASMs in the inventory of the US military and its allies. Although production ended in the late 1990s, development continues, with older versions of the weapon being upgraded to the latest standards. An improved IIR Maverick was developed for the USAF for use against hardened targets. This AGM-65G is an updated AGM-65D with the heavy warhead of the AGM-65E/F. Other changes include a new digital autopilot and expanded target selection options. After passing through the CCD upgrade, older AGM-65B/Cs become the AGM-65H, while similar changes to US Navy AGM-65Fs produce the AGM-65J. Finally, the AGM-65K refers to an AGM-65G with the new CCD seeker, which

AGM-88 targets in Operation *Allied Force*	
Target type	Missiles used
Early warning radars	125
SA-2 'Guideline' SAM	1
SA-3 'Goa' SAM	208
SA-6 'Gainful' SAM	389
Unknown	20

provides greater reliability and the ability to operate in lower light levels.

The HARM also continues to be refined, with a number of successive block updates followed by the latest Advanced Anti-Radiation Guided Missile

▼ **AGM-84H SLAM-ER**
The Standoff Land Attack Missile–Expanded Response (SLAM-ER) was delivered to the US Navy from 1998. Key features are the pop-out swept wings that increase both range and agility. The datalink had to be replaced in order to account for its extended range compared to the original SLAM, and the AGM-84H also received a heavier warhead.

Specifications

Length overall: 3800mm (12ft 7in)	Speed: 864km/h (537mph)
Fuselage diameter: 340mm (13.4in)	Powerplant: Teledyne turbojet
Wingspan: 910mm (35.8in)	Guidance system: Sea-skimming cruise
Launch weight: 691kg (1523lb)	monitored by radar altimeter/active radar
Warhead weight: 221kg (488lb)	terminal homing
Range: 124km (67 nautical miles)	

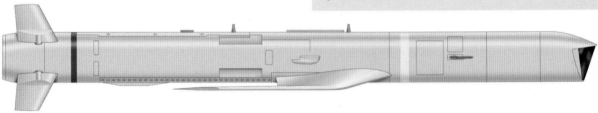

(AARGM) development. A new seeker was added in the AGM-88A Block II, while in 1987 the AGM-88B had upgraded guidance, followed by Block III software from 1990. Next version of the HARM was the AGM-88C, introduced after the 1991 Gulf War, and with a warhead with tungsten alloy fragments to increase lethality. The AGM-88C also introduced the Block IV software standard, followed by Block V, with a home-on-jam capability.

The Block VI, known in US service as the AGM-88D, is an international version used on Tornado ECRs of Germany and Italy, and including GPS navigation for much-improved accuracy. Should the target radar stop emitting, the GPS guidance brings the missile to the correct coordinates. GPS guidance was found to be necessary in light of the experience over Kosovo during Operation *Allied Force*, when the efforts of Serbian air defence systems combined with adverse weather reduced the success rate of the HARM and other guided weapons. The GPS-aided HARM is also produced through modification of older AGM-88Bs, creating the AGM-88B Block IIIB. In future, earlier weapons will gave way to the AGM-88E, or the AARGM. This new weapon, which is scheduled for deployment in 2011, combines GPS with a millimetre wave active radar seeker for terminal homing.

The AGM-84E Standoff Land Attack Missile (SLAM) was developed from 1986 on the basis of the Harpoon anti-ship missile (AShM), for precision land-attack missions. Following inertial guidance to the target area, 'man in the loop' guidance is provided for the terminal phase, using the IIR seeker from the AGM-65D, and the datalink from the Walleye. After

combat use in *Desert Storm*, the basic weapon was refined to produce the AGM-84H SLAM-ER (Expanded Response), first tested in 1997, and fitted with pop-out wings. Blurring the definition between tactical ASM and cruise missile, and with a reported range of almost 300km (186 miles), the SLAM-ER is a cruise missile according to the Missile Technology Control Regime definition. Guidance is inertial, with GPS coupled with an IIR seeker for all-weather operation. The latest versions are the AGM-84K with minor improvements and the Automatic Target Acquisition (ATA) upgrade that allows autonomous target selection using a stored image 'library'.

The AGM-130 is a rocket-assisted glide bomb for the F-15E, based on the 907kg (2000lb) GBU-15. Use of a rocket booster increases the low-altitude release range by a factor of three. The GBU-15A version differs in its use of a BLU-109 penetrating warhead rather than the standard Mk 84 in the AGM-130A, while the AGM-130D has a thermobaric warhead. All have the option of the original TV/CCD guidance, combined with GPS updates, or an alternative IIR seeker.

The AGM-154 Joint Standoff Weapon (JSOW) and the longer-range AGM-158 Joint Air-to-Surface Standoff Missile (JASSM) were developed in the 1990s to upgrade the standoff precision strike capabilities of the USAF and US Navy; both were to be true fire-and-forget weapons, with GPS/inertial guidance. JSOW is a glide bomb with pop-out wings, and it entered production in 1999. The weapon is available with two warhead options, comprising cluster dispenser with 145 Combined Effects Munition (CEM) bomblets (AGM-154A) or blast-

▲ **AGM-154 JSOW**
Although the AGM-154 carries a guided missile designation, the versions of the weapon issued to date have been unpowered. There have been efforts, however, to develop a turbojet-powered derivative, and the Williams J400 engine has already been earmarked for projected AGM-154C and D models.

Specifications

Length overall: 4100mm (13ft 5.4in)	Range: Low-altitude: 22–130km (14–81 miles)
Fuselage diameter: 330mm (13in)	Speed: Subsonic
Wingspan: 270cm (106in)	Powerplant: N/A
Launch weight: 483–497kg (1065–1095lb)	Guidance system: GPS/INS (Global
Warhead weights: Various: 1.54–25kg (3.4–	position/Inertial), Terminal infrared seeker
65lb)	(unique to 'C' model)

▼ AGM-158A JASSM

The unconventional appearance of the JASSM is governed by the requirement to reduce its radar cross-section to a minimum. Both Lockheed Martin and McDonnell Douglas developed competing designs, with the former being declared winner of the development contract in 1998.

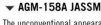

Specifications

Length overall: 4270mm (14ft)	Range: 370+ km (230+ miles)
Fuselage diameter: n/a	Speed: Subsonic
Wingspan: 2400mm (94.5in)	Powerplant: Teledyne CAE J402-CA-100
Launch weight: 975kg (2150lb)	Guidance system: INS/GPS
Warhead weight: 450kg (1000lb)	

Specifications

Length overall: 4100mm (13ft)	Range: 106km (65.9 miles)
Fuselage diameter: 254mm (10in)	Speed: 2280km/h (1420mph)
Wingspan: 1100mm (43.3in)	Powerplant: Thiokol SR113-TC-1 dual-thrust
Launch weight: 355kg (780lb)	rocket engine
Warhead weight: 66kg (150lb)	Guidance system: Active radar homing

▼ AGM-88E AARGM

The latest version of the HARM series is the AARGM. Outwardly similar to previous AGM-88s, the new weapon will likely be made compatible with the F-35 Joint Strike Fighter. HARMs are also carried by the USAF's F-16CJ Block 50 and the US Navy's EA-6B Prowler, the latter being replaced by the EA-18G Growler.

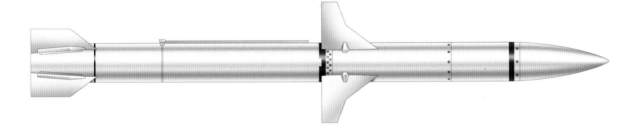

fragmentation/penetrator (AGM-154C). The anti-armour AGM-154B was cancelled. The AGM-154C also has an IIR seeker and ATA. The latest version of the latter missile introduces a moving-target capability, plus a datalink for mid-flight updates.

Stealthy JASSM

Despite its 'Joint' development, the JASSM was eventually procured only by the USAF. Using low-observable technology, the JASSM is powered by a turbojet and features pop-out wings. Terminal guidance is supplied by an IIR seeker, with a datalink. The warhead is of the penetrating type. The JASSM entered production in 2001, with service entry in 2003, initially aboard the B-52H. An extended-range version is under development as the AGM-158B JASSM-ER, with service entry planned for 2013.

The Soviet-designed Kh-59 (AS-13 'Kingbolt') was schemed as a standoff weapon for the Su-24M

strike aircraft. It is powered by a solid-fuel rocket motor and although both TV and laser guidance modules were developed, it seems that the only version to enter service was that with TV guidance. In the latter, TV imagery is transmitted from the seeker head to a screen in the cockpit of the launch aircraft, where the crew member is provided with a joystick to guide the weapon to the target, before switching to terminal homing mode. Similar in concept to the SLAM-ER, the Kh-59M (AS-18 'Kazoo') adds a turbofan under the missile body, extending range to around 115km (71 miles). The solid-fuel booster rocket is retained. A more recent development is the Kh-59MK. This differs in its use of a Russian- rather than Ukrainian-made turbofan and has an estimated range of 285km (177 miles). The missile receives the target coordinates prior to launch and flies under inertial guidance during the cruise phase, switching to TV homing for the

▼ Kh-59 (AS-13 'Kingbolt')

This Kh-59 is seen with its canard control fins in the stowed position. After launch, these control surfaces fold out. The rear end of the missile carries the solid-fuel booster motor that falls away after it has burnt out and the missile has been accelerated to cruising speed. Thereafter, the main rocket motor takes over.

Specifications

Length overall: 5700mm (18ft 8.4in)	Range: 200km (124 miles)
Fuselage diameter: 380mm (15in)	Speed: Mach 0.72–0.88
Wingspan: 1300mm (51in)	Powerplant: Two-stage rocket
Launch weight: 930kg (2050lb)	Guidance system: Inertial, then TV-guided
Warhead weight: 315kg (694lb)	

Specifications

Length overall: 3875mm (12ft 8in)	Warhead weight: 317kg (699lb)
Fuselage diameter: 380mm (14.9in)	Range: 10–12km (6.2–7.5 miles)
Wingspan: 1100m (43.3in)	Speed: 1470km/h (910mph)
Launch weight: Laser-guided 657kg (1448lb);	Powerplant: Solid rocket
TV-guided 680kg (1499lb)	Guidance system: Semi-active laser or TV

▼ Kh-29L (AS-14 'Kedge')

The laser-guided version of the Kh-29 features a different nose profile, with a housing for the semi-active seeker head. Unusually for a Soviet-era ASM, the Kh-29 was developed and built by the Vympel bureau, which was better known for its activities in the field of AAMs.

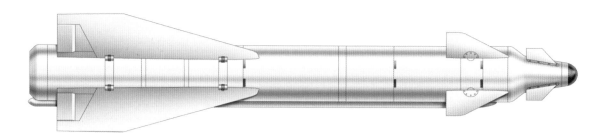

terminal phase. A two-way datalink is maintained with the launch aircraft using an APK-9 targeting pod. The Kh-59MK has also been combined with an active radar seeker. Primary launch aircraft for the Kh-59MK are the Su-24M and upgraded versions of the Su-30 and Su-35 family.

Among the most successful and versatile Soviet-designed tactical ASMs is the Kh-29 (AS-14 'Kedge'), broadly comparable to the American Maverick. Armed with a powerful warhead, the Kh-29 can be fitted with laser (Kh-29L) or TV (Kh-29T) seeker heads. A solid-fuel rocket provides the powerplant, and the missile adopts a 'pop-up' terminal flight mode. Entering operational service in the Soviet air arms in 1980, the Kh-29 series is compatible with a wide range of tactical aircraft. An extended-range Kh-29TE has also been developed, offering a range of 30km (18 miles).

More radical in its design is the Kh-31 (AS-17 'Krypton'), which is characterized by a combined solid-fuel booster and ramjet propulsion system, producing a high-speed weapon intended to defeat modern air defences. The Kh-31 was designed to fulfil a number of tactical roles, and therefore a range of seekers were provided. The first to enter service, in around 1990, were the Kh-31P ARM, with a passive radar seeker, and the Kh-31A, an AShM with an active radar seeker. The primary launch platform for the Kh-31P is the Russian Air Force's Su-24M strike aircraft, as well as advanced members of the Su-30/35 series.

Israel's experience with early American ASMs led to the development in the mid 1980s of the indigenous Popeye, a TV-guided weapon that would provide the IDF/AF with its first standoff attack capability. The Popeye was also adopted by the USAF

▶ AGM-158 JASSM

USAF aircraft armament system specialists load a Joint Air-to-Surface Standoff Missile (JASSM) into a B-1B Lancer bomber at Ellsworth AFB, South Dakota. The JASSM is a conventional air-launched standoff weapon employing low observable technology capable of destroying heavily defended, high-value, time-sensitive targets. Along with the B-1B, the B-2 Spirit, B-52 Stratofortress and F-16CJ can all carry the weapon. The first JASSM operational launch from a B-1B took place in August 2006.

as the AGM-142 Have Nap, which was acquired to provide the B-52G/H with a precision conventional attack capability. The missile was developed as a powered version of the TV-guided Pyramid glide bomb, with lock-on achieved before or after launch, in the latter scenario via a two-way datalink. The AGM-142B version differs in its use of an IIR seeker, while the TV-guided AGM-142C has a penetrator warhead. The AGM-142D allies the IIR seeker with the penetrator warhead. Other operators have their own particular versions of the missile, including the AGM-142E for Australia's F-111s, the AGM-142F for Israel, and the AGM-142G/H for South Korea. The Popeye II or Have Lite is designed for carriage by smaller tactical fighters, and is therefore of reduced weight and dimensions.

Israel's Delilah is another standoff missile, and is unusual in that it has a loitering capability, being provided with 22 minutes of flight time in order to break off its attack and then return to the target when opportune, to relocate a mobile target, or to switch to an alternative target. Powered by a turbojet, the Delilah also uses TV guidance and can be helicopter-launched.

▼ Kh-59MK (AS-18 'Kazoo')

The Kh-59M adds an underslung turbofan engine to the basic Kh-59. Illustrated is the Kh-59MK version fitted with an active radar seeker head. The forward section of the missile body is also of a greater diameter than the previous missiles. The complete Kh-59 weapons complex is named Ovod, meaning gadfly.

Specifications

Length overall: 5700mm (18ft 8in)	Range: 200km (124 miles)
Fuselage diameter: 380mm (15in)	Speed: Mach 0.72–0.88
Wingspan: 1300mm (51in)	Powerplant: Rocket then turbofan
Launch weight: 930kg (2050lb)	Guidance system: Inertial, then TV-guided
Warhead weight: 320kg (705lb)	

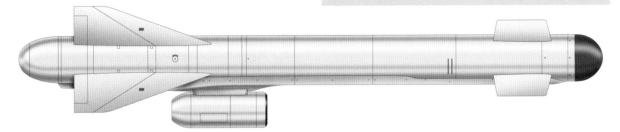

Weapons load

A Swedish JAS 39 Gripen armed with AGM-65 ASMs on underwing pylons, seen here taking part in exercises.

European cruise

The most widely used European standoff missile is the MBDA Storm Shadow and the SCALP EG family – Système de Croisière Conventionnel Autonome à Longue Portée et d'Emploi Général (Autonomous Long-range Conventional Cruise System – General Use). Both these weapons, which were primarily developed for service with the UK and France respectively, were intended as offshoots from the same company's Apache airfield attack weapon, in use with the French Air Force's Mirage 2000D fleet since 2002. The turbojet-powered Apache carries 10

separate runway-penetrating submunitions over a range of 278km (172 miles). Flight tests were completed between 1993 and 2001.

Apache, Storm Shadow and SCALP EG all use inertial and GPS navigation, together with TERCOM. An IIR seeker is provided for the terminal phase, together with an automatic target-recognition system. Developed by Matra of France and BAe in the UK in light of the experience of Operation Desert Storm, the Storm Shadow and SCALP EG are both intended to attack hardened targets, so feature a single Bomb Royal Ordnance Augmented Charge (BROACH) warhead developed in the UK. The BROACH consists of a penetration charge, a shaped precursor charge and a final blast-fragmentation warhead. Apart from their different

▼ Kh-31P (AS-17 'Krypton')

The Kh-31P ARM is part of a family of ramjet-powered missiles with differing guidance systems and applications. The air-breathing ramjet is fed by four circular-section intakes around the body, with the intakes protected by caps (here coloured blue) until the booster rocket at the rear of the missiles fires.

Specifications

Length overall: 5200mm (17ft 2in)	Range: 110km (70 miles)
Fuselage diameter: 360mm (14in)	Speed: 2160–2520km/h (1340–1570mph)
Wingspan: 914mm (36in)	Powerplant: Solid-fuel rocket in initial stage,
Launch weight: 600kg (1320lb)	ramjet for rest of trajectory
Warhead weight: 87kg (192lb)	Guidance system: Inertial with passive radar

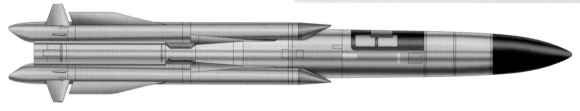

▼ **AGM-142 Have Nap**

When initially adopted for USAF service with the B-52, the Rafael-developed Popeye was named Raptor, although this name was discarded when the F-22A air superiority fighter entered service. Each B-52H can carry three AGM-142s.

Specifications

Length overall: 4820mm (15ft 10in)	I-800 penetrating warhead
Fuselage diameter: 533mm (21in)	Range: 78km (48 miles)
Wingspan: 1520mm (60in)	Speed: Mach 1.2
Launch weight: 1360kg (3000lb)	Powerplant: Single-stage solid-fuel rocket
Warhead weight: 340kg (750lb) blast-fragmentation or 360kg (800lb)	Guidance system: Inertial plus IIR or TV

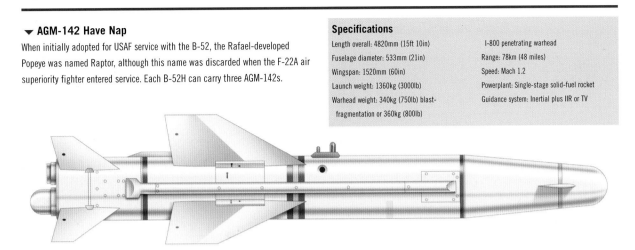

aircraft interfaces, Storm Shadow and SCALP EG are essentially similar and feature turbojet propulsion. Under its stated requirement for a Conventionally Armed Standoff Missile (CASOM), the UK ordered the Storm Shadow in 1997, and it entered RAF service on the Tornado GR.Mk 4 in time for the 2003 campaign in Iraq. The SCALP EG was ordered by France in 1997, before entering service in 2004. By this time, the missile was the responsibility of the pan-European MBDA concern. Italy joined the programme in 1999, acquiring the Storm Shadow for its Tornado IDS. The Black Shaheen is a further single-warhead version tailored for use by the United Arab Emirates Air Force (UAEAF), with which it arms the Mirage 2000-9. The weapon has also been acquired by Greece, which uses the SCALP EG for its Mirage 2000-5 fleet. Typical targets for Storm Shadow and SCALP EG are high-value static objectives with known coordinates that can be programmed into the missile before the mission.

The primary European competitor to the Storm Shadow/SCALP EG is the Taurus KEPD 350, originally developed by DASA of Germany and Bofors of Sweden, but now the responsibility of MBDA. Again, navigation is based on inertial and GPS guidance with TERCOM, with an IIR seeker provided for waypoint checks and terminal guidance. A Mephisto penetrator warhead is carried, this consisting of a precursor (shaped) charge and a high-explosive kinetic-energy penetrator. Development began in 1998 and the Taurus KEPD 350 entered service with the German Air Force's Tornado IDS fleet in 2005. The missile has also been selected by Spain, initially to arm the F/A-18.

Another, relatively little-known, European missile is the PGM family. Once again the responsibility of the MBDA missile house, the PGM was originally developed in Italy by Marconi, and is apparently only in service with the UAE. The PGM series is offered with three different seeker options (laser, TV and IIR), all of which are provided with a datalink to the launch aircraft or to another third party. Target data can be programmed on the ground, or can be uploaded from the aircraft's databus to the missile before launch, allowing the target coordinates to be modified in the course of the mission, or for targets of opportunity to be selected. Although providing fire-and-forget capability, the missile can be returned to 'man in the loop' guidance during its flight to the target. Two different blast-fragmentation warheads are available, with weights of either 227kg (500lb) or 907kg (2000lb). In UAE service, the PGM is known as the Hakim, and has been integrated on the Mirage 2000-9 fleet. It can also be used by F-16s.

Royal Air Force ALARM

The standard British anti-radar missile is the Air-Launched Anti-Radiation Missile (ALARM) that equips the RAF's Tornado GR.Mk 4. Selected in favour of the HARM, it made its combat debut in Iraq in 1991. Development first began in 1983, with the aim of the replacing the RAF's Martel in the anti-radar role. A first firing took place in 1986. The ALARM uses a passive radar seeker to prosecute its target and as well as the direct-attack LOBL mode, the missile can loiter in the area of the target by deploying a parachute after having climbed to cruise altitude. Once the radar is switched on, the missile

▲ **AGM-154 JSOW**
US Navy Aviation Ordnancemen from the Weapons Department aboard the aircraft carrier USS *Enterprise* position an AGM-154 JSOW weapon onto a trolley for transport to the flight deck during operations in the Mediterranean.

will eject the parachute, complete its descent and home in on the target. The weapon can also be launched in the general direction of the threat, where it will then select and engage the highest-priority target based on a pre-programmed threat library. The ALARM was initially adopted by the RAF's Tornado fleet, with each aircraft capable of carrying up to seven missiles.

A unique combination of Russian and Indian technology, the Brahmos is a supersonic cruise missile intended for the Indian Air Force. Produced in naval, ground-launched and air-launched versions, the Brahmos is intended to be carried by the Su-30MKI, although early tests have raised issues over the missile's excess weight in its airborne application. As well as being designed to attack important ground targets in a land-attack version, the Brahmos has an important anti-shipping function. Indeed, the design of the missile is informed by that of the Russian Navy's 3M55 Onyx (export name Yakhont) AShM, and retains this weapon's ramjet propulsion system. A first ground launch was recorded in 2003 and the IAF hopes to induct the air-launched version of the Brahmos into its inventory by 2013.

Meanwhile, Russia's NPO Mashinostroyeniya design bureau has exhibited the Yakhont with its Su-32 naval strike aircraft, as a potential AShM. The manufacturer claims a range of 300km (186 miles) and a flight speed of Mach 2.0 to 2.5. When adapted for aerial launch, the Yakhont is fitted with streamlined covers for the nose intake and the tail, and features a smaller booster motor that reduces overall weight compared to the original ship- and submarine-launched version. The booster motor takes the Yakhont up to cruising speed, whereupon the ramjet is engaged. Inertial navigation is used during the high-altitude cruise phase, before the missile descends to the target area and flies at low level using an active/passive radar seeker.

An apparent alternative to the Yakhont is the smaller Alfa, again from the NPO company, and again powered by a ramjet engine. In common with the Yakhont, the Alfa has been primarily offered with a view to its use in the anti-shipping role, but is also available for the land-attack mission. The weapon has a range of around 300km (186 miles) and cruises at Mach 3. Guidance is inertial with satellite-navigation updates, and a multi-spectral seeker head is provided for the terminal phase. The final run-in to the target is flown at a height of 10–20m (32–66ft).

Confusingly, a rival Alfa missile has been developed by the Novator design bureau, suggesting that 'Alfa' is a project name for the basic requirement. This weapon is similarly based on an existing maritime missile, in this case the 3M51 Klub, development of which began in the late 1980s. The missile features pop-out wings and a turbofan engine. Guidance is based on an inertial platform for cruise, with an active radar seeker used for the run-in to the target. In its naval form, the missile features a rocket-propelled final stage that accelerates it to Mach 2.5 in order to defeat modern air defence systems.

Neither the Yakhont nor either of the Alfa projects have yet received orders in air-launched form.

A recent addition to the ARM field is the Brazilian MAR-1, apparently intended for use on upgraded Brazilian Air Force AMX attack aircraft, and possibly also on Brazil's upgraded F-5M fighters. The MAR-1 is a medium-range weapon developed jointly by Mectron and the Brazilian Air Force. The missile uses a boost-sustain motor and a passive radar seeker head. The MAR-1 secured its first confirmed order from Pakistan, however, with an agreement reached in 2009.

Meanwhile, Pakistan has made recent efforts to develop and field indigenous air-launched standoff weapons. The Raad cruise missile was first tested in 2007 and in 2008 was launched from an upgraded Pakistani Air Force Mirage III.

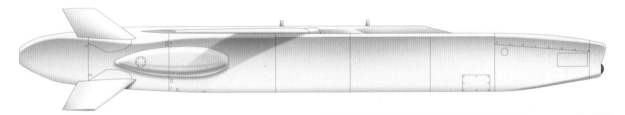

▲ **Taurus KEPD 350**

The Taurus standoff missile was introduced to operational service aboard *Luftwaffe* Tornado IDS strike aircraft. Germany also plans to arm its Eurofighter EF2000s with the weapon, which has also been tested aboard the Saab Gripen.

Specifications

Length overall: 5100mm (16ft 8.8in)	Speed: Mach 0.80–0.95
Fuselage diameter: 1080mm (42.5in)	Powerplant: Williams P8300-15 Turbofan
Wingspan: 2064mm (81in)	Guidance system: Image-Based Navigation (IBN),
Launch weight: 1400kg (3086lb)	Inertial Navigation System (INS), Terrain
Warhead weight: 499kg (1100lb)	Referenced Navigation (TRN) and GPS
Range: Over 500km (311 miles)	

MBDA **PGM 500**

Specifications

Length overall: 4620mm (15ft 2in)	Range: 50km (31 miles)
Fuselage diameter: 460mm (18.1in)	Speed: n/a
Wingspan: 1520mm (59.8in)	Powerplant: Solid fuel
Launch weight: 1060kg (2337lb)	Guidance system: INS, Semi-active laser
Warhead weight: 910kg (2006lb)	

▲ **PGM-500**

Once a Marconi product, and now handled by MBDA Missile Systems, the PGM-500 is the smaller of the two PGMs, with a 227kg (500lb) warhead. The manufacturer claims an accuracy of within 1m (3ft), and there are two available fusing options: impact or proximity.

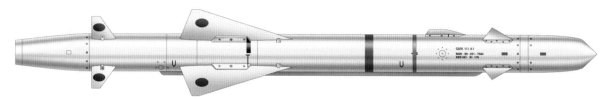

▲ ALARM

A unique feature of the RAF's ALARM is the loiter mode, which is designed to counter threat radars that are switched off as they come under attack. Hanging under a parachute, the ALARM loiters until the operator reactivates the radar, then discards its parachute and completes the attack profile.

Specifications

Length overall: 4240mm (13ft 10in)	Speed: 2455km/h (1525mph)
Fuselage diameter: 230mm (9.1in)	Powerplant: Bayern Chemie two-stage solid fuel
Wingspan: 730mm (29in)	rocket motors
Launch weight: 268kg (590lb)	Guidance system: Pre-programmed/passive
Range: 93km (58 miles)	radar seeker

Ultimately it is expected that the missile will be integrated on the JF-17 fighter. Powered by a turbofan engine and utilizing inertial, GPS and TERCOM guidance modes, the Raad is reported to be capable of carrying a nuclear warhead. The Raad is also known by the alternative name Hatf 8, part of the designation sequence for the country's strategic missile programme.

The South African connection

Unconfirmed reports suggest that Pakistan may have called upon South African expertise in the development of the Raad cruise missile. This is based on the similarity in its appearance to the South African Multi-Purpose Standoff Weapon (MUPSOW) and Torgos standoff weapons, and the fact that South Africa supplied the PAF with the Raptor 2 powered glide-bomb.

Following early experience with the AS.20 and AS.30 missiles supplied by France for use on its Mirage III, Mirage F.1 and Buccaneer aircraft, South Africa began development of an indigenous series of standoff weapons. The first of these to see service and combat was the unpowered Raptor 1 (H-2)

glide-bomb, which was further developed as the powered Raptor 2. This simply added a rocket motor to the original weapon, increasing range and agility. Although apparently never adopted for front-line service by the South African Air Force (SAAF), the Raptor 2 was exported, and examples were delivered to Pakistan. Guidance options comprised autonomous, waypoint or inertial with GPS.

Powered by a solid-propellant rocket motor, the MUPSOW was a further development of the Raptor, with a range of 50km (31 miles) and either a TV or IR seeker head. Development began in 1991, and unpowered flight tests commenced in 1997. In the mid 1990s the MUPSOW was revised, with a turbojet engine and range extended to around 150km (93 miles). The new version represents a considerably more advanced air-to-ground weapon, with optional TV, IIR or radar seekers, together with inertial/GPS guidance and a datalink. Depending on the type of target to be attacked, the missile can accept a unitary warhead, anti-runway submunitions or a tandem-charge penetrator for use against hardened facilities. A conventional 454kg (1000lb) Mk 83 warhead had been installed in the early version. The MUPSOW

▼ Brahmos

The name 'Brahmos' is derived from India's Brahmaputra river and the Moskva river in Russia. The first version of this hypersonic standoff missile was the ship-launched form that entered service on Indian Navy warships, followed by a land-based army variant. The IAF hopes to introduce an air-launched model for both land attack and anti-shipping missions.

Specifications

Length overall: 8400m (27ft 6in)	Range: 290km (180 miles)
Fuselage diameter: 600mm (24in)	Speed: Mach 2.8–3.0
Wingspan: 1700mm (67in)	Powerplant: Two-stage integrated rocket/ramjet
Launch weight: 2500kg (5512lb)	Guidance system: Inertial, GPS, active and
Warhead weight: 300kg (661lb)	passive radar

was associated with the SAAF's Cheetah fighter, which has now been retired, suggesting that the weapon is also no longer in service.

The Torgos, which first appeared in 1999, represents a further evolution of the MUPSOW, with the range extended to 300km (186 miles) to put it into the true cruise missile category. The Torgos relies on inertial and GPS guidance for the initial phase of the flight, with an IR seeker used for the terminal phase. Mid-course updates can be provided by remote datalink.

Iranian programmes

Iran's years of isolation during the Iran–Iraq War prompted it to embark on a number of guided weapons programmes. In terms of air-to-surface weapons, the Sattar series represents a laser-guided missile that was informed by technology from the AGM-65A and the AS.30L and is associated with a locally developed targeting pod based on the ATLIS. It is likely that technology for the Sattar was obtained

from several examples of unexploded IrAF AS.30Ls that were recovered on Iranian territory. The original Sattar-1 had a range of 20–30km (12-18 miles) but proved to be aerodynamically deficient. The Sattar-2 was the first to offer supersonic performance, and also introduced reconfigured control surfaces. The ultimate version in service is believed to be the Sattar-3, carried by Iranian F-4Es, but a Sattar-4 has also been identified.

In addition to the laser-guided Sattar, Iranian industry has developed a range of electro-optically guided missiles based on combinations of AGM-65 Maverick seeker heads and Mk 80-series warheads. The first of Iran's indigenous TV-guided ASMs was the GBU-67 Zoobin, a supersonic weapon with guidance derived from that of the Maverick. Carrying a blast-fragmentation warhead, the Zoobin has a range in excess of 30km (18 miles). Among the TV-guided weapons, it is reported that the only design to have entered quantity production and front-line service is the (unpowered) Qassed guided bomb.

▼ MAR-1

The Brazilian-made MAR-1 has been acquired by Pakistan, likely for use on its JF-17 fighters. The weapon was developed jointly by Mectron (responsible for the Piranha AAM) as well as the Brazilian Air Force's Centro Técnico Aeroespacial (CTA). The weapon is also associated with Brazil's upgraded AMX attack aircraft.

Specifications

Length overall: 4030mm (13ft 2.7ft)	Range: 25km (15.5 miles)
Fuselage diameter: 230mm (9in)	Speed: n/a
Wingspan: n/a	Powerplant: Rocket motor
Launch weight: 274kg (600lb)	Guidance system: Passive radar homing, home-
Warhead weight: 90kg (200lb)	on-jam

▼ Delilah

The Delilah draws upon Israeli combat experience with attack drones, which are typically used to loiter in the vicinity of enemy air defence systems, waiting for threat emissions before homing on the target. In the 2006 Lebanon War, Delilah missiles were used by Israel to seek out vehicles supplying Hezbollah forces.

Specifications

Length overall: 3310mm (10ft 11in)	Range: 250km (160 miles)
Fuselage diameter: 330mm (13iin)	Speed: Mach 0.3–0.7
Wingspan: 1150mm (45.3in)	Powerplant: Turbojet
Launch weight: 250kg (550lb)	Guidance system: CCD\IIR with GPS\INS
Warhead weight: n/a	

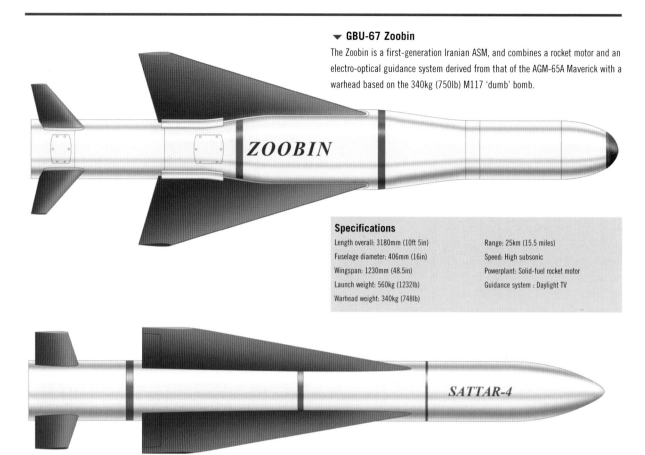

▼ GBU-67 Zoobin

The Zoobin is a first-generation Iranian ASM, and combines a rocket motor and an electro-optical guidance system derived from that of the AGM-65A Maverick with a warhead based on the 340kg (750lb) M117 'dumb' bomb.

Specifications

Length overall: 3180mm (10ft 5in)	Range: 25km (15.5 miles)
Fuselage diameter: 406mm (16in)	Speed: High subsonic
Wingspan: 1230mm (48.5in)	Powerplant: Solid-fuel rocket motor
Launch weight: 560kg (1232lb)	Guidance system : Daylight TV
Warhead weight: 340kg (748lb)	

▲ Sattar-4

The Sattar has been identified in four different versions, each of which present significant external differences. The Sattar-1 had an appearance similar to the MIM-23 HAWK SAM, while the Sattar-3 has canard control surfaces. The Sattar-4 reverted to a mid-wing and tailfin configuration.

Specifications
Unavailable

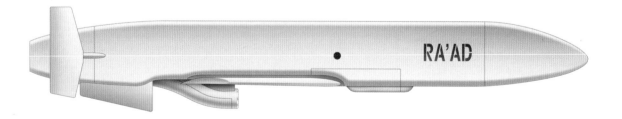

▲ Raad

Pakistan's semi-stealthy air-launched Raad cruise missile (also known as the Hatf 8) was developed by the Pakistan Air Weapons Complex and the National Engineering and Scientific Commission (NESCOM). The Raad also has strategic potential, since it is able to be configured to carry a nuclear warhead.

Specifications

Length overall: 4850mm (15ft 10in)	Range: 350km (217 miles)
Fuselage diameter: n/a	Speed: Subsonic
Wingspan: n/a	Powerplant: n/a
Launch weight: 1100kg (2425lb)	Guidance system: INS, TERCOM, DSMAC, GPS,
Warhead weight: n/a	COMPASS

ASMs in Desert Storm

While the vast majority of air-launched ordnance expended during the 1991 Gulf War was of the unguided or 'dumb' variety, the conflict was also notable for its use of some advanced ASMs.

THE MOST POWERFUL ASM employed by the Coalition air arms during *Desert Storm* was the AGM-86C Conventional Air-Launched Cruise Missile (CALCM), which became operational in January 1991 and made its debut over Iraq. In *Desert Storm*, all 35 CALCMs were launched by B-52Gs during the first night of the war. Flying from Barksdale Air Force Base in the US, the seven B-52Gs were responsible for the longest known aircraft combat sorties in history, each involving 35 hours of flight. Later in the same decade, the CALCM was used again against Iraq in Operations *Desert Strike* (1996) and *Desert Fox* (1998) and during NATO's *Allied Force* campaign against Serbia in 1999.

Maverick to the fore

With the USAF flying the bulk of the almost 50,000 fixed-wing attack missions flown during the conflict, the key air-launched missiles comprised the AGM-65 Maverick and AGM-88 HARM. Numerically by far the most important missile was the AGM-65, with more than 5000 examples launched, in five different variants. Of those employed by the USAF, over 90 per cent were launched by A-10 Thunderbolt IIs, reflecting the importance of the anti-armour mission during the campaign. A-10s typically fired their Mavericks from a range of 5–6km (3–4 miles), eliminating the need to overfly the target. A typical A-10 load-out consisted of two electro-optical Mavericks, four Rockeye cluster bombs and a full load of 30mm (1.18in) ammunition for the cannon.

The Maverick was also used by F-16s that were assigned the close air support and battlefield air interdiction roles. In total, 116 AGM-65s were launched by F-16s in the conflict, and these contributed to the destruction of 360 armoured vehicles claimed by this aircraft. Overall, the USAF's Maverick was credited with a hit rate of between 80 and 90 per cent.

Slightly less successful were the AGM-65Es launched by the USMC, which achieved hit rates in the region of 60 per cent. The IIR seeker of the AGM-65D was found to be ineffective in certain situations as a result of thermal clutter caused by the heat of the desert. Following the war, a new CCD seeker was developed for the Maverick by Raytheon.

Iraq's highly integrated air defence system was tackled by the USAF's 'Wild Weasel' F-4Gs armed with AGM-88B Block III missiles. A total of 116 USAF F-4Es were converted to F-4G standard, becoming the ultimate 'Wild Weasel' platform, armed with AGM-65 and AGM-88 missiles and with the AN/APR-38 radar homing and warning system, with no fewer than 52 antennas. The HARM had

US air-to-surface missiles in Operation *Desert Storm*

Missile	Number used
AGM-62B Walleye II	133
AGM-65 Maverick	5296
AGM-84E SLAM	7
AGM-86C CALCM	35
Total	**5471**

US anti-radar missiles in in Operation *Desert Storm*

Missile	Number used
AGM-45 Shrike	78
AGM-88 HARM	1961
Total	**2039**

AGM-65 variants used in Operation *Desert Storm*

Variant	Guidance	Number used
AGM-65B	EO	1673
AGM-65C	Laser	5
AGM-65D	IR	3405
AGM-65E	Laser	36
AGM-65G	IR	177
	Total	**5296**

▲ **Cruise missile**

A right side view of an AGM-86C Conventional Air-Launched Cruise Missile (CALCM) during a test flight. The AGM-86C was used very successfully during Operation *Desert Storm* in 1991, and in NATO operations against Serbia in 1999.

made its combat debut in US Navy hands in the course of raids on Libya's Gulf of Sidra in 1986, but *Desert Storm* was the first time the weapon had been deployed in considerable numbers. In total, almost 2000 HARMs were employed during the air war, with some 40 per cent of these launched at Iraqi air defence installations by F-4Gs. Other HARM carriers included the US Navy's F/A-18, EA-6B, A-7 (over 140 HARMs launched) and A-6E, the latter also launching ADM-141 Tactical Air Launched Decoy (TALD) defence suppression drones. HARM tactics saw large number of missiles 'lobbed' against Iraqi air defences in a pre-emptive manner, immediately before a conventional strike package arrived in the area. Once the air defence operators detected the incoming attack aircraft, they either switched on their radars, which were then targeted by the HARMs, or were forced to keep their systems shut down in anticipation of the HARM threat. In some instances, the launch signal for the HARM was enough in itself to keep the Iraqi radars silent.

Supporting the HARM in the anti-radar mission over Iraq was the RAF's ALARM system, with 112 examples being expended by Tornado GR.Mk 1s, the conflict marking the debut of this missile. Compared to the HARM, which typically flew a shallow dive trajectory onto its target, the ALARM climbed steeply following launch, before diving vertically and at great speed upon the emitting radar. A number of anecdotes suggest that the ALARM was so feared by Iraqi radar operators that on occasions it was sufficient for RAF Tornado aircrew to report a launch over an open radio frequency, at which point the radar shut down.

Also used in *Desert Storm* was the USMC's AGM-123 Skipper II, which had been developed as a low-cost solution for extending the range of the Paveway laser-guided bomb. Entering service in 1985, the Skipper II added the rocket motor of the HARM to a GBU-16 LGB. The launch aircraft for the three Skipper IIs expended in the Gulf was the A-6E of VMFA-224 and VMFA-533.

Walleye finale

One weapon to see its swansong in *Desert Storm* was the US Navy's Walleye guided bomb. Phase-out of the weapon had began in the late 1980s, but the Walleye was pressed into combat service in the Gulf, primarily being launched by A-7E Corsair IIs.

A weapon that made its debut in the Gulf was the AGM-84H SLAM, examples of which were launched by US Navy A-6s and F/A-18s before the weapon had even been officially cleared for service. The debut SLAM mission was conducted by an A-6E, which launched two examples of the missile that were then guided to their target – an Iraqi powerplant – by an A-7E. Both aircraft were operating from the carrier USS *John F. Kennedy*.

Finally, the French Air Force Jaguar fleet expended around 60 examples of the laser-guided AS.30L missile, using the ATLIS targeting pod. Targets against which the AS.30L were employed included hardened shelters in Kuwait and southern Iraq. Using the ATLIS in an aft-facing installation, the Jaguars could execute a hard turn after releasing the weapon, flying away from the target with the pod continuing to designate.

Specifications

Length overall: 4100mm (13ft)	Range: 106km (66 miles)
Fuselage diameter: 254mm (10in)	Speed: 2280km/h (1420mph)
Wingspan: 1100mm (43.3in)	Powerplant: Thiokol SR113-TC-1 dual-thrust
Launch weight: 355kg (780lb)	rocket engine
Warhead weight: 66kg (150lb)	Guidance system: Passive radar

▼ AGM-88B HARM

The major HARM version used by the USAF during Operation *Desert Storm* was the AGM-88B Block III, this weapon being characterized by its improved in-flight reprogramming capabilities, allowing new threats to be added to the missile's database at short notice. The US Navy meanwhile retained the earlier Block II missile, which was considered safer for operations on carrier decks.

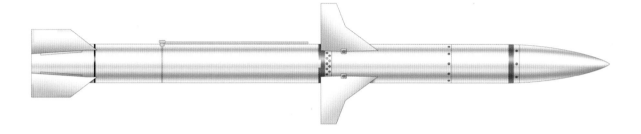

▼ AGM-86C CALCM

Seen here in prototype form, the conventionally armed AGM-86C had entered service only weeks before the Gulf War broke out. The first of the CALCMs to go operational were in Block 0 (or Baseline) configuration, armed with a blast-fragmentation warhead and employing an early form of GPS guidance.

Specifications

Length overall: 6350mm (20ft 10in)	Range: 1100km (680 miles)
Fuselage diameter: 620mm (24in)	Speed: 890km/h (550mph); Mach 0.73
Wingspan: 3650mm (143.7in)	Powerplant: Williams International F107-WR-101
Launch weight: 1429kg (3200lb)	turbofan
Warhead weight: 1400kg (3000lb)	Guidance system: INS-GPS

▼ AS.30L

The AS.30L that armed French Air Force Jaguars deployed to the Gulf proved to be a very useful weapon. Features include the Thomson-CSF Ariel laser seeker, a gyro unit for mid-course correction, and a hardened case penetrator warhead with a delayed fuse. The combination of supersonic performance and hardened warhead allow the AS.30L to defeat over 6ft (2m) of reinforced concrete.

Specifications

Length overall: 3700mm (12ft 1in)	Speed: 1700km/h (1056mph)
Fuselage diameter: 340mm (13in)	Powerplant: Two-stage solid-fuel rocket motors,
Wingspan: 1000mm (39.4in)	composite booster, double-based sustainer
Launch weight: 520kg (1146lb)	Guidance system: Semi-active laser homing
Warhead weight: 240kg (529lb)	
Range: 11km (6.8 miles)	

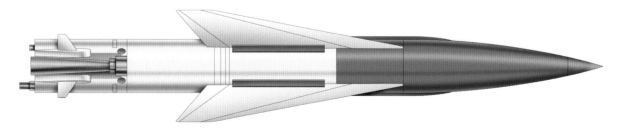

ASMs in the Global War on Terror

Wars in Afghanistan and Iraq in the early 21st century have seen an increasing reliance on precision air-to-ground weaponry, with the aim of reducing collateral damage.

IN ADDITION TO long-established US-developed missiles such as the AGM-65 and AGM-88, the conflicts waged by Coalition air power in Afghanistan from 2001 and in Iraq from 2003 have seen the use of a number of new and increasingly accurate air-to-ground weapons. At the same time, the shift towards close air support missions, the frequent close proximity of allied troops, and the drive to introduce lower-cost GPS-guided weapons such as the Joint Direct Attack Munition (JDAM) has seen the more expensive and more lethal ASMs restricted to attacks on only the most hardened or high-value targets.

Of the established weapons, a total of 918 Mavericks were used in Operation *Iraqi Freedom* in 2003, these missiles now being increasingly applied against urban targets. Also utilized were 408 HARMs, 153 air-launched AGM-86C/D CALCMs and three US Navy SLAM-ERs. In Operation *Enduring Freedom*, which began over Afghanistan in 2001, Coalition air commanders have repeatedly demonstrated their preference for using laser- and GPS-guided bombs rather than missiles. Indeed, by December 2001, 6546 US air strike sorties had been flown, although only four of these involved the use of ASMs (AGM-65G, AGM-130 and AGM-142). Overall, however, Afghanistan demonstrated the

ever-increasing importance of precision-guided ordnance, with some 56 per cent of all air-launched weapons being precision guided. This figure is in contrast to around 35 per cent during Operation *Allied Force* over the former Yugoslavia, and just 7–8 per cent during Operation *Desert Storm* in 1991.

The first official combat use of the AGM-130 occurred during 1999 against Iraqi air defence installations (unsuccessfully) during Operation *Northern Watch* and against a railway bridge in Serbia in the same year; it was also credited with destroying two Serbian MiG-29s on the ground. The missile, a powered version of the GBU-15 glide-bomb, was used in 2001 during *Enduring Freedom* and later over Iraq. In total, the USAF launched four AGM-130s during *Iraqi Freedom*.

JSOW debut

The AGM-154 JSOW saw its combat debut during *Allied Force* in Kosovo before being employed in Afghanistan and over Iraq. The very first combat use of the JSOW was recorded by F/A-18s flying from the carrier USS *Carl Vinson* when three such weapons were used to attack missile sites in southern Iraq in 1999. When US forces returned to Iraq in 2003, a total of 253 JSOWs were expended.

▼ **AGM-130**

In USAF service, the AGM-130 is deployed only by the F-15E, and in the 'Global War on Terror' it has been the only powered air-to-surface weapon employed by this aircraft. Each F-15E normally carries a single AGM-130 under the wing.

Specifications

Length overall: 3920mm (12ft 10.5in)	Warhead weight: 240kg or 430kg
Fuselage diameter: 380–460mm (15–18in)	(520lb or 950lb)
Wingspan: 1500mm (59in)	Range: More than 60km (40 miles)
Launch weight: 1323kg (2917lb)	Powerplant: Solid-fuel rocket engine
	Guidance system: Inertial, GPS

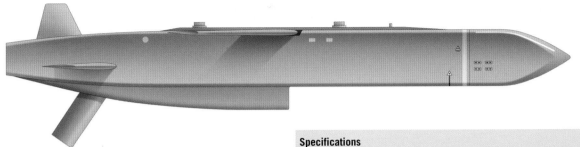

▲ Storm Shadow

The RAF's Storm Shadow made its combat debut during the invasion of Iraq in March 2003, carried by Tornado aircraft flying from Ali Al Salem in Kuwait. The standoff missile was used against hardened targets of the Iraqi High Command.

Specifications

Length overall: 5100mm (16ft 8in)	Range: 250km (155 miles)
Fuselage diameter: 1660mm (65.4in)	Speed: 1000km/h (621mph)
Wingspan: 2840mm (111.8in)	Powerplant: Turbomeca Microturbo TRI 60-30
Launch weight: 1230kg (2710lb)	turbojet
Warhead weight: 450kg (992lb)	Guidance system: Inertial, GPS, TERPROM

The Storm Shadow was successfully deployed by Tornado GR.Mk 4s of No. 617 'Dambusters' Squadron during Operation *Telic*, the RAF's contribution to *Iraqi Freedom*, in 2003. A total of 27 missiles were fired during the conflict. The only other British ASM used during *Telic* – 47 in total – was the ALARM. Meanwhile, RAF Harriers launched 38 US-supplied AGM-65G Maverick missiles.

The Have Nap was first used in *Allied Force* (two missions) before being employed in small numbers during *Enduring Freedom* in Afghanistan in 2001. In the latter instance, a handful of the missiles were launched from USAF B-52Hs against fortified targets.

SLAM-ERs deployed over Afghanistan were fired from US Navy P-3 Orion maritime surveillance aircraft during the first night of attacks. Around 10 SLAM-ERs were directed against high-priority Taliban and al-Qaeda targets including key buildings and an air defence site.

▼ Test run

A US Air Force F-15E Strike Eagle aircraft releases a specially painted AGM-130 missile over the Utah Test and Training Range, 2002.

Chapter 3

Anti-Ship Missiles

Air-launched AShMs (anti-ship missiles) were employed with notable success by Germany in the Mediterranean theatre in World War II, and the importance of these weapons grew as a powerful counter to aircraft carriers and other capital ships during the Cold War years. In the Soviet Union in particular, a potent range of air-launched AShMs were fielded as a means of challenging the threat posed by the growing US Navy carrier fleet. By the early 1980s, events in the Persian Gulf and the South Atlantic demonstrated that the air-launched AShM also presented small navies with an important tool to challenge the supremacy of larger maritime powers.

◀ **Soviet ship-buster**
The Swedish Air Force intercepted this Soviet Navy Tu-22M-2 armed with a single Kh-22 (AS-4 'Kitchen') AShM during the Cold War. The Baltic Sea was of critical importance during the superpower standoff, and its geography meant that AShM would have been key to its control. The supersonic Kh-22 entered service in 1967 and became the primary weapon for the 'Backfire' bomber.

Cold War anti-ship missiles

Early efforts to develop air-launched AShMs took place in the USSR and in France, the former stressing larger, nuclear-capable weapons, and the latter lighter, wire-guided types.

THE FIRST SUCCESSFUL Soviet AShM was the KS-1 Komet (AS-1 'Kennel'), developed from 1947. Powered by an RD-500 turbojet engine, the KS-1 entered service with Tu-4 bombers of the Soviet Navy's Black Sea Fleet in 1954. At one point the Soviet authorities considered using the Tu-4 and KS-1 against US Navy carriers involved in the Korean War, but sufficient trained crews were not available in time. Also in 1954, the Tu-16 jet bomber began to be adapted for carrying the KS-1, with a first launch recorded in 1957. The target for the KS-1 was detected and then tracked by the launch aircraft's Kobalt radar and the missile was guided to the target using beam-riding guidance, before the missile's own passive radar seeker achieved a lock-on for the terminal phase. Although this form of guidance was primitive and could be susceptible to countermeasures, the KS-1 was a success and remained in service with the Tu-16 into the 1970s.

The K-10 (AS-2 'Kipper') was the first supersonic Soviet air-launched AShM, with development beginning in 1955. The carrier aircraft for the new turbojet-powered missile was again the Tu-16, which could carry a single example of the weapon under its fuselage. The missile guidance utilized the carrier aircraft's YeN radar for target detection, the K-10 flying to the vicinity of the target using its autopilot, with mid-course guidance from the Tu-16. Terminal guidance was achieved through the missile's active radar. Either a shaped-charge high-explosive or nuclear (in the K-10S version) warhead was carried, and the missile dived onto the target to strike the ship at low level. The K-10 entered service in 1961 and was also produced as an ECM drone.

New weapon for the Tu-16

The KSR-2 (AS-5 'Kelt') was intended to succeed the KS-1 and was powered by a liquid-fuel rocket motor, with high-explosive or nuclear warhead options. The carrier aircraft was the Tu-16, which could accommodate two of the high-subsonic KSR-2s underwing. The target was acquired by the aircraft's Rubin search radar, and the missile incorporated inertial guidance with an autopilot receiving command updates, and an active radar seeker for the terminal phase of the attack. The Soviet Navy

Specifications

Length overall: 1870mm (6ft 1.6in)	Range: 7–8km (4.3–5 miles)
Fuselage diameter: Body 180mm (7in); warhead 210mm (8.3in)	Speed: 370km/h (230mph)
	Powerplant: Solid-fuel rocket
Wingspan: 650mm (25.6in)	Guidance system: Wire Manual Command to Line of Sight (MCLOS)
Launch weight: 76kg (167.5lb)	
Warhead weight: 28kg (62lb)	

▼ **AS.12**

The AS.12 was a basic weapon utilizing wire guidance, which required launch from a height of 122m (400ft) to maintain line of sight, and to prevent the control wires contacting the water. It was used with some success, however, both in the Iran–Iraq War and during the Falklands campaign. When fired by Wasp helicopters against an Argentine submarine in the Falklands, the missiles passed directly through the submarine's conning tower without exploding.

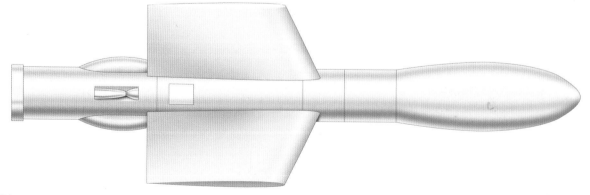

introduced the KSR-2 missile into operational service in 1965.

Developed for carriage by the Tu-22 supersonic bomber, the Kh-22 (AS-4 'Kitchen') retained the liquid-fuel rocket propulsion of the KSR-2, but was capable of high-supersonic performance in order to penetrate more capable air defences. The anti-shipping version of the missile used an active radar seeker (with the designation PG) that acquired the target while the missile was still on the aircraft, and carried a shaped-charge high-explosive or nuclear warhead. There was also a version of the missile with an inertial Doppler dead-reckoning system (known as PSI) and a nuclear-only warhead. The latter could be used for attacks on area targets, such as large groups of ships. After launch, the anti-ship Kh-22 climbs to an altitude of 22,500m (73,820ft), where it cruises at Mach 3.4. After activation of the homing system, the seeker tracks the target before the missile executes a 30° terminal dive. With the area-target version, the

bomber's radar provides the target location, the missile's radar emitting a signal in the target's direction, following the radar returns to home in on the coordinates.

The original Tu-22K missile-carrier and Kh-22 combination entered service in 1967 and was followed in 1975 by a modernized missile, the Kh-22M, which was optimized for the variable-geometry Tu-22M bomber that entered service in 1979. The new missile had a three-stage motor and a modified autopilot, and could also be carried by the earlier Tu-22K and Tu-95K-22. The Kh-22N, meanwhile, was a version with optional high- or low-altitude launch parameters, providing improved chances of penetrating enemy air defence systems. Guidance and warhead options were as before.

▼ **Westland with Sea Skua**

A British Royal Navy Westland Super Lynx helicopter armed with Sea Skua missiles undergoes training somewhere on the British coast, early 1980s.

Development of the KSR-5 (AS-6 'Kingfish') was informed by the Kh-22 and was authorized in 1974. Arming upgraded Tu-16s, a single KSR-5 was carried under each wing (with a K-10 under the fuselage in some versions). The missile was provided with an active radar homing guidance system, with the target acquired prior to missile launch, coordinates being delivered by the carrier aircraft's Rubin or Yen radar. The flight profile was similar to that of the Kh-22 with inertial guidance, and there was also an anti-radar version with passive radar homing. This KSR-5P could also be used against ship-based radars. As with the Kh-22, a KSR-5N version was provided with improved low-altitude performance, and

therefore featured modifications to its guidance system. The motor had five different altitude modes.

French anti-shipping

In France, development of a dedicated air-launched AShM began with the lightweight Nord AS.12, an airborne version of the SS.12 wire-guided anti-tank missile. First fielded in 1960 by French Navy Etendard carrier-borne fighters, the solid-fuel AS.12 retained the wire guidance, with tracking flares at the rear to serve as an optical aid. Key to the success of the AS.12 was the fact that its light weight made it suitable for carriage by helicopters. This fact was exploited by the AS.15TT, an improved AShM optimized for launch from rotary-wing platforms. Developed by Aérospatiale with Saudi Arabian funding, the 'TT' indicated *tous temps* (all-weather), and the missile used radio command guidance, with

▼ KS-1 (AS-1 'Kennel')

When the KS-1 entered Soviet Navy service in 1954, the carrier aircraft was the Tu-4 piston-engined bomber of the Black Sea Fleet. Subsequently the KS-1 was used by the Tu-16 missile-carrier, which began trials in 1954 and which was operated by the Black Sea, Baltic and Northern Fleets. In both cases, the bombers carried two examples of the missile underwing.

Specifications

Length overall: 8290mm (27ft 2in)	Range: 100km (60 miles)
Fuselage diameter: 1150m (45.3in)	Speed: 1060km/h (659mph)
Wingspan: 4900m (192.9in)	Powerplant: RD-500K turbojet
Launch weight: 2735kg (6030lb)	Guidance system: Semi-active radar with
Warhead weight: 1000kg (2200lb)	passive terminal homing

▼ Kormoran

The Kormoran fire-and-forget missile was optimized for use in the Baltic Sea, where the German Navy would have been tasked with closing down the approaches to Warsaw Pact shipping. The missile was also exported to Italy, who put the weapon to use within a single Tornado IDS unit, 36° Stormo.

Specifications

Length overall: 4400mm (14ft 4.8in)	Range: 35km (22 miles)
Fuselage diameter: 344mm (13.5in)	Speed: Mach 0.9
Wingspan: 1220mm (56.7in)	Powerplant: Solid-fuel rocket motor
Launch weight: 630kg (1388lb)	Guidance system: INS, active radar homing
Warhead weight: 220kg (485lb)	

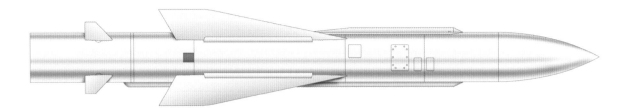

missile and target tracking carried out by the launch helicopter's Agrion 15 radar. A first full test launch took place in 1982 and the missile is used by Panther maritime helicopters in Saudi Arabia and the UAE.

Another Aérospatiale anti-shipping product, the revolutionary fire-and-forget Exocet, gained notoriety on account of its contribution to the Falklands War and the Iran–Iraq conflict. Developed in the late 1960s to meet a French requirement, the Exocet has been produced in surface-, submarine- and air-launched versions. The airborne version is the AM.39 Exocet, a two-stage solid-fuel missile applicable for launch from both fixed-wing aircraft and larger helicopters. Target acquisition is conducted by the launch aircraft's radar, and then provided to the missile guidance system. The cruise

phase of the flight is undertaken using inertial guidance, with an active radar seeker switched on for the terminal phase, which is conducted using a sea-skimming flight profile. Manufacturer's trials of the airborne Exocet began in 1973, initially in preliminary AM.38 form, followed by production of the definitive, lighter-weight AM.39, testing of which was completed in 1978. The original platform for the AM.39 was the French Navy Super Etendard fighter, but it was soon adapted to many other aircraft.

Based on the Nord AS.34 design, the Kormoran was developed from 1964 for West Germany, and entered service on German Navy F-104G Starfighters before being adopted by German and Italian Tornado IDS aircraft. A fire-and-forget weapon, the Kormoran used the inertial guidance system from

▼ K-10 (AS-2 'Kipper')

Most examples of the K-10 were issued with nuclear warheads, which resulted in the designation K-10S. The live firing of nuclear-armed examples was initiated by a Northern Fleet Tu-16K-10 over Novaya Zemlya in August 1962. The 'Kipper' was also fielded as an ECM drone, to provide protection for strike aircraft.

Specifications

Length overall: 9750mm (32ft)	Range: 200km (125 miles)
Fuselage diameter: n/a	Speed: 2030km/h (1260mph)
Wingspan: 4180mm (164.6in)	Powerplant: n/a
Launch weight: 4500kg (9920lb)	Guidance system: n/a

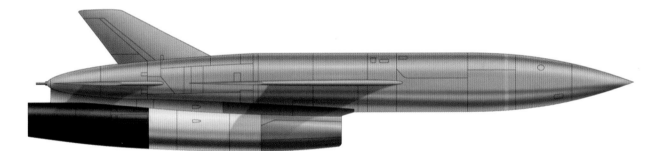

▼ Kh-22PG (AS-4 'Kitchen')

The Kh-22 is seen here in flight configuration, with the folding ventral fin in the deployed position. The different seeker heads can be distinguished by their external appearance: the PG active radar seeker has a dielectric radome, while the PSI with Doppler dead-reckoning has a metal nose, with a ventral dielectric panel.

Specifications

Length overall: 11.3m (37ft)	Range: 400km (248.5 miles)
Fuselage diameter: n/a	Speed: 3600km/h (2237mph)
Wingspan: 3350mm (131.9in)	Powerplant: Liquid-fuelled
Launch weight: 5900kg (13,007lb)	Guidance system: Inertial + active radar
Warhead weight: 1000kg (2205lb)	

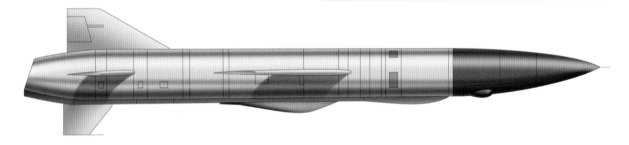

the experimental Franco-German AS.33 project, becoming an MBB-led project with assistance from Aérospatiale. The first flight trials were undertaken in 1970, with deliveries in 1977. The Kormoran has twin solid-fuel boost motors and a single sustainer, cruise flight using inertial guidance before the missile adopts a sea-skimming attack profile under the guidance of its onboard radar, which has pre-set active or passive modes. The definitive Kormoran 2 has longer range, a multiple-launch capability, an improved warhead and improved ECM resistance.

In Italy, AShM development initially focused on ship-based weapons, before the introduction of the Marte medium-range missile intended for use by Italian Navy AB.212 and SH-3 helicopters. The original Marte Mk 1 was based on the surface-launched Contraves Italiana Sea Killer Mk 2 AShM, with initial development by Sistel from 1970. Service entry followed in 1977. The Marte 2 was upgraded by Otobreda through the addition of a new active terminal seeker (taken from the Otomat surface-launched AShM), resulting in a reprofiled, bulbous nose. The Marte 2 entered service on Italian Navy SH-3Ds in the mid 1980s. An air-launched version for fixed-wing platforms was the Marte 2/A, first tested in 1995.

In the UK, two AShM programmes were launched to replace the AS.12 and the Martel. These resulted in BAe's Sea Eagle and Sea Skua respectively. Introduced on the Royal Navy's Lynx helicopter fleet in time to see combat in the Falklands, the Sea Skua was developed to tackle small and agile naval vessels, such as missile-armed fast attack craft, and requires target illumination by the launch helicopter. In the case of the Lynx, this is achieved using the Seaspray surveillance and target-tracking radar. The missile carries a semi-active radar homing seeker, which picks up the reflected energy from the target.

Sea Eagle for the Buccaneer

The Sea Eagle was a heavyweight fire-and-forget weapon with over-the-horizon range, designed to arm the RAF's Buccaneer fleet. Developed by BAe in response to a request of the early 1970s, the Sea Eagle started launch trials in 1980, and initial deliveries began in 1985. Subsequently, the Sea Eagle was adopted by the Tornado GR.Mk 1 fleet when this took over the maritime attack role. The weapon was also cleared for the Nimrod and Sea Harrier, and remains in use with Indian Navy Jaguars and Sea King Mk 42Bs.

The Sea Eagle uses the basic airframe of the Martel, but adapted with an underslung air intake to feed a turbojet engine. An autopilot provides initial guidance, based on the last known coordinates of the target. For the terminal phase, guidance switches over to an active radar seeker.

During the 1967 Six-Day War, Israel was on the receiving end of some of the first successful post-war AShM attacks. The loss of the destroyer *Eilat* to Egyptian fast attack craft armed with Soviet-made AShMs prompted the development of indigenous weapons in this class to supersede the lightweight French weapons previously in Israeli use. The result was the Gabriel family, which initially equipped the 'Saar' class of missile craft. The Gabriel III was the first to feature a fire-and-forget capability, this replacing the semi-active radar homing previously

▼ KSR-5 (AS-6 'Kingfish')

Similar in outward appearance to the Kh-22, the KSR-5 was carried operationally only by variants of the Tu-16. In its basic form, the KSR-5 approached the enemy warship in a dive, which was initiated at a distance of around 60km (37 miles) from the target, after having climbed to cruise level at full power.

Specifications	
Length overall: 10.56m (8ft 6in)	Range: 300–700km (185–435 miles)
Fuselage diameter: 900mm (34.4in)	Speed: Mach 3
Wingspan: 2600m (102.3in)	Powerplant: n/a
Launch weight: 4500kg (9920lb)	Guidance system: (Mid-course) INS, (terminal)
Warhead weight: 1000kg (200lb)	either active or passive radar seeker

▼ Marte Mk 1

The Marte was evolved from the surface-launched Sea Killer Mk 2, developed as a private-venture AShM and not adopted by the Italian Navy. In this respect, the air-launched Marte proved more successful, and was selected in the mid 1970s as the primary missile armament for Italian Navy AB.212 and SH-3D helicopters. Compared to the Marte 2, the Mk 1 had a smaller-diameter nose.

Specifications

Length overall: 3790mm (12ft 5in)	Range: 25km (15.5 miles)
Fuselage diameter: 320mm (12.6in)	Speed: Mach 8–9
Wingspan: n/a	Powerplant: n/a
Launch weight: 324kg (713lb)	Guidance system: GPS, INS radar
Warhead weight: 70kg (154lb) HE	

▼ Gabriel III/AS

Originally developed as a counter to Egyptian P-15 (SS-N-2 'Styx') ship-launched missiles, the Gabriel first entered service in 1972, but an air-launched derivative was not offered until 1981, and emerged as an altogether more sophisticated weapon, with an active radar terminal seeker and twice the range of its predecessor. An extended-range (ER) version has a range of 60km (37 miles).

Specifications

Length overall: 3350mm (11ft)	Range: Mk II 20km (12.4 miles); 36km (22.4
Fuselage diameter: 340mm (13.3in)	miles)
Wingspan: 1350mm (53.1)	Speed: 386km/h (240mph)
Launch weight: Mk I 430kg (948lb); Mk II 522kg	Powerplant: n/a
(1151lb)	Guidance system: Semi-active radar and manual
Warhead weight: 100kg (220lb)	

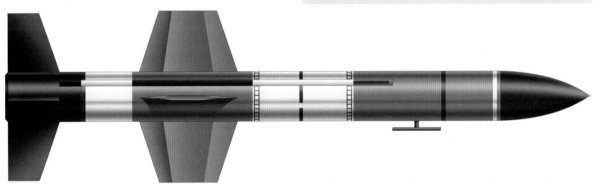

employed. It was this version that served as the basis for the first air-launched model, the Gabriel III/AS. The primary carrier aircraft associated with the Gabriel was the F-4E. The basic air-launched Gabriel IIIA/S was followed by the Mk IIIA/S ER, with a lengthened sustainer motor to provide an extended range of 60km (38 miles). The air-launched versions retain the guidance of the standard Gabriel III, with terminal homing using an active radar seeker.

Japan's first indigenous AShM was the ASM-1, developed from 1973 by Mitsubishi to arm the F-1 attack fighter, as well as the F-4EJ and P-3. Also known as the Type 80, this is a solid-propellant

missile with inertial guidance for the cruise phase, an active radar seeker for terminal homing and a semi-armour-piercing warhead. The ASM-1C (Type 91) was introduced in 1991, and it featured an extended range capability.

For many years the primary Chinese weapon in this class was the YJ-6 (exported as the C-601), before a new generation of lighter and more capable weapons became available to aircraft of the PLA. The C-601 was developed from the Soviet surface-launched P-15 from the late 1970s and entered service in 1985, arming the H-6B missile-carrier. Powered by a liquid-fuel rocket motor, guidance is a combination of inertial with an active radar seeker.

Specifications

Length overall: 4140m (13ft 7in)	Range: More than 110km (68 miles)
Fuselage diameter: n/a	Speed: More than Mach 0.85
Wingspan: 1200mm (47.2in)	Powerplant: Turbojet
Launch weight: 580kg (1279lb)	Guidance system: Inertial, with active radar
Warhead weight: 230kg (507lb)	homing

▼ Sea Eagle

Using the Sea Eagle, salvo attacks are possible against a single target, with missiles approaching the warship from different directions. Another option is for the missile to overfly one warship in order to prosecute an attack against a higher-priority target. As of 2010, India was the only remaining operator.

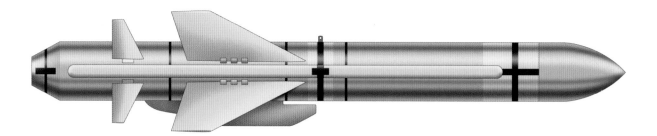

▼ ASM-1

The ASM-1 was designed to be compatible with the J/AWG-11 fire-control system of the Japanese F-1 attack fighter. After the air-launched model had been fielded, development of a coastal defence system (SSM-1 or Type 88) followed, while the ASM-1C (Type 91) was optimized for launch by the P-3C maritime patrol aircraft.

Specifications

Length overall: 4000mm (13ft 1in)	Range: 50km (31 miles)
Fuselage diameter: 350mm (14in)	Speed: n/a
Wingspan: 1200m (47.2in)	Powerplant: Solid-fuel engine
Launch weight: 600kg (1323lb)	Guidance system: Inertial and active radar
Warhead weight: 150kg (331lb)	

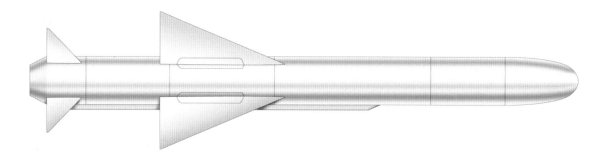

▼ YJ-6 (C-601)

The C-601 is the export version of the YJ-6. Both weapons have the reporting name CAS-1 'Kraken'. Although design work began in 1966, the YJ-6 was not introduced to service for another two decades. After target detection by the H-6D carrier aircraft, the YJ-6 flies to the target under inertial guidance, with active radar terminal homing conducted at one of three pre-set flight levels.

Specifications

Length overall: 7100mm (23ft 3.5in)	Range: 90–100km (56–62 miles)
Fuselage diameter: 760mm (30in)	Speed: n/a
Wingspan: 2400m (94.5in)	Powerplant: Liquid-fuel rocket engine
Launch weight: 2988kg (6587lb)	Guidance system: Automatic control + homing
Warhead weight: n/a	

C 601

Anti-ship missiles in the Tanker War

During the Iran–Iraq War, both combatants made considerable efforts to disrupt each others' shipping and oil supplies, and air-launched anti-ship missiles played a key role in this campaign.

THE TANKER WAR began in 1981 with Iraqi efforts to weaken Iran's ability to continue the war, and initially targeted vessels that were bringing military supplies for onward transit to the battlefield, with Iraq stating its intention to attack any vessel entering or leaving an Iranian port in the northern part of the Gulf. Subsequently the campaign extended to vessels that were carrying Iran's vital exports.

Among the Iraqi Air Force aircraft used for anti-shipping strikes were Mirage F.1EQ-5 fighter-bombers equipped with Agave radar and SA.321GV Super Frelon helicopters, and both were capable of launching Exocet missiles.

In October 1981 a Super Frelon used an Exocet to sink the Liberian-registered bulk carrier *Al-Tajdar*, in the first successful use of this missile. Ultimately, of all the attacks prosecuted by both sides against shipping in the campaign, anti-ship missiles (whether air- or surface-launched) were used in more than half of these instances. For Iraq, the percentage was even higher, with anti-ship missiles employed in around 80 per cent of that country's attacks against commercial shipping in the Gulf. Exocets proved to be the most effective weapon, with around 600 launched during the conflict, and several pilots scored dozens of hits each. Also employed in an anti-ship role was the AS.30L, in use from early 1986.

After two years in which Iraq maintained the initiative in the Tanker War, Iran formulated a response and began to target shipping belonging to Iraq's trading partners and to nations that provided financial support to Iraq during the war, chiefly Kuwait and Saudi Arabia.

The catalyst for this widening of the campaign was Iraq's escalation of anti-shipping efforts in 1984, by which time the IrAF had introduced five Super

▼ **USS *Stark* damaged**

A port quarter view of the guided missile frigate USS *Stark* (FFG-31) listing to port after being struck by an Iraqi-launched Exocet missile.

Etendards leased from the French Navy. Acquired as a stopgap in 1983, the Super Etendard was first used in February 1984, attacking a Greek tanker, by which time Western reports noted that there had been 24 ship sinkings in the Gulf. The Super Etendard remained in use until 1985, when anti-shipping Mirages became available.

Extemporized response

Since Iran lacked dedicated AShMs, it was forced to adopt several creative solutions to the anti-ship mission. Instead, the IRIAF used AGM-65A Maverick ASMs to great effect, together with 'dumb' bombs, cluster weapons and rockets. Early Iranian use of the AGM-65 in a maritime context – and especially during Operation *Morvarid* in late 1980 – served to encourage development of the AGM-65F variant for the US Navy, engineers adding an IR seeker head and a more powerful warhead.

Attacks with these weapons were driven home with precision, but even dedicated AShMs were not necessarily powerful enough to disable a target as large as an oil tanker. Of all the vessels attacked during the campaign, more than 60 per cent were oil tankers, but of these only 23 per cent were sunk or completely put out of action. Bulk carriers and freighters, however, proved far more vulnerable to attacks.

The IRIAF's campaign saw clashes with the Royal Saudi Air Force. In May 1984, IRIAF F-4Es targeted a Liberian ship with Mavericks and were in turn pursued by RSAF F-15s, with two Phantoms claimed shot down. By the end of 1984, 67 major vessels had been hit in attacks prosecuted by both sides. The year also saw the first use of the AS.12 AShM by Iranian AB.212 helicopters. In 1985, the Iranian Navy began using Maverick missiles launched from SH-3D Sea King helicopters that were reportedly stationed on the Rostam platform in the lower Gulf.

In the context of increasing Iranian attacks, the Tanker War took a significant turn in 1987, when the US Navy launched Operation *Earnest Will* and began to provide escorts to Kuwaiti oil tankers, and security to other tankers transporting oil to and from other countries in the Gulf.

In May 1987 an IrAF Mirage F.1 launched an Exocet that hit and damaged the US Navy frigate USS *Stark*. The Iraqi regime apologized for the incident, claiming that the intended target was a tanker. Throughout 1987, a total of 178 ships were hit, compared to around half that number in the previous year. The IRIAF also resumed its attacks on shipping in 1987, with F-4s targeting vessels in retaliation for an IrAF raid on Kharg Island. F-4Es deployed AGM-65As as well as general-purpose bombs and, more unusually, AIM-9 Sidewinder AAMs and RIM-66B Standard naval SAMs adapted for use as air-launched AShMs.

The US Navy ultimately began to attack Iranian shipping, and A-6s sunk the Iranian frigate *Sahand* with AGM-84D and AGM-123 missiles after she engaged US Navy warships in the Strait of Hormuz.

Anti-ship missiles in the Falklands

The naval war in the South Atlantic in 1982 saw the use of AShMs old and new, with the Exocet in particular highlighting deficiencies in Western naval defences and early warning systems.

THE EXOCET became a signature weapon in the Falklands, it had in the Tanker War. Only five air-launched AM.39s were available to the Argentine Navy's fleet of Super Etendards, but these succeeded in inflicting considerable damage and disruption upon the British Task Force. On 4 May 1982, an Argentine Navy SP-32H Neptune found the destroyer HMS *Sheffield*, against which three Super Etendards were then launched. Two aircraft were armed with AM.39s, with the third acting as a target designator. After being refuelled by the two remaining Super Etendards, the attackers launched their missiles at a range of 43km (27 miles). Target data was supplied by the unarmed aircraft, which had climbed, while the two strike jets flew at low level. The first missile arrived without warning and hit *Sheffield* above the waterline, causing severe damage and setting the warship ablaze. The second Exocet, which was directed at the frigate HMS *Yarmouth*, was successfully decoyed away from its target. *Sheffield*

▼ Sea Skua

The Sea Skua is powered by a solid-propellant boost/sustain motor, and once launched the missile adopts one of four sea-skimming flight profiles, depending on sea state. After approaching the target at low level, the missile then 'pops up' to allow the semi-active radar homing seeker to gain a lock-on.

Specifications

Length overall: 2500mm (8ft 2.4in)	Range: 25km (15.5 miles)
Fuselage diameter: 250mm (9.8in)	Speed: Mach 0.8+
Wingspan: 720mm (28.3in)	Powerplant: Solid-fuel booster/solid-fuel
Launch weight: 145kg (320lb)	sustainer
Warhead weight: SAP 30kg (66.1lb); RDX 9kg	Guidance system: Semi-active radar
(19.8lb)	

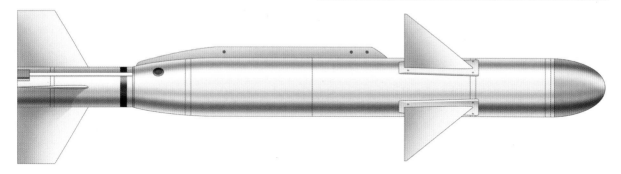

▼ AM.39 Exocet

Flying at low level, in 1982 the Exocet achieved surprise against an ill-prepared Royal Navy Task Force that lacked adequate AEW assets. Only five air-launched rounds were available to the Argentines, although use was also made of an extemporized ground launcher that was deployed to the Falkland Islands.

Specifications

Length overall: 4700mm (15ft 5in)	Range: 70–180km (43–110 miles)
Fuselage diameter: 348mm (13.7in)	Speed: 1134km/h (704.6mph)
Wingspan: 1100mm (43.3in)	Powerplant: Solid-fuel engine turbojet (MM40
Launch weight: 670kg (1500lb)	Block 3 version)
Warhead weight: 165kg (360lb)	Guidance system: Inertial, active radar homing

had to be abandoned, and 21 sailors were killed in the shocking attack.

Two more Super Etendards were launched with Exocets on 25 May, supported by a KC-130H Hercules tanker. The aircraft discovered a target northeast of the Falklands, although the Task Force this time detected the attackers. All warships in the area deployed ECM and opened fire with their air defence systems. The two Exocets were decoyed away from the warships, but instead locked on to the stores ship *Atlantic Conveyor*, which was hit by both missiles and had to be abandoned, with 12 sailors killed. The vessel went down, taking with it vital Chinook and Wessex helicopters, as well as other equipment.

The final AM.39 was launched on 30 May, when two Super Etendards accompanied by four A-4C

Skyhawks launched a strike against the HMS *Invincible* carrier task group, sailing east of the Falklands, again with KC-130H tanker support. The Argentines claimed that the missile inflicted damage upon *Invincible*, but the weapon seems to have been decoyed, or perhaps destroyed by gunfire from HMS *Avenger*, which also claimed a Skyhawk downed.

Sea Skua in action

The Sea Skua debuted in the South Atlantic on 3 May, when a Royal Navy Lynx from HMS *Coventry* attacked a converted tug in Argentine service. This vessel, the *Comodoro Somerella*, was in the Total Exclusion Zone (TEZ) around the Falklands, and had earlier fired upon an RN Sea King. The Lynx ripple-fired two Sea Skuas, which destroyed the vessel. Another Lynx, this time from HMS *Glasgow*, sent to look for survivors was then fired upon by another vessel. In response, the Lynx fired another two Sea Skuas, which inflicted serious damage upon the *Allerez Sobral*, sister vessel to *Somerella*. Four more Sea Skuas were launched by Lynxes against the cargo ship *Rio Carcarania* on 21 May, setting it ablaze. The Royal Navy also armed its Wasp helicopters with the older AS.12 missiles in the Falklands, and this combination succeeded in seriously damaging the Argentine submarine *Santa Fé* off South Georgia on 25 April, helping to prevent the submarine from making its escape.

▼ **HMS *Sheffield* damaged**
The Royal Navy Type 42 destroyer burns following a hit by an Exocet missile.

Modern anti-ship missiles

Israeli success in defeating Egyptian AShMs in the Yom Kippur War demonstrated the importance of electronic warfare at sea, also reflected in the next generation of naval missiles.

THE SIGNIFICANCE OF the AShM in campaigns in the Middle East prompted the US to accelerate its developments in this area. The AGM-84 Harpoon had originally been developed from 1965 as an air-launched weapon for use against surfaced submarines, but became a family of anti-ship weapons for air, surface and submarine launch. The first AGM-84A was flown in 1972, with turbojet propulsion. Production began in 1975, and the AGM-84A entered service on the P-3 in 1979. Guidance is based on an Attitude Reference Assembly, a type of inertial system, with an active

radar seeker for the terminal phase. The Harpoon Block 1B, or AGM-84C, flies at low level, without a 'pop-up' attack profile. The Block 1C (AGM-84D) offers increased range and either a pop-up or sea-skimming attack profile. Subsequent versions include the Block 1G (AGM-84G) with a re-attack capability and improved resistance to ECM, and the Block II with GPS guidance, and some elements from the SLAM. The Block II is an export-only project, designated AGM-84L in air-launched form, or AGM-84J when produced via the conversion of older variants. In development since 2008 is the Block III,

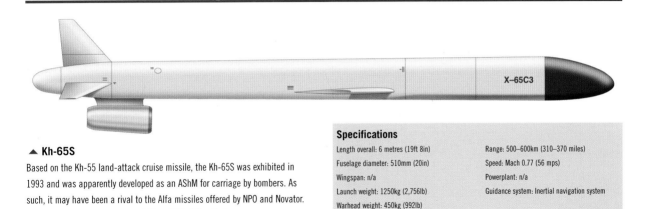

▲ Kh-65S

Based on the Kh-55 land-attack cruise missile, the Kh-65S was exhibited in 1993 and was apparently developed as an AShM for carriage by bombers. As such, it may have been a rival to the Alfa missiles offered by NPO and Novator. The Kh-65S had a range of 250–280km (155–174 miles).

Specifications

Length overall: 6 metres (19ft 8in)	Range: 500–600km (310–370 miles)
Fuselage diameter: 510mm (20in)	Speed: Mach 0.77 (56 mps)
Wingspan: n/a	Powerplant: n/a
Launch weight: 1250kg (2,756lb)	Guidance system: Inertial navigation system
Warhead weight: 450kg (992lb)	

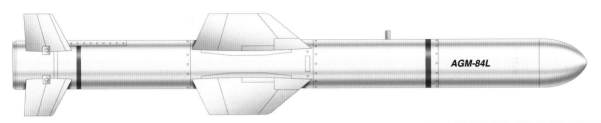

▲ AGM-84L Harpoon

Although the US Navy did not adopt the GPS-aided Harpoon Block II, the missile found export success. The air-launched Block II is the AGM-84L, used by Saudi Arabia and South Korea for their F-15 Strike Eagles, while India has ordered the weapon for its P-8I Poseidon.

Specifications

Length overall: 3800mm (12ft 7in)	Speed: 864km/h (537mph)
Fuselage diameter: 340mm (13.38in)	Powerplant: Teledyne solid-fuel turbojet
Wingspan: 910mm (35.8in)	Guidance system: Sea-skimming cruise
Launch weight: 691kg (1523lb)	monitored by radar altimeter/active radar
Warhead weight: 221kg (488lb)	terminal homing
Range: 124km (77 miles)	

or AGM-84M. This includes GPS guidance and a new seeker, as well as a two-way datalink to provide target updates and mid-course guidance.

Enhanced European missiles

Improvements continue to be made to the European Marte and Exocet AShMs, principally in order to arm a new generation of more sophisticated launch platforms. Now an MBDA product, the latest Marte Mk 2/S is optimized for more modern maritime helicopters, including the AW101 and NH90. The missile adds a greater use of digitalization, a refined radar seeker and it can follow pre-programmed trajectories to the target. Although a more powerful warhead is carried, overall weight and dimensions are actually reduced. The missile is also made more compact thanks to its folding wings and the replacement of the original co-axial booster by two smaller lateral boosters.

The latest Exocet version is the Block 2, this standard being used across the fleet, and including air-, surface- and submarine-launched models. Block 2 was introduced in 1990 and features a greater use of computers as part of a full electronics upgrade. In addition, the seeker includes improvements in its ability to discriminate between targets, and the missile is more resistance to ECM. The latest Block III version, with turbojet powerplant, is not adapted for air launch.

The Soviet-developed Kh-31A (AS-17 'Krypton') was the first in-service, air-launched AShM to feature a ramjet propulsion system, and the programme was launched in 1977. Using a solid-fuel booster and a ramjet sustainer, the Kh-31A can penetrate naval defences at low level, and at speeds of around Mach 4.5. Guidance is provided by an active homing radar seeker. Somewhat less exotic than the Kh-31A is the subsonic Kh-35 (AS-20 'Kayak'), development of

Specifications

Length overall: 4700mm (15ft 6in)	Range: 25–50km (15.5–31 miles)
Fuselage diameter: 360mm (14in)	Speed: 2160–2520km/h (1340–1570mph)
Wingspan: 1150mm (45in)	Powerplant: Solid-fuel rocket in initial stage,
Launch weight: 610kg (1340lb)	ramjet for rest of trajectory
Warhead weight: 94kg (207lb)	Guidance system: Inertial with active radar

▲ Kh-31A (AS-17 'Krypton')

On account of its ramjet propulsion system, the Soviet-designed Kh-31A remains in a class of its own as far as air-launched AShMs are concerned. As well as flying at a speed of Mach 4.5, the missile ensures it reaches its target by employing terminal manoeuvres, during which it can pull loads of up to 10g.

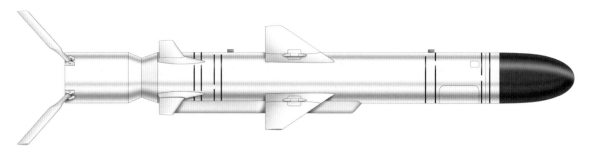

▲ Kh-35 (AS-20 'Kayak')

Originally intended to arm small missile boats and patrol vessels, the 3M24 Uran was later developed as an air-launched weapon. When employed by maritime helicopters such as the Ka-32 family, a strap-on solid-fuel booster is required. The missile is seen here in flight configuration, with the control surfaces deployed.

Specifications

Length overall: 2600mm (8ft 6.4in)	Range: 10km (6.2 miles)
Fuselage diameter: 250mm (9.84in)	Speed: Mach 1.7
Wingspan: 800mm (31.5in)	Powerplant: n/a
Launch weight: 143kg (315lb)	Guidance system: MCLOS via radio link
Warhead weight: 33kg (73lb)	

which began in 1978. The Kh-35 is powered by a turbofan engine, with a ventral air intake. The guidance system utilizes an inertial platform with an active radar seeker for the terminal phase. The missile uses a sea-skimming flight profile and has also been adopted by surface warships and as a coastal defence system. The Kh-35 can be carried by a variety of tactical aircraft and maritime helicopters, with a solid-fuel launch booster being used by the latter.

With Sweden's key strategic position, maritime and littoral warfare is a priority for the Swedish military, and its defensive posture relies upon securing key naval objectives. As a result, the RBS 15 was developed specifically for use in this environment, and is provided to fast attack craft, coastal batteries and aircraft. The predecessor to the RBS 15 was the Rb 04, an active radar homing

weapon available for the A 32 Lansen from 1958 (Rb 04C/D) and which remained in service on the AJ 37 Viggen until 1978 (by then, the Rb 04E was the major version).

The Rb 05A, meanwhile, was an all-purpose ASM developed from 1960. It utilized radio command guidance, and armed the AJ 37 Viggen and Saab 105. Powered by a liquid-fuel rocket motor, the Rb 05A was mainly to be used in littoral environments, but also had a limited air-to-air role. Derived from the Rb 04 (and originally named Rb 04 Turbo), the RBS 15 was ordered from Saab Bofors in 1979, with the air-launched RBS 15F selected in 1982. The initial firing trials of the surface-launched version took place in the same year, and after the first air launch in 1986 the Swedish Air Force adopted the weapon for its AJ 37s, with service entry in 1989.

The missile was subsequently integrated on the new JAS 39 Gripen fighter in the mid 1990s. In common with the Rb 04, the RBS 15F has inertial mid-course guidance with an active radar terminal phase, but replaces the solid-propellant rocket with a turbofan. The RBS 15F is armed with a blast-fragmentation warhead and a sea-skimming attack profile is used for the final run-in to the target.

Norway has also fielded its own AShM in the form of the Penguin, another weapon with coastal defence, ship-based and air-launched applications. The Penguin Mk 1 was developed in the 1960s by Kongsberg Våpenfabrikk and entered service with the Royal Norwegian Navy in 1972. The missile was designed for use within narrow and steep-sided fjords, so radar guidance was not considered viable, and instead IR guidance was adopted. The ship-launched Penguin Mk 2 was introduced in 1980, with increased range thanks to a new seeker. First of the air-launched versions was the Penguin Mk 3, which arms Royal Norwegian Air Force (RNoAF) F-16 fighters.

The development contract was awarded in 1982 and live firings began in 1984. The missile entered service in 1987 and was also acquired by the US Navy as the AGM-119 Penguin for the SH-60B Seahawk. The missile can be launched towards the area of the target, using one of a range of target search options. Initially flying under the control of an INS, the IR

Specifications

Length overall: 4330mm (14ft 2.4in)	Range: 250km (155 miles)
Fuselage diameter: 500mm (19.7in)	Speed: Subsonic
Wingspan: 1400mm (55.1in)	Powerplant: Turbojet
Launch weight: 800kg (1764lb)	Guidance system: Inertial, GPS, active radar (J
Warhead weight: 200kg (441lb)	band)

▼ RBS 15F

Developed by Saab Bofors from 1979, the heavyweight RBS 15 was first deployed on Swedish Navy missile craft. The air-launched version differs in its deletion of the strap-on booster rockets. The 'F' in the designation denotes Flyg (flight), while RBS signifies 'Robot system'. An AJ 37 made the first air-launched test in 1986.

▼ Penguin

The Kongsberg-developed Penguin is unusual for an AShM in employing IR guidance. The missile was developed for use in the Norwegian littoral environment, and can navigate through archipelagos and across terrain.

Specifications

Length overall: 3200mm (10ft 6in)	Range: 55km (34 miles)
Fuselage diameter: 280mm (11in)	Speed: Mach 1.2
Wingspan: 1000mm (39.3in)	Powerplant: Solid-fuel rocket motor and booster
Launch weight: 370kg (815lb)	Guidance system: Passive infrared, radar
Warhead weight: 130kg (286lb)	altimeter

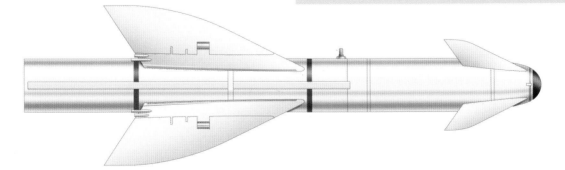

seeker is activated during the target search phase. The US Navy's AGM-119 differs in its use of folding wings for helicopter carriage and became operational in 1994.

Successor to the Penguin is the Kongsberg Naval Strike Missile (NSM), the only new Western AShM design currently under development. In development since the mid 1990s, and intended to arm coastal batteries, naval vessels and aircraft from 2015, the turbofan-powered NSM uses entirely passive guidance, flies a sea-skimming profile and makes use of terminal-phase manoeuvres. The Penguin's electro-optical seeker is retained, but combined with much greater range and stealth technology. A first ballistic test firing took place in 2000, with a full test launch by a surface-launched NSM in 2009.

The Far East

The next-generation Japanese air-launched anti-ship weapon is the Mitsubishi ASM-2 (Type 93), which is superficially similar to the earlier ASM-1 but with a new turbojet powerplant, with the result that range is effectively doubled. The missile is also equipped with a IR terminal seeker instead of the active radar seeker of the ASM-1. Optimized for carriage by the F-2 attack fighter, the ASM-1 entered service in 1995.

China's first air-launched AShM was the YJ-6. Although it was based on primitive technology, programme delays meant it was not until 1986 that the missile entered service. The YJ-6 uses Doppler inertial guidance with an active radar seeker for the terminal phase. An improved version known as the YJ-61 (C-611) was introduced in the mid 1990s, again arming the H-6D missile-carrier. This later

Specifications

Length overall: 3950mm (13ft)	Speed: High subsonic
Fuselage diameter: n/a	Powerplant: Solid fuel rocket booster, Microturbo
Wingspan: n/a	TRI-40 turbojet
Launch weight: 410kg (904lb)	Guidance system: Inertial, GPS, terrain-reference
Warhead weight: 125kg (276lb)	navigation, IIR homing, target database
Range: More than 185km (115 miles)	

▼ NSM

Kongsberg's NSM is among the most advanced AShMs currently under development and has been proposed as armament for the F-35 Joint Strike Fighter. A titanium warhead ensures penetration of hardened targets, and the guidance system makes use of GPS and an in-flight datalink, with an IIR seeker and automatic target recognition facility.

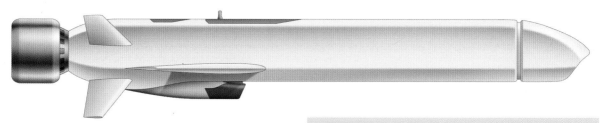

▼ Hsiung Feng II

Taiwan's Hsiung Feng II has been deployed in ship-launched, coastal defence and airborne variants. Terminal active homing is provided using dual active and IR imaging seekers. The use of an IIR seeker (mounted in the fairing above the nose) suggests that the missile may also have a land-attack capability.

Specifications

Length overall: 4800mm (15ft 9in)	Speed: 0.85 Mach
Fuselage diameter: 400mm (15.7in)	Powerplant: Solid-fuel booster, turbojet in-flight
Wingspan: n/a	Guidance system: Inertial guidance mid-flight,
Launch weight: 685kg (1510lb)	terminal active homing with dual RF and IR
Warhead weight: 180kg (397lb)	imaging seekers
Range: 160km (99.4 miles)	

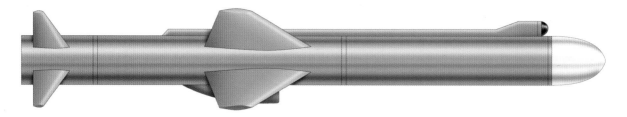

▼ ASM-2

The Mitsubishi ASM-2, seen here in tracking markings used for instrumented test launches, is Japan's second-generation AShM and was derived from the earlier ASM-1C, key differences relating to the powerplant and guidance.

Specifications

Length overall: 4000mm (13ft 1.6in)	Range: 150km (93.2 miles)
Fuselage diameter: 350mm (13.8in)	Speed: n/a
Wingspan: n/a	Powerplant: Turbojet engine
Launch weight: 530kg (1168lb)	Guidance system: Inertial and IR image
Warhead weight: n/a	

version uses a new liquid-fuel rocket motor that extends range to around 200km (124 miles). Targets are normally acquired by the H-6D, using its target acquisition/illumination radar. After missile launch, the aircraft can turn away immediately.

More advanced Chinese AShMs are the YJ-81 and KD-88, better known by their export designations C-801K and C-802KD respectively. Designed as an air-launched AShM, the YJ-8 was ultimately cancelled, but became a successful surface-launched weapon with the PLA Navy. Development of an air-launched version resumed in the 1980s and led to the YJ-81, which entered service in the mid 1990s, arming the JH-7 fighter-bomber.

The KD-88 is a further development of the YJ-83 (C-802) surface-launched AShM. It has been

reported that the air-launched weapon is optimized for land attack, making it a Chinese counterpart to the SLAM. The lack of electro-optical or laser guidance for the terminal phase, however, suggests it would be better suited to warship targets. Alternatively, different guidance modes may be under study. Powered by a small turbojet engine, the missile likely uses an inertial navigation system, with datalink for mid-course updates and active radar homing for terminal guidance. Carrier aircraft comprise the JH-7 and the H-6 bomber.

Nationalist China has fielded the Hsiung Feng II air- and surface-launched AShM. The air-launched version was developed from 1983. This turbojet-powered missile first appeared in the early 1990s and is associated with the F-CK-1 fighter. Similar in appearance to the American Harpoon, it is a sea-skimming missile and is unusual in its use of a dual IR/radar seeker for the terminal phase.

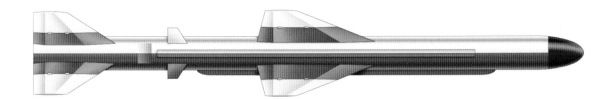

Specifications

Length overall: 6392mm (20ft 11.6in)	Range: 120km (74.6 miles)
Fuselage diameter: 360mm (14in)	Speed: (attacking) Mach 1.6; (cruising) Mach 0.9
Wingspan: (unfolded) 1220mm (48in); (folded) 720mm (28.3in)	Powerplant: Turbojet engine
	Guidance system: Inertial and terminal active radar
Launch weight: 715kg (1576lb)	
Warhead weight: 165kg (364lb)	

▲ YJ-82 (C-802)

Seen here with the solid-propellant rocket booster associated with surface-launched versions, the YJ-82 is a further development of the air-launched YJ-81, which was itself derived from the surface-launched YJ-8. An air-launched land-attack version of the YJ-82 has been produced under the KD-88 designation.

Chapter 4

Anti-Tank Missiles

Development of air-launched anti-tank (AT) missiles followed two distinct paths during the Cold War. Faced by the numerical superiority of Warsaw Pact armour, Western nations fielded helicopters armed with AT missiles as a means of redressing the balance on the battlefield. In the Soviet Union, however, such weapons were ultimately intended to be used in an offensive capacity, arming assault helicopters that would serve as breakthrough weapons in support of armour. Today, the changing face of the battlefield means that traditional air-launched AT missiles are being modified to counter a more diverse range of 'soft' and 'hardened' targets, both on the open battlefield and in an urban warfare environment.

◀ **Ground attack**
A front view of a US Army YAH-64 Apache helicopter prototype during a demonstration flight. It is equipped with an M230A1 30mm (1.18in) automatic cannon and AGM-114A Hellfire tactical ASMs.

Cold War anti-tank missiles

The first generation of air-launched ATGMs were invariably adaptations of ground-based systems, and suffered from the inherent limitations of early command guidance systems.

THE FIRST TACTICAL missile to enter service anywhere in the world was the French Nord SS.10. This dated back to an experimental project of 1946, which intended to provide the infantryman with a portable anti-armour weapon. Spin-stabilized, and with a solid-propellant rocket motor, the SS.10 (or Nord 5203) utilized wire guidance, and was aimed at the target by the operator, who used a tracking flare at the rear for visual reference. A first ground launch in 1949 was followed by service entry with the French Army in 1953, and the SS.10 also became the first anti-tank guided missile (ATGM) to be launched from a slow-flying aircraft (an MS.500 Criquet, in 1951) and from a helicopter (Alouette II, 1952). Adding thrust vectoring for improved manoeuvrability, plus extending the range and upgrading the warhead of the SS.10, created the SS.11 (Nord 5210, but later an Aérospatiale product). This entered service in 1959, and was also adapted for air launch. The air-launched model was designated AS.11, and was carried by both helicopters and light fixed-wing aircraft.

A new guidance concept was heralded by the Euromissile HOT, which emerged as a heavyweight,

longer-range counterpart to the Franco-German MILAN infantry ATGM. Both weapons introduced semi-automatic command line-of-sight (SACLOS) guidance, with an IR tracking system, meaning the operator only had to keep the target centred in his sight in order for the missile to reach its objective, with a consequent improvement in first-hit probability. The spin-stabilized, tube-launched HOT was fielded from 1978 in both vehicle- and helicopter-launched forms, in the latter version equipping the French Gazelle and German BO 105. Improvements in the armour of Soviet tanks prompted the development of the HOT 2, with a hollow-charge warhead of 150mm (6in), compared to 136mm (5.4in) on the original HOT. The new missile also used a more powerful explosive, guaranteeing penetration of 1250mm (49.2in) of armour, compared to 850mm (33.5in). The new missile entered service in 1985. In order to defeat reactive armour, the HOT 2 was also available with a tandem warhead, as the HOT 2T of 1992.

TOW dominance

The US initially adopted the SS.11 as its first air-launched ATGM, before developing the successful BGM-71 TOW (Tube-launched, Optically tracked,

▼ SS.11

The wire-guided SS.11 represented a major improvement over the SS.10, with penetration capability increased to 610mm (24in) and twice the range. This red-and-white trials weapon was in use at the US Army's Redstone testing grounds.

Specifications

Length overall: 1890mm (6ft 2in)	Range: 500–3000m (1640–9842ft)
Fuselage diameter: 165mm (6.5in)	Speed: 190m/sec (623ft/sec)
Wingspan: 500mm (19.69in)	Powerplant: n/a
Launch weight: 30kg (66.1lb)	Guidance system: MCLOS
Warhead weight: 6.8kg (15lb)	

Specifications

Length overall: 1300mm (4ft 3in)	Range: 4300m (14,107ft)
Fuselage diameter: 150mm (6in)	Speed: 864km/h (537mph)
Wingspan: 310m (12.2in)	Powerplant: Two-stage solid-fuel rocket
Launch weight: 24.5kg (54lb)	Guidance system: SACLOS
Warhead weight: n/a	

▲ HOT

The HOT (*Hautsubsonique Optiquement Téleguidé Tiré d'un Tube*, or High-subsonic Optical Remote-guided, Tube-fired) missile was the result of a successful Franco-German development programme that also led to the MILAN infantry ATGM and the Roland SAM. As well as air-launched applications, the HOT was ground-launched from French Army VAB and German Army Jaguar vehicles.

Wire-guided) missile. Developed for ground or helicopter launch, the BGM-71 became the standard Western weapon in its class. Design work began for the US Army in 1961, and the missile emerged with SACLOS guidance, with an IR sensor tracking the missile signal in order to send automatic correction commands via a guidance wire link. The initial-production BGM-71A was introduced in 1970, with a high-explosive shaped-charge warhead and range of 3000m (9843ft). From 1972, efforts began to integrate the TOW with the weapons system of the AH-1 Cobra.

A further development of the original TOW (without nose probe) was the BGM-71B or Extended-Range TOW, which became the basic production model in 1976. It had a longer guidance wire and was optimized for air launch. In order to improve armour penetration, the BGM-71C Improved TOW (ITOW) of 1981 featured a larger-diameter warhead fitted with a telescopic nose probe fuse. The BGM-71D TOW 2 of 1983 introduced an even larger warhead, plus digital guidance for improved resistance to ECM, and a revised powerplant. In 1987, the TOW 2 was superseded by the BGM-71E TOW 2A, designed to defeat tanks equipped with explosive reactive armour (ERA). This added a small shaped-charge warhead in the nose probe. The BGM-71F TOW 2B entered service in 1992, bringing with it an overflight top attack (OTA) capability and a revised nose section carrying downwards-fired warheads activated by a new dual laser/magnetic fuse.

Serious development of a Soviet air-launched ATGM began in the early 1960s, initial trials pairing the Mi-1 helicopter with the 3M11 Falanga (AT-2 'Swatter'), a radio command guided weapon that had entered service in vehicle-launched form in 1960. Accurate guidance from a helicopter proved to be difficult to achieve, and further development was required, resulting in the Mi-4 helicopter being allied with the improved 9M17M Falanga-M. This system met with approval and was adopted for service in 1967. The 9M17M was retained for use by assault versions of the Mi-8, which entered service from the early 1970s, and also provided the initial armament for the Mi-24A combat helicopter. The improved Mi-24D introduced the 9M17P Falanga-P. This system differed in its use of the Skorpion missile, in which manual control guidance was replaced by SACLOS guidance. In this form, the air-launched 'Swatter' was widely exported to international markets, serving across the Warsaw Pact and with Soviet client states around the world.

The Soviet 9K11 Malyutka (AT-3 'Sagger') ATGM became a signature weapon for ground forces of the Red Army and Soviet allies, but in air-launched form its wire-guided 9M14M missile was restricted to service on export variants of helicopters, including Mi-8 assault transports and Mi-2s configured for anti-armour missions. In addition, a locally produced version of the 9M14M armed Yugoslavia's licence-built Partizan (Gazelle) helicopters.

One further Cold War-era ATGM was Sweden's Bofors Bantam, a first-generation lightweight wire-guided weapon that was also adapted for carriage by helicopters, such as the Swedish Army's AB.204. The Bantam was introduced into service in 1963.

▼ 9M14M (AT-3 'Sagger')

The 'Sagger' gained notoriety in its ground-launched form when it was used with great success by the Egyptian Army during the Yom Kippur War. The Soviets did not adopt the weapon in air-launched form, but it was supplied to export customers as an alternative to the radio command-guided Falanga.

Specifications

Length overall: 860mm (2ft 10in)	Range: 500–3000m (1640–9843ft)
Fuselage diameter: 125mm (4.9in)	Speed: 115m/sec (49ft/sec)
Wingspan: 393mm (15.5in)	Powerplant: n/a
Launch weight: 10.9kg (24lb)	Guidance system: MCLOS
Warhead weight: 2.6kg (5.7lb)	

Early anti-tank missiles in combat

Air-launched AT missiles saw considerable combat during the years of the Cold War, as the armed helicopter emerged as a key influence in small-scale and counter-insurgency wars.

THE FRENCH PIONEERED the use of the armed helicopter during their post-war conflict in Algeria, which broke out in 1954. In particular, the H-34 proved suitable for adaptation as a helicopter gunship, being outfitted with cannon and rockets in order to counter rebel attacks. Among a number of armed helicopters trialled in combat, the French Navy armed its HSS (navalized H-34) with the SS.10 missile. The SS.11 also had its combat debut in North Africa, and in 1956 it was experimentally adapted for air launch from a French Air Force MD.311 fixed-wing utility transport. After these trials, the weapon became widely adopted by French aircraft in Algeria. Rather than attacking armour, these missiles were primarily used against fortified caves. Fixed-wing aircraft were not ideal platforms for wire-guided missiles, and the AS.11 went on to see more considerable use in Algeria from Alouette II and Alouette III helicopters from 1958 to 1962.

The AS.11 was also used in combat by the US Army in Vietnam, first being deployed by UH-1B Iroquois helicopters of the 1st Cavalry Division in 1966. Around 22,000 examples of the air-launched SS.11 (the air-launched AS.11 designation was apparently not used) were ordered by the US in 1964. When integrated on the UH-1B, the weapons installation was known as the M22, while the missile itself later received the US military designation AGM-22. In combat, the US Army found the AS.11 to be less than reliable, primarily on account of its manual command guidance, which required the missile operator to track the missile visually, with manual guidance commands inputted via a joystick. Despite its limitations, the AGM-22 was again used in Vietnam in 1967 and 1972.

The British took the AS.11 to the Falklands, where it was used in action in support of ground troops by British Army Scout helicopters. Eight Argentine troops surrendered after a Scout launched an AS.11 against a suspected observation post on 7 June 1982. The AS.11 was also used by Iraq during the Iran–Iraq War, equipping Iraqi SA.316C Alouette IIIs. Iraqi Alouettes had previously been applied with great effect against Kurdish insurgents, but by the time of the Iran–Iraq War, these helicopters were primarily used for liaison and artillery spotting.

ANTI-TANK MISSILES

The Soviet-developed Falanga system proved relatively effective in combat, and saw heavy use both with Soviet forces in Afghanistan and in Iraqi hands during the Iran–Iraq War. In one mission flown by eight Iraqi Mi-25s, the helicopters claimed destruction of 17 Iranian tanks.

TOW and HOT in action

The TOW was first tested in combat by UH-1Bs of the 1st Combat Aerial TOW Team against North Vietnamese Army (NVA) targets in summer 1972, two years after the first examples of the BGM-71A missile had been issued to front-line US Army ground troops. Initial targets included NVA PT-76 amphibious tanks and T-54 main battle tanks. A year later, the TOW was delivered to Israel during the Yom Kippur War. The missile saw only limited use during the 1973 conflict, but by the time of the 'Peace for Galilee' operations in Lebanon, the TOW had become the standard Israeli ATGM. Air-launched versions were used with great success against Syrian armour by AH-1S Cobra and Hughes 500MD Defender helicopter gunships, these being credited with the destruction of 29 tanks and around 60 other armoured vehicles. In one unusual encounter, an Israeli Cobra claimed the destruction of a Syrian Gazelle using an air-to-air TOW shot.

The TOW was also used in combat against Iraqi armour by Iranian AH-1J Cobras, which typically operated in groups of three to four, flying nap-of-the-earth profiles, with forward air control provided by an O-2A. In a matter of days in November 1982,

Iranian AH-1s reported the destruction of at least 106 Iraqi tanks and 70 armoured personnel carriers (APCs), an impressive tally.

The HOT missile has likewise seen widespread combat service. In the Iran–Iraq War, when it was deployed by Iraqi SA.342L Gazelles, which frequently operated alongside Mi-25s as hunter-killer teams, Iraqi HOT missiles proved capable of defeating Iranian M60 and Chieftain armour. Typically, the Mi-25 would be used to provide suppressive rocket fire against enemy artillery and anti-aircraft defences, while the Gazelles would pick off armour with their HOTs.

Syria used the HOT from its SA.342L/M Gazelles during 'Peace for Galilee', with up to 100 sorties and 30 vehicle kills reported in the first four days of fighting in June. The Gazelle/HOT combination was to have been supported by Syrian Mi-25s with the Falanga, but the Syrians found the reliability of the Falanga left a lot to be desired. Indeed, following the Iraqi model, the Syrians instead armed their Mi-25s with bombs and rockets, and the type saw little or no action during 'Peace for Galilee'. Ultimately, the Gazelle crews claimed 71 Israeli tanks, five APCs, three trucks, two artillery pieces and nine jeeps.

The HOT was used by France for the first time in combat in January 1984, when a French Army Gazelle helicopter used an example of the missile to destroy a Libyan anti-aircraft gun during French operations in Chad.

Specifications

Length overall: 1160mm (3ft 9.7in)	Range: 500m–2.5km (1640ft–1.55 miles)
Fuselage diameter: 148mm (5.8in)	Speed: 150–170m/sec (492–558ft/sec)
Wingspan: n/a	Powerplant: n/a
Launch weight: 27kg (59.5lb)	Guidance system: Radio command MCLOS
Warhead weight: 5.4kg (11.9lb)	

▲ **9M17P Skorpion (AT-2 'Swatter')**
The Falanga-P system, and its Skorpion missile, was the primary armament of the Mi-24D assault helicopter. In this application, the Falanga-P was allied with the helicopter's SPSV-24 fire-control system and Raduga F missile-control system, with an optical observation device and a radio-command transmitter.

125

Modern anti-tank missiles

The latest air-launched AT missiles are far more flexible weapons than their predecessors, with fire-and-forget guidance and the ability to be used against a wider range of targets.

THE US RACE TO keep abreast of improvements in Soviet tank armour led to the development of a new generation of ATGMs in the late 1980s. The signature Western weapon remained the TOW, later joined by the AGM-114 Hellfire. The laser-guided Helicopter-Launched Fire-and-Forget Missile (Hellfire) project was launched in 1971, and was declared operational with the US Army's AH-64A Apache helicopter gunship in 1985. Powered by a solid-propellant rocket motor, the Hellfire's laser seeker can lock on before or after launch, and carries a shaped-charge warhead.

The AGM-114B was tailored for shipboard use by US Navy and Marine Corps AH-1s, with a reduced-smoke motor and improved seeker and autopilot. The similar AGM-114C was adopted by the US Army. The next production version was the AGM-114F, with a dual warhead to defeat reactive armour.

The AGM-114 was subject to a major update in 1989, leading to the Hellfire II. Key features of the weapon are a new digital autopilot, more powerful warhead, enhanced seeker and reprogrammable software that allows a range of attack profiles to be selected. The initial-production Hellfire II was the AGM-114K introduced in 1994 and followed by

the Navy's AGM-114M with a new blast-fragmentation warhead, and the AGM-114N with a thermobaric warhead. Meanwhile, in order to arm AH-64Ds equipped with the Longbow battlefield radar, the AGM-114L was developed with a new millimetre-wave (MMW) active radar seeker. The seeker can be used in LOBL mode, with target data supplied by the launch helicopter, or can fly to the target under inertial guidance before the seeker locks on for terminal guidance. The AGM-114L entered service in 1998. The latest AGM-114R has a new warhead, combining the effects of a shaped-charge and a blast-fragmentation charge. The 'Romeo' can engage targets within a wider envelope and can be used to arm both helicopters and UAVs.

Further, faster

Recent TOW development efforts have focused on extending range and expanding the target set. The BGM-71H TOW Bunker Buster has a new warhead to defeat bunkers, while the TOW 2B Aero has its range increased to 4500m (14,763ft), with a longer guidance wire. The latest TOW 2B Aero is a wireless missile, instead using a radar frequency datalink.

The Third-Generation Anti-Tank (TRIGAT) family of weapons was originally developed as a

Specifications

Length overall: 1630mm (5ft 4.2in)	Range: 500m–8km (1638ft–5 miles)
Fuselage diameter: 178mm (7in)	Speed: Mach 1.3
Wingspan: 330mm (13in)	Powerplant: Solid-fuel rocket
Launch weight: 45.4–49kg (100–108lb)	Guidance system: Semi-active laser homing;
Warhead weight: 8–9kg (17.6–19.8lb)	MMV radar seeker

▼ **AGM-114K Hellfire II**

First of the Hellfire II family, which incorporated lessons learnt during the 1991 Gulf War, was the AGM-114K. The use of lightweight components allowed the maximum range to be extended, while returning to the original smaller dimensions of the AGM-114B/C. Production versions of the AGM-114K began to be delivered in 1994.

pan-European project, although the land-based portion of the programme was abandoned in 2000. This left Germany to pursue the air-launched, long-range TRIGAT development, or PARS 3 LR, for its Tiger UHT combat helicopter. This weapon uses IR guidance. Other Tiger operators have opted for more established solutions, selecting either the Hellfire or the Israeli Spike. Meanwhile, development of HOT continued, with the HOT 3 of 1998.

A further development of the Hellfire is the British Brimstone, typical of the latest generation of anti-armour weapons and capable of all-weather attacks by day or night, with an autonomous fire-and-forget capability and standoff range. The project was launched in 1994, with a joint venture between Boeing and GEC Marconi selected in

1996. Tested from 1999, with a first guided firing in2000, the Brimstone uses active radar guidance, with the MMW seeker providing high-resolution target imagery. Firing can be conducted in direct or indirect modes, and coordinates can also be passed to the launch aircraft from another aircraft. Armed with a tandem hollow-charge warhead, the Brimstone arms the RAF's Tornado GR.Mk 4.

A Soviet second generation

The Soviet successor to the Falanga was the 9K113 Shturm system, in which the missile received the designation 9M114 Kokon (AT-6 'Spiral'). Once again, SACLOS guidance was used, with a radio link passing guidance commands to the missile, but the weapon was now tube-launched and was capable of supersonic performance.

▼ Brimstone

Based on the AGM-114F, the MBDA Brimstone is supplied on a three-round launcher. The first of the operational rounds with the original MMW radar guidance were delivered to the RAF in November 2004, with operational capability declared the following March.

Specifications

Length overall: 1800m (5ft 10.9ft)	Range: 12km (7.5 miles)
Fuselage diameter: 178mm (7in)	Speed: Supersonic
Wingspan: n/a	Powerplant: Solid-fuel rocket
Launch weight: 48.5kg (107lb)	Guidance system: Radar and INS autopilot
Warhead weight: n/a	

▼ 9M114 Kokon (AT-6 'Spiral')

Successor to the Falanga, the Kokon missile that formed part of the Shturm-V system was the first Soviet weapon of its type to use a tandem warhead to defeat contemporary reactive armour. Unlike its predecessor, the Kokon was tube-launched, and was equipped with SACLOS guidance from the outset.

Specifications

Length overall: 1625mm (5ft 4in)	Range: 400m–5km (1312ft–3.1 miles)
Fuselage diameter: 130mm (5.1in)	Speed: 345m/sec (1131ft/sec)
Wingspan: 360mm (14.1in)	Powerplant: n/a
Launch weight: 31.4kg (69.2lb)	Guidance system: Radio command link SACLOS
Warhead weight: 5.3kg (11.7lb)	

The system was developed for both vehicle and helicopter launch, the Shturm-V initially being integrated on the Mi-24V combat helicopter, which entered operational service in 1976. The missile was spin-stabilized and carried a tandem warhead. The subsequent 9M114M missile offered improved levels of armour penetration.

The Shturm-V was widely exported with the Mi-24V, and was also retained by this helicopter's successor, the Mi-24P. It is also integrated on the Russian Navy's Ka-29 assault helicopter, which can also use the 9M120 Ataka (AT-9 'Spiral 2') missile. This ATGM was developed to arm the Mi-28 anti-armour helicopter, and was based on the Shturm-V.

Although similar to the Shturm-V, when combined with the Mi-28, the Ataka is provided with an optical and low-light-level TV fire-control system, allowing use at night and in poor weather. The 9M120 Ataka missile has also been cleared for use on upgraded versions of the Mi-24P series. Compared to the 9M114, the 9M120 is outwardly similar but has a larger and more penetrative tandem warhead, and its range is increased to 6km (3.7 miles).

Attack helicopters

The next stage in Soviet air-launched ATGM development was the 9M120M Vikhr-M (AT-16 'Scallion') intended to arm the Ka-50 combat helicopter and the Su-25T attack aircraft. The Vikhr is a long-range weapon that can be launched outside the range of hostile air defence systems. The missile is supersonic and uses semi-active laser guidance, requiring the target be continuously illuminated by a laser signal. Tested in the 1990s, the missile is apparently still to enter large-scale service, with initial Ka-52s instead utilizing the earlier 9M120 Ataka.

China's current air-launched ATGM is the HJ-8 carried by the PLA's Z-9G, Z-9W and Z-11 battlefield helicopters. Developed from the early 1970s, the missile is used in conjunction with an optical sight unit mounted on the roof of the helicopter, and guidance is of the SACLOS type. Since the late 1980s, the HJ-8 has been deployed by the PLA in man-portable, vehicle-mounted and helicopter-launched versions. An all-new air-launched ATGW is now under development for carriage by the Z-10 attack helicopter. Designated HJ-10, this weapon is likely to be in the Hellfire class of performance and capability.

South African missiles

South Africa's extensive combat experiences during the border conflicts in the 1980s saw the development of indigenous anti-armour missiles for both vehicle and helicopter launch systems. The tube-launched ZT-3 Swift ATGM was developed in the mid 1980s and was combat-tested in Angola in 1987 before being mounted for further testing on a Puma helicopter.

The air-launched Swift was then superseded by the laser-beam-riding ZT-35 Ingwe, tested from

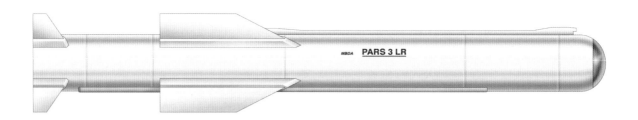

Specifications

Length overall: 1500mm (4ft 10.8in)	Range: 500–6000m (1640–19,685lb)
Fuselage diameter: 150mm (6in)	Speed: 2000km/h (1243mph)
Wingspan: 370mm (14.6in)	Powerplant: Solid-fuel rocket
Launch weight: 49kg (108lb)	Guidance system: Passive IR CCD sensors
Warhead weight: 9kg (19.8lb)	

▲ PARS 3 LR

The air-launched version of the abortive TRIGAT LR, the PARS 3 LR is on order to arm the German Army's Tiger UHT combat helicopters. A fire-and-forget missile, the PARS 3 LR's IR seeker locks onto the target before launch, after detection and identification by the Tiger UHT's mast-mounted sight. The missile is carried in a four-round launcher.

▲ Mokopa

The Mokopa, or ZT-6, is the most advanced air-launched ATGM developed to date by South Africa's Denel. Although the weapon has not been procured for use by the South African Rooivalk attack helicopter, the laser-guided missile is still offered for export, and the manufacturer reports that it is capable of defeating 1350mm (53in) of armour thanks to its tandem warhead.

Specifications

Length overall: 1995mm (6ft 6.5in)	Range: 10km (6.2 miles)
Fuselage diameter: 178mm (7in)	Speed: 530m/sec (1739ft/sec)
Wingspan: n/a	Powerplant: Solid-fuel composite rocket motor
Launch weight: 49.8kg (110lb)	Guidance system: Semi-active laser
Warhead weight: n/a	

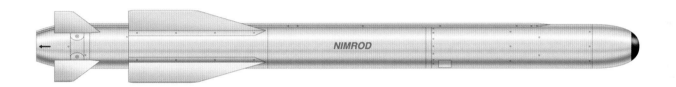

▲ Nimrod

The IAI Nimrod is a medium-range laser-guided missile that can be used against personnel and buildings as well as armour. The weapon was likely developed from the mid 1980s and is associated with the CH-53 assault helicopter, each of which can carry eight missiles in place of the normal external fuel tanks.

Specifications

Length overall: 1679mm (5ft 6in) (with launcher)	Missile weight: 34kg (74.8lb)
Fuselage diameter: 170mm (6.7in) (with launcher)	Range: 800–25,000m (2600–82,000ft)
Wingspan: n/a	Speed: n/a
Launcher weight: 55kg (121lb)	Powerplant: Solid-fuel rocket
	Guidance system: Infrared homing

1998 and ordered by Algeria for its upgraded Mi-24s. The heavyweight Mokopa, by contrast, was intended to arm the Denel AH-2 Rooivalk attack helicopter and utilized semi-active laser guidance, with a MMW seeker option. Armed with a tandem warhead, it was to be capable of lock-on before or after launch. The first guided tests of the missile took place in 2000, but the missile was cancelled thereafter.

Spike family

Israel employed both French- and US-supplied air-launched ATGMs before fielding indigenous weapons. The Spike comprises a family of weapons, in which the Spike-ER is a stand-alone system that can be integrated on helicopters and is also the

version with the longest range: around 8000m (26,246ft). The missile carries a tandem warhead and combines electro-optical (IR and TV) guidance with a fibre-optic datalink for fire-and-forget and directed launch modes. The Spike-ER can be used in LOBL or LOAL modes. In helicopter-launched form, the Spike-ER is used by Romania (IAR-330 SOCAT) and Spain (Tiger HAD).

The Israeli Nimrod is a laser-guided all-weather weapon intended for use against armour or infantry targets and offers a much longer standoff range than typical ATGMs. In air-launched form the Nimrod is associated with the Israeli CH-53. In a normal operating scenario, the missile is guided to its target by a forward scouting team equipped with a laser designator.

Modern anti-tank missiles in combat

While the 1991 Gulf War saw air-launched ATGMs used to destroy armour on the battlefield, more recent conflicts have seen these weapons adapt to the demands of asymmetric warfare.

TOGETHER WITH EARLIER versions, the TOW 2A saw significant use during Operation *Desert Storm* in 1991. In total, more than 3000 examples of the TOW were launched by ground and air assets, with most missiles being of the BGM-71D/E variants. The TOW was also the primary air-launched ATGW deployed by British Army helicopters during *Desert Storm*, arming the Lynx battlefield helicopter. TOWs were launched before the onset of the ground offensive, when four US Marine Corps AH-1Ts destroyed an Iraqi command post near the Saudi/Kuwaiti border on 18 January 1991.

The HOT 2 also saw its baptism of fire during *Desert Storm*. In total, 337 HOT rounds were fired in the Gulf, these being launched by Gazelle helicopters in service with France, Kuwait, Qatar and the United Arab Emirates.

Hellfires were used in the Gulf War by US Army AH-64As, and like the TOW were employed in some

of the first engagements of the war. In the early hours of the campaign on 17 January, Apaches used Hellfires and Hydra rockets to clear a path through Iraqi air defence systems, preparing the way for the initial air attack. In addition to being employed against Iraqi armour, Hellfires were launched at bunkers, bridges and artillery positions, the missile demonstrating a hit rate of around 65 per cent, with some performance limitations brought about by dust and sand interfering with sighting systems. An estimated 2900–4000 Hellfire missiles were fired in total during the conflict.

Following *Desert Storm*, air-launched ATGMs have increasingly been used to destroy targets other than

▼ **Laser-guided Brimstone**
Inspection of a Dual-Mode Seeker (DMS) Brimstone on its triple launcher under a Tornado GR.Mk 4 deployed in Afghanistan. The DMS Brimstone is favoured for use against moving targets and for minimizing collateral damage.

▲ **BGM-71 TOW 2**

After a very-short-duration rocket motor ejects the TOW from its launch tube, the mid-body fins and the tail control fins flip out and the solid-fuel main boost motor is lit. The rocket exhausts are on the side of the missile, so as not to damage the guidance wire that trails from the rear of the missile.

Specifications

Length overall: 1170mm (3ft 9in) (probe folded);	Warhead weight: 3.9–5.9kg (8.6–13lb)
1510mm (4ft 11in) (probe extended)	Range: Up to 3750m (12,303ft)
Fuselage diameter: 152mm (6in)	Speed: n/a
Wingspan: 460mm (18.1n)	Powerplant: n/a
Launch weight: n/a	Guidance system: Optically tracked, wire-guided

armour, including lighter vehicles, bunkers and urban structures. The repurposing has been established in Coalition campaigns in Afghanistan and Iraq, and also in Israel's counter-insurgency operations, in which helicopter-launched Hellfire and Spike missiles have been used to target individual Hamas and Hezbollah insurgents.

Hellfire at war

When Coalition air forces returned to Iraq for the 2003 invasion under Operation *Iraqi Freedom*, the Hellfire was established as the most important air-launched ATGM. Although originally designed for AT work, the Hellfire's lightweight high-explosive/fragmentation warhead makes it eminently suitable for urban engagements, where the premium is on accurate fire and also the limitation of collateral damage effects.

Versions of the Hellfire used by the US Army and Marine Corps in both *Iraqi Freedom* and *Enduring Freedom* in Afghanistan have included the AGM-114K for use against armoured targets, the AGM-114M for use against buildings, bunkers and urban targets, and the AGM-114N thermobaric round for destroying enclosed structures. The US Army also employed the AGM-114L, or Longbow Hellfire.

The RAF's Brimstone saw its combat debut during *Iraqi Freedom*, after being declared operational in 2005. An updated version, the Dual-Mode Seeker (DMS) Brimstone, was first used in action over Iraq in early 2009, having been fitted with a laser

US helicopter-launched missiles in Operation *Desert Storm*

Missile	Number used
AGM-114 Hellfire (US Navy)	30
AGM-114 Hellfire (USMC)	159
BGM-71 TOW	293
	Total 482

guidance system in place of the original millimetre-wave radar sensor, as a result of an urgent operational requirements in Afghanistan and Iraq.

One key development during the 'Global War on Terror' has been the use of UAVs to prosecute air attacks. The Hellfire missile has been one of the primary UAV weapons, and the AGM-114P has been fielded as a variant of the AGM-114K, optimized for use by high-flying combat drones. Operated by the USAF and Central Intelligence Agency (CIA), the unmanned Predator drone can carry two Hellfire missiles that are guided to a laser spot on the target provided by the UAV's own Multi-spectral Targeting System (MTS), video imagery from which is transmitted to the ground control station, typically located back in the US. MTS imagery, however, can also be provided to other land and air assets. The Hellfire has been adapted for carriage by the USMC's KC-130J 'Harvest Hawk' close air support aircraft, first used in combat over Sangin, Afghanistan, in November 2010.

Chapter 5

Bombs

Bombs were among the very first weapons delivered by aircraft. First employed on a large scale during World War I, these weapons rapidly grew in size and destructive capacity, changing the face of military aviation and the way that wars were fought. The end of World War II saw the dawn of the atomic age, and the first generation of nuclear bombs would be delivered exclusively by aircraft. Throughout the Cold War, nuclear and conventional bombs were refined and developed for a wider spectrum of missions, while the arrival of the missile age saw the first guidance systems introduced to free-fall bombs. The latest guided bombs use a range of sophisticated guidance types, ensuring that they are as accurate as powered missiles. And, through the use of aerodynamic surfaces, guided bombs now also possess genuine standoff range.

◀ **Ground-attack Eurofighter**

Demonstrating the continued importance of unpowered weaponry in the missile age, this RAF Typhoon carries six inert Enhanced Paveway II laser-guided bombs. Developed at the time of the Vietnam War, the Paveway family remains the pre-eminent guided bomb, although the latest versions combine the original laser guidance with inertial/GPS guidance kits in order to ensure accuracy, even in adverse weather.

Free-fall bombs

Unguided free-fall bombs are one of the longest-established aerial weapons. Ranging from strategic nuclear bombs to anti-armour weapons, they are characterized by their adaptability.

THE DEVELOPMENT OF the atomic bomb changed the face of air-launched weapons development in the years after 1945, although the conventional 'dumb' or 'iron' bomb – more properly, the general-purpose (GP) bomb – retained its relevance, and was the primary offensive weapon in major post-war conflicts, including Korea and Vietnam. In addition to GP weapons filled with conventional high-explosive, free-fall conventional bombs have also been developed with specialized fragmentation, demolition, armour-piercing and semi-armour-piercing, shaped-charge/fragmentation, incendiary or smoke, training, and leaflet warheads. Cluster munitions and dispensers form a separate category within free-fall bombs, and are discussed separately.

In the US, the M-series were the primary weapons of their class in the years immediately after World War II, although many of them dated from the pre-1945 period. In order of weight, operational (as opposed to practice) weapons of the early Cold War period included: the 100lb (45.4kg) M30A1 GP bomb, 100lb M47 incendiary/smoke bomb, 115lb (52.5kg) M70 chemical bomb, 120lb (54.5kg) M86 fragmentation bomb, 125lb (56.7kg) M113 chemical bomb, 220lb (100kg) M88 fragmentation bomb, 250lb (113kg) M57 GP bomb, 260lb (117.9kg) M81 fragmentation bomb, 500lb (227kg) M58 semi-armour-piercing bomb, 500lb M64 GP bomb, 500lb M76 incendiary bomb, 500lb M78 chemical bomb, 750lb (340kg) M116 napalm bomb, 1000lb (454kg)

▼ M117

Introduced into service in the early 1950s, the M117 carries a Minol 2 or Tritonal explosive filling. Currently the M117 is only used by the USAF's B-52 Stratofortress, with tactical aircraft now using the more streamlined Mk 80 series bombs, as well as guided weapons.

Specifications

Length overall: 2160mm (7ft)	Weight: 340kg (750lb)
Body diameter: 408mm (16in)	Guidance system: None
Stabilizer span: 520mm (20in)	

Specifications

Length overall: 1880mm (6ft 2in)	Weight: 119kg (262lb)
Body diameter: 229mm (9in)	Guidance system: None
Filling weight: 44kg (96lb)	

▼ Mk 81

Smallest of the Mk 80 series, the Mk 81 has a nominal weight of 250lb (113kg). Although lighter weapons are now favoured, the Mk 81 fell from favour during the Vietnam War, when the power of its 44kg (96lb) Composition H6, Minol or Tritonal explosive was found to be lacking for most tactical applications. Today, the Mk 81 remains in service with various export operators.

Specifications

Length overall: 2200mm (7ft 2.6in)	Weight: 227kg (500lb)
Body diameter: 273mm (10.75in)	Guidance system: None
Filing weight: 89kg (192lb)	

▲ Mk 82

This Mk 82 is fitted with the Snakeye retarding fin kit. These fins flick out immediately after release from the launch aircraft, increasing drag and slowing the fall of the bomb. The 'Snake' allows delivery from very low level and at lower speeds, providing a safer drop envelope that makes the weapon particularly suitable for the close air support role.

▲ Mk 83

The Mk 83 has a nominal weight of 1000lb (454kg), and consists of a streamlined steel casing containing Tritonal high-explosive. Widely operated by the US Navy, the Mk 83 is used as the warhead for a variety of PGMs, and has also been developed as the Quickstrike sea mine.

Specifications

Length overall: 3000mm (9ft 10.1in)	Weight: 447kg (1014lb)
Body diameter: 256mm (14in)	Guidance system: None
Filing weight: 202kg (385lb)	

M52 armour-piercing bomb, 1000lb M59 semi-armour-piercing bomb, 1000lb M65 GP bomb, 1000lb M79 chemical bomb, 2000lb (907kg) M66 GP bomb, 2000lb M103 semi-armour-piercing bomb, 3000lb (1361kg) M118 low-drag ('slick') GP bomb, 4000lb (1814kg) M56 light-case demolition bomb, 10,000lb (4536kg) M121 GP bomb, 12,000lb (5443kg) M109 GP bomb, and the 22,000lb (9979kg) M110 GP bomb. Other World War II-era weapons that survived in service after 1945 included the Mk 1 1600lb (726kg) and the 1000lb Mk 33 bombs, both armour-piercing types.

The heaviest weapons in the above category were retained for carriage by SAC bombers, before giving way to the first generation of free-fall nuclear bombs. Among the M-series, the most important and enduring weapon was the 750lb M117, also available in retarded form. This bomb was a signature weapon of the B-52 (as well as tactical warplanes) in Vietnam, and later in the Persian Gulf, and remains in use with the Stratofortress today. The M117 also served as the basis for the MC1 chemical bomb.

While napalm bombs are no longer in use with the US military, modern incendiary bombs include the Mk 77, which weighs around 750lb (Mod 0) or 500lb (Mods 1, 4 and 5), the 750lb Mk 78 and the 1000lb Mk 79. All of these later fire bombs use a filling consisting of petroleum oil. While the Mks 78 and 79 have now been withdrawn, the Mk 77 has seen notable use in recent operations in Afghanistan and Iraq from 2001.

Mk 80 series

The M-series gave way to the low-drag Mk 80 series in the early 1960s, and these remain the most important US conventional free-fall bombs, as well as serving as the warheads for a wide variety of precision-guided munitions. The smallest of these is the 250lb Mk 81, a GP bomb frequently fitted with the Snakeye retarding tailfin kit, providing stability and slowing the bomb's descent after release.

The Mk 82 is a 500lb-class weapon, also frequently fitted with the Snakeye; the 1000lb Mk 83 can also be fitted with a retarding tailfin kit. Largest of the family is the 2000lb Mk 84. The Mk 82 was

▲ AN-M65

Dating from 1942, the US-made M65 1000-lb general purpose (GP) bomb was mainly used against reinforced targets like dams and concrete or steel railroad bridges. The P-47 Thunderbolt ground attack fighter could carry two M65s, while the B-26 medium bomber could carry four. The bomb continued in service with NATO countries until 1960, when it was withdrawn from service.

Specifications

Length overall: 1700mm (66in)	Explosive weight: 269kg (595lb)
Body diameter: 480mm (18.8in)	Guidance system: Aerial, free-fall
Weight: 471kg (1040lb)	

▼ BLU-82

The BLU-82 'Daisy Cutter' demolition bomb was for many years the most powerful conventional weapon in the US inventory. In Vietnam the weapon was used to clear helicopter landing zones in the jungle, being delivered from the rear door of a C-130 Hercules transport.

Specifications

Length overall: 3597mm (11ft 9.6in)	Weight: 6804kg (15,000lb)
Body diameter: 1372mm (54in)	Guidance system: None
Stabilizer span: n/a	

Specifications

Length overall: 3280mm (10ft 9.1in)	Weight: 925kg (2039lb)
Body diameter: 458mm (18in)	Guidance system: None
Explosive weight: 429kg (945lb)	

▲ Mk 84

With a nominal weight of 2000lb (907kg), the Mk 84 is the most powerful of the Mk 80 bombs. The weapon was popular in Vietnam, where it was second only to the 15,000lb (6804kg) BLU-82 'Daisy Cutter' in terms of the heaviest GP bombs. It can penetrate up to 3.4m (11ft) of concrete, depending on launch profile.

also adapted during the Vietnam War to serve as a mine, the Mk 36 destructor having a thermal or seismic trigger. The Mk 40 and Mk 41 were similar adaptations of the Mk 83 and Mk 84, respectively.

Other derivatives of the ubiquitous Mk 80 series included the Mk 94, essentially a Mk 82 casing with a non-persistent Sarin gas filling. Meanwhile, remaining members of the post-war series of US free-fall weapons included the 750lb Mk 116 Weteye chemical bomb and the 750lb Mk 122 Fireye incendiary bomb.

American nuclear bombs

Following the first-generation 'Little Boy' and 'Fat Man' bombs dropped on Japan in 1945, the initial

in-service free-fall US nuclear weapon comprised a handful of Mk I weapons, productionized derivatives of the gun-assembly-type Little Boy, with a yield of 15–16 kilotons (KT). The Mk III that followed this was similarly a mass-produced version of the Fat Man; a total of 120 examples of this plutonium implosion bomb were completed, with yields ranging from 18 to 49 KT. All of these early weapons had been retired from SAC service by 1950. Revised designations were introduced with the Mk 4, the first US nuclear bomb to see quantity production, and a product-improved version of the Fat Man, with a variable yield. Introduced in 1952, the Mk 5 was the first nuclear bomb to introduce a major reduction in size and weight, and could be used in airburst or contact profiles, with a yield ranging from 6 to

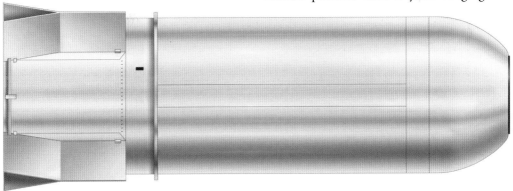

▲ **B53**

The B53 employed a similar warhead to the W53 device used in the Titan II intercontinental ballistic missile, with a yield of 9 MT. The tail section of the bomb was fitted with four fins and a parachute array, which comprised one pilot chute and four canopies of two different sizes. It was mainly replaced by the B83.

Specifications

Length overall: 3800m (12ft 6in)	Weight: 4015kg (8850lb)
Body diameter: 1.27m (50in)	Parachute system: 350–400kg (800–900lb)
Stabilizer span: n/a	

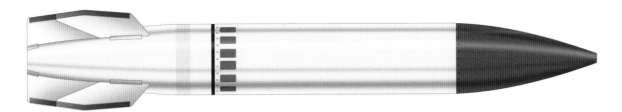

▲ **B57**

The tactical B57 saw widespread use across NATO, and armed nuclear-tasked Alliance fighter-bombers under the 'dual key' arrangement, in which maintenance and security of the bombs remained the responsibility of the USAF. The B57 was also carried by anti-submarine warfare aircraft, including the Sea King helicopter.

Specifications

Length overall: 3000mm (9ft 10in)	Parachute retarder (optional):
Body diameter: 37.5mm (14.75in)	3800mm (12ft 6in) diameter
Weight: 227kg (500lb)	

120 KT. The Mk 6 was another 'lightweight' weapon, based on the Mk 4, and it was in production throughout the first half of the 1950s. The Mk 7 was the first US nuclear bomb designed for tactical use. Also known as Thor, this weapon was in service from 1952 to 1967, with variable yields of between 8 and 61 KT. The Mk 8 was designed as an earth-penetrating bomb, with a delayed fuse and a yield of 25 to 30 KT. It remained in use for only a brief period until superseded by the improved Mk 11. The Mk 12 was optimized for carriage by tactical fighters, with a 12–14 KT yield, and was in use from 1954 until its eventual withdrawal in 1962.

The thermonuclear age was heralded by the Mk 14 of 1954, the first such weapon in the megaton (MT) class. Only five examples of the Mk 14 were produced during 1954, before the Mk 15 was introduced as the first 'lightweight' thermonuclear bomb. This had a yield of between 1.7 and 3.8 MT, compared to 5–7 MT for the Mk 14 that preceded it. Heaviest of all US nuclear weapons was the Mk 17, with a yield of 10–15 MT. This weapon was so large that it could only be accommodated by the B-36

Peacemaker bomber, and it saw service for just three years, between 1954 and 1957.

The Mk 18 was the largest US fission weapon, and saw brief service in the second half of the 1950s, with a yield of 500 KT. From the Mk 20 onwards the designation system was again revised. The Mk 20 (or B20) was an improved high-yield Mk 13, but was cancelled in 1954. It was followed by the B21, a 4–5 MT weapon deployed in the late 1950s. The B24 was very similar to the Mk 17, with a yield of 10–15 MT. The B36 was among the most prolific weapon of its type, and was another megaton-class weapon retired in the early 1960s in favour of the B41. The B39, meanwhile, represented an improved Mk 15, with a low-level retarded (laydown) delivery option.

Second-generation US nuclear bombs

Primary US nuclear weapons fielded in the later Cold War period included the B28, which was first introduced by SAC in 1958, mainly as a weapon for the B-52. The thermonuclear B28 was produced in numerous versions, with five different yields including 70 KT, 350 KT, 1.1 MT and 1.45 MT; the

▼ B61

By the mid 1980s, the B61 was the most numerous nuclear bomb in the NATO inventory, and the weapon remains in service today, including on USAF bases in Western Europe. A number of variants have been fielded, including the latest B61 Mod 11, which is a ground-penetrating 'bunker buster'.

Specifications

Length overall: 3580mm (11ft 8in)	Weight: 320kg (700lb)
Body diameter: 330mm (13in)	Parachute retarder: 7300mm (24ft) diameter
Stabilizer span: n/a	

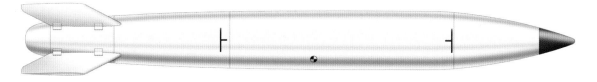

▼ B83

The B83 entered service in the early 1980s as the successor to the B28, B43 and some of the ultra-high-yield B53 weapons. A variable yield means the weapon can be used against strategic or tactical targets, and the weapon is also suitable for external carriage by supersonic fighters, with the parachute capable of slowing the bomb down to 96km/h (60mph) from a launch speed of Mach 2.

Specifications

Length overall: 3670mm (12ft)	Weight: 1100kg (2400lb)
Body diameter: 457mm (18in)	Parachute retarder: 14m (46ft)
Stabilizer span: n/a	

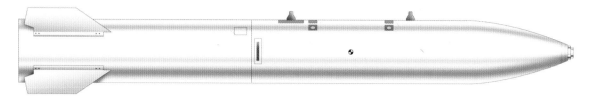

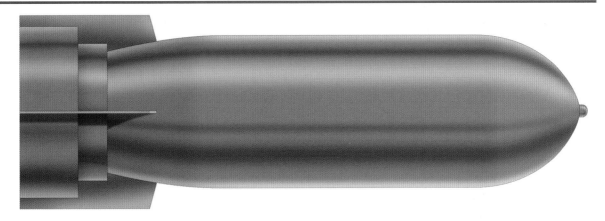

Specifications

Length overall: 2210mm (7ft 3in)	Weight: 515kg (1135lb)
Body diameter: 450mm (17.7in)	Guidance system: None
Stabilizer span: 570mm (22.4in)	

▲ **FAB-500Sh**

The 'Sh' of this bomb's designation indicates a weapon designed for carriage by a Shturmovik, or assault aircraft. The FAB-500Sh is intended for low-level use, and therefore features a parachute and a different fuse to ensure detonation, despite the reduced force of the impact.

warhead was also used to arm the AGM-28 Hound Dog ASM. The B28EX was a streamlined version that was tailored for supersonic external carriage, while the compact B28IN was for internal carriage. The B28RE was an externally carried weapon with a parachute retarding system, and the B28FI was a version with a parachute for laydown delivery, and with air, ground and delayed-action burst options. Finally, the B28RI was similar to the B28FI, but with options for air or contact burst only. Withdrawal of the B28 began in the early 1980s, but

▼ **FAB-500M-54**

The Soviet M-54 pattern of bombs were high-drag weapons that featured conical noses with a prominent ballistic ring. These weapons were primarily intended for internal carriage and were superseded by the low-drag M-62 pattern that could be carried externally by high-speed aircraft.

was not completed until 1991. Replacement for the B28 was the B83, a high-yield bomb developed for the B-1B Lancer, as well as the B-52 and FB-111. The B83 was the first laydown-type weapon in the megaton class, and could be dropped at speeds of Mach 1 for a groundburst detonation. It entered service in 1983 and remains within America's 'Enduring Stockpile' of nuclear weapons. Despite its primary strategic tasking, the B83 can also be carried by tactical aircraft.

The high-yield B43 saw widespread use with the US Air Force, Navy and Marine Corps, with most

Specifications

Length overall: 1500mm (4ft 11in)	Weight: 477kg (1052lb)
Body diameter: 457mm (18in)	Guidance system: None
Stabilizer span: 570mm (22.4in)	

▲ ODAB-500

The ODAB series comprises fuel/air explosive (thermobarbic) bombs of the type used by the Soviets in Afghanistan and by Russia during its campaigns in Chechnya. Reports suggest that the early versions were unreliable, and as a result their use in Afghanistan was limited. When they functioned, however, these weapons were extremely destructive.

Specifications

Length overall: 2200mm (7ft 2.6in)	Weight: 392kg (864lb)
Body diameter: 450mm (17.7in)	Guidance system: None
Stabilizer span: n/a	

Specifications

Length overall: 1065mm (4ft 6in)	Weight: 123kg (271lb)
Body diameter: 273mm (10.75in)	Guidance system: None
Stabilizer span: 345mm (13.6in)	

▲ OFAB-100-120

OFAB bombs are high-explosive/fragmentation weapons intended for use against light armoured vehicles, artillery, radar sites and personnel. Unlike standard GP bombs, the steel body is designed to create splinters on detonation. The OFAB-100-120 can be fitted with a parachute that can be allied with a standoff detonation device for mid-air detonation.

examples being optimized for external carriage; some examples were also provided for use by RAF heavy bombers. Manufacture began in 1961 and the last examples were retired in 1991. The weapon could be delivered in free-fall or retarded modes, for laydown or toss delivery, and could be set for airburst or ground detonation. Five different yields were provided for the weapon, ranging from 70 KT to 1 MT.

SAC's largest ever nuclear bomb was the B53, a 9-MT weapon that armed the B-47 Stratojet, B-52 and B-58 Hustler from 1962. Fielded in four versions, the B53 could be delivered in free-fall or parachute-retarded form. It was eventually phased

out in favour of the B61, the most numerous bomb within NATO air forces by the 1980s, also being supplied for use by other Alliance members. Intended for external, supersonic carriage, the B61 is a lightweight store, but it can also be carried internally by the B-52 (and by the B-1B, before this aircraft lost its nuclear role). Production began in 1968, and the weapon is available with variable tactical or strategic yield, ranging from 0.3 to 340 KT – the yield can be selected in flight. Laydown delivery is an option, for which the B61 can be dropped from altitudes down to 15m (50ft), and both free-fall or parachute delivery can be used, with airburst, contact or time-delay fuses. The B61 remains in USAF service.

Entering production in 1963, the B57 nuclear bomb was widely used as a depth charge by naval aircraft, but also had a role arming various US and NATO fixed-wing tactical aircraft. Yield was variable between 5 and 10 KT, with options for laydown, toss or loft delivery, and as well as airburst and groundburst. A depth pressure fuse was available for use as an anti-submarine weapon. The B57 was removed from the inventory in 1993.

The Soviet Union developed a range of different free-fall bombs during the Cold War, and many of these remain in use. The standard free-fall GP bomb is the FAB series, which has been provided in various weights ranging from the 50kg (110lb) FAB-50 to the 9000kg (19,840lb) FAB-9000, together with smaller bomblets for use in weapons dispensers. The FAB-9000 was one of the heaviest conventional bombs ever fielded, and was primarily associated with the Tu-22 supersonic bomber. The first major series introduced after World War II was the M-46 type

Specifications

Length overall: 362mm (14.2in)	Weight: 2.23kg (4.9)
Body diameter: 60mm (2.4in)	Guidance system: None
Stabilizer span: 90mm (3.5in)	

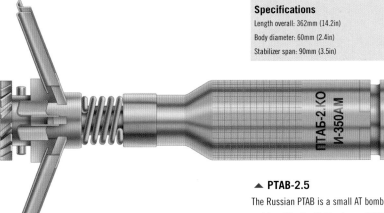

▲ PTAB-2.5

The Russian PTAB is a small AT bomb that is usually carried by a submunitions pod (see Chapter 7). Two types of PTAB are currently available, the PTAB-2.5 and the larger PTAB-10.5. The PTAB-2.5 illustrated here is capable of penetrating 65mm (2.6in) of armour thanks to its shaped-charge warhead, which creates a powerful and directional high-velocity stream of hot gases and liquid metal.

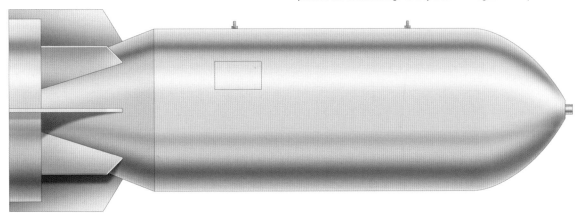

▲ OFAB-500ShN

The OFAB series also includes the OFAB-500ShN, with a nominal weight of 500kg (1100lb) and provision for low-level delivery by close-support aircraft. The basic version is intended to be dropped from an altitude of 50–500m (164–1640ft), while the OFAB-500ShR version is equipped with multiple warheads within an elongated body.

Specifications

Length overall: 2493mm (8ft 1in)	Weight: 525kg (1157lb)
Body diameter: 450mm (17.7in)	Guidance system: None
Stabilizer span: 570mm (22.4in)	

◀ **Full load of 'slicks'**
An underside view of an F-111 aircraft banking over the Nellis Air Force Base range in Nevada. The aircraft, assigned to the USAF's 391st Tactical Fighter Training Squadron, 366th Tactical Fighter Wing (TFW), is carrying 24 500lb Mk 82 low-drag bombs.

(indicating 1946), these adding the suffix M-46 to their designations and being available in weights ranging from 250kg (551lb) to 3000kg (6613lb).

▼ AN.52

France's AN.52 was a tactical nuclear weapon that armed the Mirage IIIE, and later the Jaguar A and Super Etendard. The weapon was first tested and entered service in 1972 and had two yield options: 6–8 KT or 25 KT. The AN.52 was finally retired in 1992 in favour of the ASMP standoff missile.

The later M-54 was available in weights ranging from 250kg to 9000kg. In the early 1960s the USSR introduced a new design of streamlined low-drag bombs, these M-62 weapons being provided in 250kg and 500kg forms only.

In addition to the FAB series, the OFAB family are high-explosive/fragmentation weapons, intended for

Specifications

Length overall: 4200mm (13ft 9in)	Weight: 455kg (1003lb)
Body diameter: n/a	Guidance system: None
Stabilizer span: n/a	

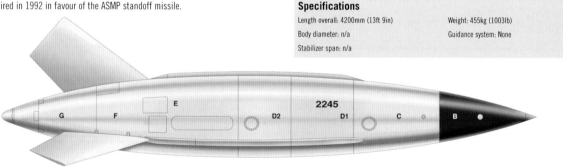

Specifications

Length overall: 2940mm (115in)	Weight: 500kg (1340lb)
Body diameter: 360mm (14.2in)	Guidance system: None
Stabilizer span: n/a	

▼ Expal BR-250

The Spanish-made Expal (Explosivos Alaveses) bombs were widely used during the 1982 Falklands War, these weapons arming the Argentine Mirage III and IAI Dagger. Two sizes were available: 250kg (550lb) BR-250 and 400kg (880lb) BRI-400. The BRP and BRIP were parachute-retarded versions.

use on soft-skinned vehicles, artillery, personnel and similar targets. Soviet-designed incendiary bombs include the ZB series of napalm tanks. The BrAB series of bombs are designed for applications against armoured vehicles, and rely on kinetic energy for their penetration. For attacking hardened targets, the BetAB series is fitted with a solid-fuel rocket booster that allows it to penetrate concrete and other hardened structures. One free-fall weapon that found particular favour in the USSR was the thermobaric bomb, or fuel/air explosive (FAE). Designated ODAB in Soviet use, these weapons contain a liquid fuel that is atomized to create a highly volatile cloud. This cloud is then ignited, creating a mid-air explosion and devastating vacuum effect.

British high-explosive GP bombs fielded after 1945 were produced primarily by Royal Ordnance, with major production types being fielded in 245kg (540lb) and 454kg (1000lb) weights, some of which could be fitted with retarding fins.

British nuclear bombs

The UK's first nuclear weapon was codenamed Blue Danube, which was employed for the first British nuclear test, Operation *Hurricane*, in 1952. Issued to the RAF in 1953 as Britain's initial operational nuclear weapon, the free-fall Blue Danube bomb had a yield of 10 KT. Production was limited, however, and it was withdrawn in 1962. A second-generation fission weapon, introduced in 1961 and named Red Beard, was a lightweight 5–20 KT tactical device that was also issued to the Royal Navy.

The interim Violet Club weapon of around 500 KT yield was deployed in small numbers from 1958, before being converted to Yellow Sun Mk 1 bombs, the UK's first genuine hydrogen bomb, although this was later discarded in favour of the US-supplied Mk 28. A first British hydrogen bomb was tested in 1957, but failed to achieve a megaton yield.

Thereafter the US supplied the British with vital nuclear technology, and by using a US design the UK

▲ **Long-lived 'dumb' bomb**
Maintainers from the USAF's 2nd Bomb Wing load M117 bombs on to a B-52H on the flight line at Andersen Air Force Base, Guam.

WE177B

Britain's final free-fall nuclear bomb was the WE177, which armed the RAF
Tornado fleet until 1998. The prominent red canister strapped to the tail of the
bomb contained a wiring harness that connected the weapon to the release
circuits. The WE177B version was a 450-KT thermonuclear weapon.

Specifications

Length overall: 3378mm (11ft 1in)

Body diameter: n/a

Stabilizer span: n/a

Weight: 457kg (1006lb)

Guidance system: None

Specifications

Length overall: 2500mm (8ft 2in)

Body diameter: 212mm (8.35in)

Warhead weight: 150kg (330lb)

Weight: 204kg (450lb)

Guidance system: None

Durandal

Developed by Matra of France, the Durandal anti-runway weapon was adopted by
a number of export customers, including the USAF. The definitive production
version falls under a parachute before a solid-fuel motor ignites, driving the
weapon through up to 400mm (15.75in) of reinforced concrete. The warhead then
detonates, or is detonated at a later time via a delayed-action fuse.

'Blue death'

A maintainer tightens down
a Mk 76 inert GP bomb on a
USMC AV-8B Harrier II on
the flight deck of a US Navy
amphibious assault ship.
The Mk 76 is known by the
ironic nickname 'Blue
death' — this 11.3kg
(25lb) practice bomblet
contains only just enough
explosive content (in the
form of a signal cartridge)
to create a visible 'puff' on
the target range.

fielded the megaton-yield Yellow Sun Mk 2 device from 1961, this incorporating the Mk 28-derived Red Snow warhead. British air-launched nuclear weapons culminated in the WE177, introduced by the RAF and Royal Navy in 1966. Three variants were fielded, comprising high-yield strategic, lower-yield tactical and depth bombs. The last nuclear store in RAF service, the WE177, was retired in 1998.

French free-fall bombs include the BAP series of runway-cratering bombs, which are delivered by parachute before a solid-fuel rocket motor accelerates the weapon, increasing velocity in order to penetrate up to 300mm (1ft) of reinforced concrete. The BAP-100 weighs just 32.5kg (71.65lb) and can be carried in clusters of up to 18 weapons. The Durandal is a similar 'runway dibber' weapon, also provided with rocket assistance.

HE bombs

High-explosive GP bombs, meanwhile, are produced in France by SAMP in a variety of nominal weights up to 1000kg (2204lb). Thomson-Brandt is responsible for the 125kg (275.5lb) TBA high-explosive/fragmentation anti-personnel bomb. French free-fall nuclear weapons were the strategic AN.11 and improved AN.22 provided for the Mirage IVA bomber, and the AN.52 that was issued to French Air Force and Navy tactical strike aircraft.

▼ **Bomb load**
Weapons specialists from the 509th Aircraft Maintenance Squadron, Whiteman Air Force Base, Missouri, prepare to load a BDU-56 bomb on a B-2 Spirit bomber from the 509th Bomb Wing (also based at Whiteman), during their deployment at Andersen Air Force Base, Guam, on 11 April 2005.

US guided bombs

Although the US employed guided bombs in World War II and Korea, it was the emergence of the Paveway family in the mid 1960s that introduced the age of the precision-guided bomb.

THE ORIGINS OF the modern US 'smart bomb' date back to the guided 'Bomb Gliders' (Guided Bomb, or GB series) that began to be fielded during World War II by the US Army Air Force (USAAF) and Navy, albeit initially in entirely unguided form. After the war, development focused on the Vertical Bomb (VB) family of free-fall guided weapons, early versions of which had seen service during the war. Subject to operational use in Korea was the 1000lb (454kg) VB-3 Razon, employed by B-29s against North Korean bridges, but lacking destructive power. The final member of the series, the VB-13 (later ASM-A-1) Tarzon, was also used in combat in Korea, against road and rail bridges and reservoirs. Weighing 12,000lb (5443kg), the Tarzon, like the Razon, employed radio command guidance.

Interest in guided bombs was revived during the Vietnam War, when the Paveway programme began with the aim of fielding accurate air-to-surface weapons by teaming free-fall bombs with laser guidance. As well as improving accuracy, the laser guidance kit provided a standoff range through its fin kit, although the weapon remained unpowered.

In 1965, Texas Instruments (TI) teamed up with the USAF's Armament Development and Test Center for collaborative development work on the Paveway family. A first laser-guided bomb (LGB) with TI guidance kit was dropped in April 1965 and the programme ultimately combined 30 related systems, including airborne navigation, target marking and identification, and all-weather and night-vision guidance systems.

By 1971, the initial Paveway I family included eight different guidance kits. All of these were basically similar, with the primary distinctions relating to the sizes of the canard fins and the rear control fins, which were adapted depending on the weight and dimensions of the bomb.

Key features of the Paveway series bombs include their 'bolt-on' guidance unit, comprising a gimble-mounted silicon detector array mounted in the nose. The seeker homes on a laser light source of the correct wavelength, provided by the launch aircraft,

another aircraft appropriately equipped or by a forward air controller (FAC) on the ground. Early aircraft designator systems included Pave Knife, Pave Spike and Pave Tack. Signals from the seeker are processed by a guidance computer that sends commands to the bomb's control surfaces, provided in the form of enlarged tailfins at the rear of the weapon. Critically, the guidance package and tail kit can be added to most standard free-fall GP bombs.

Paveway I

Individual weapons within the Paveway series received a Guided Bomb Unit (GBU) designation. The Paveway I family included guidance packages compatible with the M117 demolition bomb (creating the 'BOLT-117'), the Mk 84 GP bomb in high- and low-drag forms, the M118E1 demolition bomb, the Mk 82 GP bomb in high- and low-drag forms, the US Navy's Rockeye Mk 20 Mod 2 cluster bomb (which carried AT fragmentation bomblets) and the Pave Storm I cluster munition for the USAF. The last weapon mentioned here consisted of an SUU-54 dispenser carrying about 1800 AT fragmentation bomblets. The Rockeye and M117-based Paveway I LGBs were soon discontinued, and instead the Mk 83 GP bomb as used by the US Navy and Marine Corps was added to the options. The GBU-2, GBU-10 and GBU-12 were provided with two different wing kits, with longer wings being tailored for slower-speed delivery and increased range. A full inventory of the various Paveway incarnations is provided in the table on p.151.

Design work on the simplified Paveway II series began in 1972, and the weapon was introduced in the late 1970s. It features a cheaper and less complex seeker array and guidance computer, and a new folding-wing (rather than fixed) aerofoil group that improves manoeuvrability. Primary bombs used in Paveway II applications are the Mk 82, Mk 83 and Mk 84/BLU-109 bombs, as well as the British 1000lb Mk 13/18 for RAF service. The Paveway II entered testing in 1974, with the first production models being introduced in 1977. Early production

Specifications

Length overall: 3331mm (10ft 11.1in)	Weight: 227kg (500lb)
Body diameter: 273mm (10.75in)	Guidance system: Laser and GPS/INS
Stabilizer span: 457mm (18in)	

▲ GBU-49 Paveway II

Typical of the latest Raytheon Enhanced Paveway II versions is the GBU-49, which is essentially similar to the 500lb GBU-12, but which adds an INS/GPS guidance package to become a dual-guidance weapon. The weapon is also unofficially known as the EGBU-12. In addition to use by US tactical aircraft, the GBU-49 has been cleared for use by the MQ-9 Reaper UAV, and export versions have been sold to various operators including France, for integration with the French Air Force Mirage 2000D and French Navy Super Etendard strike aircraft.

Specifications

Length overall: 7600mm (24ft 11in)	Weight: 2268kg (5000lb)
Body diameter: 356mm (14in)	Guidance system: Laser seeker
Stabilizer span: 1700mm (67in)	

▼ GBU-15

The electro-optically guided GBU-15 glide bomb is intended to destroy high-value enemy targets and is currently carried by the F-15E. In 1999 and 2000, a large number of GBU-15 weapons were given an adverse-weather capability through the addition of inertial/GPS navigation guidance.

▲ GBU-28 Paveway III

Codenamed 'Deep Throat', the GBU-28 was hurriedly developed for use in Operation *Desert Storm*, where it was employed on two occasions by USAF F-15Es. The 'bunker buster' weapon was intended to be used against hardened Iraqi bunkers and needed to be dropped from high altitude to maximize its kinetic energy. The original BLU-113 warhead case was made of former US Army M201 howitzer gun barrels, while the guidance package was taken from the GBU-24/B Paveway III.

Specifications

Length overall: 3900mm (12ft 10in)	Weight: 907kg (2000lb)
Body diameter: 457mm (18in)	Guidance system: TV or infrared
Stabilizer span: 1500mm (59in)	

was handled by Raytheon, but later Paveway IIs are also built by Lockheed Martin.

A drawback of the Paveway II is the limitations of its laser seeker in poor weather, which can result in a terminal break in the guidance. In order to address this, a GPS-aided inertial guidance kit can be added, resulting in the Enhanced Paveway (EGBU series).

An alternative to the Raytheon EGBU is the Lockheed Martin Dual-Mode LGB (DMLGB) upgrade, which also adds an inertial/GPS package. Since 2005 the DMLGB has been produced for the US Navy's Paveway II.

The Paveway III was developed from 1980 and can be dropped within a wider altitude envelope, adding

▼ GBU-44 Viper Strike

Primarily intended for carriage by UAVs, the Northrop Grumman
Viper Strike glide-bomb is a GPS-aided laser-guided variant of the
Brilliant Anti-Tank (BAT) munition that originally incorporated a
combined acoustic and IR seeker. The weapon is also integrated on
close air support versions of the C-130 in order to add a precision
standoff capability.

Specifications

Length overall: 900mm (36in)   Weight: 20kg (42lb)

Body diameter: 140mm (5.5in)   Guidance system: GPS-midcourse/terminal laser

Stabilizer span: 900mm (36in)   homing

Specifications

Length overall: 4320mm (14ft 2in)   Weight: 453kg (1000lb)

Body diameter: 457mm (18in)   Guidance system: Laser seeker

Stabilizer span: 490mm (19in)

▼ 1000lb British Paveway II

Sometimes erroneously described as the 'GBU-13', this British Paveway consists
of a locally produced Mk 13 bomb with a Paveway II kit. The British also adopted
the Paveway II in conjunction with the Mk 18 of the same weight. These weapons
were used by RAF Harrier strike aircraft during the Falklands War in 1982. British
Paveways are sometimes also referred to by the designation CPU-123, although
this technically only describes the guidance package.

▼ GBU-16 Paveway II

Paveway II LGBs in the 1000lb class are known as GBU-16s. In terms of
warheads, these can be armed with either a standard Mk 83 low-drag GP bomb or
the BLU-110, which is externally similar but includes a thermally insensitive
explosive. The BLU-110 is the version used by the US Navy, and these weapons
also feature a grey external protective coating (as seen here). The thermally
insensitive explosive is designed to withstand fuel fire in case of an accident on
an aircraft carrier.

Specifications

Length overall: 3700mm (12ft)   Weight: 454kg (1000lb)

Body diameter: 360mm (14.7in)   Guidance system: Laser seeker

Stabilizer span: n/a

▼ GBU-22 Paveway III

A blue casing for this GBU-22 signifies an inert version, normally filled with concrete in order to preserve the ballistic qualities for test launches. The 500lb GBU-22 is based on a Mk 82 bomb, and although it has not been supplied to the US military, the weapon has been produced by Raytheon for export customers and is cleared for use by the F-16 and Mirage 2000.

Specifications

Length overall: 3505mm (11ft 6in)	Weight: 327kg (720lb)
Body diameter: 270mm (10.8in)	Guidance system: Laser seeker
Stabilizer span: 490mm (19.3in)	

▼ GBU-24 Paveway III

Seen here with its tailfins deployed, the GBU-24 is a Paveway III LGB with a 907kg (2000lb) warhead. The warhead is typically a Mk 84 low-drag GP bomb, a BLU-109 penetrator warhead or a BLU-116 Advanced Unitary Penetrator (AUP) warhead. The GBU-24 can also be outfitted with Enhanced Paveway inertial/GPS guidance.

Specifications

Length overall: 4320mm (14ft 2in)	Weight: 907kg (2000lb)
Body diameter: 370mm (14.6in)	Guidance system: Laser seeker
Stabilizer span: 1650mm (65in)	

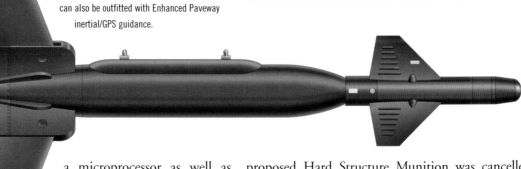

a microprocessor as well as pop-out lifting wings. In particular, the Paveway III is better suited to launch at low level. A deficiency of earlier Paveways was the fact that the lofted trajectory required to permit standoff range from a low-level launch was compromised by the original 'bang-bang' autopilot. With the 'bang-bang' guidance, the control surfaces were either at full deflection, or at zero deflection, and the weapon would therefore depart its lofted trajectory as soon as the seeker locked on to the target. In contrast, the Paveway III uses the new Low-Level LGB (LLLGB) guidance system. A digital autopilot ensures accuracy even in poor weather conditions or within a low cloudbase. Also capable of being dropped in a dive, at high altitude or using a loft technique to extend range, the Paveway III uses proportional terminal guidance to provide optimum impact angles.

The initial Paveway III guidance kits were allied with the Mk 82, Mk 83 or Mk 84 warheads, while a proposed Hard Structure Munition was cancelled. The first Paveway IIIs were delivered in 1983. In common with the Paveway II, the Paveway III is also provided with inertial/GPS packages to improve accuracy in adverse weather. The first inertial/GPS-enabled Paveway III (EGBU) was tested in 1999 and issued in 2000. Typically, the inertial/GPS package is used to provide mid-course guidance, with the laser seeker providing terminal homing.

The latest Paveway IV series has been developed for export, as an alternative to the Small Diameter Bomb, and has been adopted by the RAF. The Paveway IV uses a penetrating Mk 82 warhead allied with dual-mode laser and inertial/GPS guidance. A key advantage of the Paveway IV is its selectable fusing, allowing the pilot to choose impact, airburst or groundburst options, depending on the target.

Electro-optical weapons

As well as driving work on LGBs, the war in Vietnam focused development on electro-optical guided

Specifications

Length overall: 3890mm (12ft 9in)	Weight: 924kg (2036lb)
Body diameter: 458mm (18in)	Guidance system: Inertial and GPS
Stabilizer span: 640mm (25in)	

▲ GBU-31 JDAM

The GBU-31 is a 2000lb-class JDAM that can carry various different warheads, including the Mk 84 low-drag GP, BLU-109 penetrator, BLU-117 with thermally insensitive explosive or BLU-119. The latter is a blast-fragmentation type designed to destroy biological/chemical targets.

bombs, using TV guidance. Under the Pave Strike programme, Rockwell International engineered the Homing Bomb System (HOBOS) for the USAF, this being an add-on kit based on a TV image-contrast tracker. Later, improved TV and IR guidance seekers were added, enhancing night and adverse-weather targeting. The HOBOS kit could be fitted to the Mk 84 or M118E1 bombs.

As well as a guidance kit on the nose, the HOBOS added a control module with four fins at the rear of the bomb and four strakes attached to the body of the weapon. Production versions were the GBU-8 with the Mk 84 bomb, and the GBU-9 with the M118. An extension of the HOBOS concept, the

GBU-15, was developed by Rockwell as the Modular Glide Weapon System, also known as the Cruciform-Wing Weapon (CWW). The GBU-15 consists of a guidance package, a cruciform wing module, a datalink module, and two warhead options. The datalink introduced the option of attacking targets indirectly as well as directly. Depending on target

▼ Strike Eagle on the range

An F-15E Strike Eagle from the USAF Fighter Weapons School at Nellis Air Force Base, Nevada, drops inert 2000lb Paveway LGBs over the ranges north of Nellis during a training mission. The F-15E is carrying five 2000lb Paveways: four on the left and right conformal stations and one on the centreline.

Specifications

Length overall: n/a

Body diameter: n/a

Stabilizer span: n/a

Weight: 227kg (500lb)

Guidance system: Laser guided

▼ Paveway IV

The Paveway IV has been adopted by the RAF and introduces a selectable fusing option coupled with dual-mode guidance. Fusing options can be chosen in flight, and comprise airburst, impact and post-impact detonation. The weapon can be released from low, medium or high level, and in loft or dive attacks. The Paveway IV entered service in late 2008 and has been deployed by the RAF in Afghanistan.

GBU series laser- and electro-optical-guided munitions

Name	Guidance	Bomb	Weight
GBU-1	laser	M117	750lb
GBU-2 Pave Storm	laser	CBU-75 cluster	2000lb
GBU-3	laser	CBU-74	n/a
GBU-5	laser	Mk 7 Rockeye	n/a
GBU-6 Pave Storm I	laser	CBU-79 cluster	n/a
GBU-7 Pave Storm I	laser	CBU-80 cluster	n/a
GBU-8 HOBOS	electro-optical	Mk 84	2000lb
GBU-9 HOBOS	electro-optical	M118	3000lb
GBU-10 Paveway I/II	laser	Mk 84 or BLU-109	2000lb
GBU-11 Paveway I	laser	M118	3000lb
GBU-12 Paveway I/II	laser	Mk 82	500lb
GBU-15	electro-optical	Mk 84 or BLU-109	2000lb
GBU-16 Paveway II	laser	Mk 83	1000lb
GBU-21 Paveway III	laser	Hard Structure Munition	2000lb
GBU-22 Paveway III	laser	Mk 82	500lb
GBU-23 Paveway III	laser	Mk 83	1000lb
GBU-24 Paveway III	laser	Mk 84 or BLU-109	2000lb
GBU-27 Paveway III	laser	BLU-109	2000lb
GBU-28 Paveway III	laser	BLU-113 or BLU-122	4500–5000lb
GBU-44 Viper Strike	laser	n/a	42lb
GBU-48 Enhanced Paveway II	laser/INS/GPS	Mk 83 or BLU-110	1000lb
GBU-49 Enhanced Paveway II	laser/INS/GPS	Mk 82 or BLU-111	500lb
GBU-50 Enhanced Paveway II	laser/INS/GPS	Mk 84 or BLU-117	2000lb
GBU-51 Paveway II	laser	BLU-126	500lb
Paveway IV	laser/GPS	Mk 82	500lb

GBU series Joint Direct Attack Munitions and GPS-guided weaponry

Name	Guidance	Bomb	Weight
GBU-31 JDAM	GPS	Mk 84 or BLU-109	2000lb
GBU-32 JDAM	GPS	Mk 83	1000lb
GBU-34 JDAM	GPS	BLU-109 or BLU-116	2000lb
GBU-36 GAM	GPS	Mk 84	2000lb
GBU-37 GAM	GPS	BLU-113	4500lb
GBU-38 JDAM	GPS	Mk 82 or BLU-126	500lb
GBU-39 SDB	GPS	n/a	285lb
GBU-43 MOAB	GPS	BLU-120	21,700lb
GBU-53 SDB	GPS	n/a	250lb
GBU-54 Laser JDAM	GPS/laser	GBU-32	1000lb
GBU-55 Laser JDAM	GPS/laser	GBU-31	2000lb
GBU-57 MOP	GPS	n/a	30,000lb

type and weather conditions, the guidance kit can be of the electro-optical TV or, for night attack, an imaging IR type. The first was introduced to service in 1983, with the IIR kit following in 1987. The warhead options comprise the Mk 84 low-drag GP bomb or the SUU-54 dispenser containing AT/fragmentation bomblets.

The GBU-15 is intended for launch at medium to very-low altitude, the former using a direct line of sight to the target, and the latter relying on the datalink, the weapon being dropped in the direction of the target, and the aircraft turning back. In datalink mode, the operator is provided with a TV image of the target on a display screen in the cockpit. The GBU-15 climbs to acquire the target, before entering a terminal dive. The operator can steer the weapon to the target, or achieve a lock-on via the seeker head.

Development of the Joint Direct Attack Munition (JDAM) was launched by the USAF and US Navy in 1991, with the aim of exploiting the accuracy offered by GPS-aided inertial guidance to produce a low-cost precision-guided bomb. In 1995 McDonnell Douglas was selected as prime contractor for the JDAM, and flight testing began in 1996. The JDAM entered service in 1998, initially on the USAF's B-52H, and subsequently the weapon was integrated with all tactical and strategic warplanes. It is provided in kit form for fitting to weapons such as the Mk 80 series GP bombs and the BLU series of penetrating weapons. A full list of variants is provided in the table on this page. Each kit consists of a guidance and control section, attached to the rear of the bomb, and coupled with cruciform tailfins. Also attached to the bomb body or nose are strakes, which improve stability and glide performance.

▼ GBU-38 JDAM

JDAMs in the 500lb class are different in appearance to the 1000lb and 2000lb versions, since they lack the centre-body strakes. Instead, the GBU-38 has strakes fitted on the nose. The GBU-38 can accommodate the Mk 82 low-drag GP bomb, the BLU-111 with thermally insensitive explosive, or the BLU-126 Low Collateral Damage Bomb (LCDB).

Specifications

Length overall: 3040mm (9ft 11.7in)

Body diameter: 590mm (15in)

Stabilizer span: 500mm (19.6in)

Weight: 459kg (1013lb)

Guidance system: Inertial and GPS

Laser guidance

The Laser JDAM introduces a laser guidance kit to complement the original all-weather fire-and-forget mode. Laser guidance allows moving targets to be engaged, and the first add-on kits were fielded from 2007, initially for the USAF and US Navy, with Germany later becoming the first export customer.

GPS guidance has also been adopted for the Small Diameter Bomb (SDB), studies of which began in the mid 1990s in order to produce a precision-guided bomb in the 250lb class. The programme was launched in earnest in 1998, and before long Boeing and Lockheed Martin were in competition to field an

▼ GBU-43 MOAB

Dubbed the 'Mother Of All Bombs', the GBU-43 was developed from mid 2002 by the Air Force Research Laboratory (AFRL). The GBU-43 combines the BLU-120 bomb body (with 8480kg/18,700lb of explosive) and an inertial/GPS guidance kit. The only aircraft capable of delivering the MOAB is the MC-130 Hercules. Gliding range is increased by two low-aspect-ratio wings.

▲ Low-cost precision

USAF munitions specialists from the 28th Air Expeditionary Wing unload a GBU-31 2,000lb Joint Direct Attack Munition (JDAM) from a B-52 bomber and place it on a munitions cart during Operation Enduring Freedom. The B-52H was the first aircraft cleared to carry the JDAM, in 1998.

operational SDB design. The Boeing GBU-39 was first tested in 2003 and was selected for production in the same year. After operational testing in 2006, the SDB was declared operational on the F-15E Strike Eagle. The GBU-39 carries a multi-purpose warhead for penetration and blast/fragmentation, and uses inertial/GPS guidance. The pop-out wings adopt a diamond configuration, and allow standoff range.

Specifications

Length overall: 9100mm (30ft)	Filling weight: 8480kg (18,700lb)
Body diameter: 1030m (40.5in)	Guidance system: Inertial and GPS
Weight: 9840kg (21,700lb)	

The forthcoming SDB II adds a multi-mode terminal seeker with autonomous target recognition capabilities and a two-way datalink. Competing designs for the SDB II contract were the Boeing and Lockheed Martin GBU-53 and the Raytheon GBU-40. In 2010, the USAF selected the Raytheon design, with initial deliveries expected to begin in 2013.

An even lighter guided bomb is the GBU-44 Viper Strike, derived from the Brilliant Anti-Tank (BAT) guided AT submunition. The GBU-44 is an unpowered glide-bomb with folding wings and uses semi-active laser guidance. A tandem shaped-charge warhead is carried. Viper Strike is light enough for carriage by UAVs.

At the other end of the scale to the SDB and Viper Strike are the Massive Ordnance Air Blast (MOAB) and the Massive Ordnance Penetrator (MOP), conceptual successors to the 'Earthquake bombs' fielded against hardened targets during World War II.

Development of the GBU-43 MOAB began in mid 2002, with the original aim of adding a guidance package to the 15,000lb (6800kg) BLU-82 bomb, the USAF's largest air-dropped bomb. The new weapon was even larger, with an aerodynamic body and inertial/GPS guidance. Such are the dimensions of the weapon that delivery is only possible using an MC-130 Hercules, with the bomb released from the cargo hold using a parachute extraction system. The weapon is then guided to the target using grid-type control fins on the tail, with standoff range provided by two wings. The MOAB was first tested in 2003.

While the MOAB relies on the destructive force of its explosive filling to destroy deep and hardened targets, the GBU-57 MOP is a penetrator weapon, and is developed for carriage by the B-2 Spirit and B-52H bombers. Once again using inertial/GPS guidance, the MOP was revealed in 2003 as a successor to the MOAB. Around 50 per cent heavier than the MOAB, the 30,000lb (13,636kg) GBU-57 was formulated under the Direct Strike Hard Target Weapon (DSHTW) programme and is primarily intended to destroy underground facilities that are buried up to 30m (100ft) below the surface.

▼ **Stealth delivery**

USAF personnel raise a 2000lb GBU-31 Joint Direct Attack Munition (JDAM) into the bomb bay of a B-2 Spirit bomber at Whiteman Air Force Base, Missouri, prior to a mission over Iraq. A single B-2 can carry 16 GBU-31s, or 80 500lb GBU-38s.

Guided bombs in Vietnam

Despite their primitive nature, early LGBs enjoyed great success in Southeast Asia, with the USAF alone dropping more than 25,000 such weapons, and achieving a kill rate of 68 per cent.

THE LASER-GUIDED BOMB went into action in the Vietnam War in 1968, when the initial examples of what was to become known as the Paveway I saw operational use. The first of the type to be issued was based on the M117 bomb and was fitted with a KMU-342/B laser guidance kit. These weapons were also known as the BOLT-117, in which BOLT indicated Bomb, Laser, Terminal Guidance.

Prior to the widespread adoption of the GBU-series designation, the early Paveway LGBs as used in combat in Vietnam were typically named using designations in the KMU- series, which specifically referred to the guidance kits. Meanwhile, the codename 'Pave Storm' described LGBs that were outfitted with a cluster bomb munition, and in particular the GBU-2.

Phantoms were the primary platforms for Paveway LGB delivery in Vietnam, with these weapons carried by both F-4D and F-4E models. In typical scenarios, the target would be illuminated by another Phantom, equipped with a 'buddy' Pave Light system. The back-seat Weapons System Operator (WSO) in the 'buddy' aircraft was provided with a laser marking device mounted on the canopy to illuminate the target. Meanwhile, the Paveway-equipped F-4 would complete the attack profile in a dive-bomb run. As a result of the large fixed guidance fins on the Paveway I, the F-4 could carry only two 2000lb LGBs, depending on fuel loads. Later in the campaign, the Pave Knife pod became available, allowing one aircraft to illuminate a target that could then be attacked by multiple bombs. By 1973, the Pave Spike pod was available, this offering a combined TV/laser tracking and targeting system and a bomb-release computer. Pave Spike was normally carried in one of the Phantom's forward Sparrow missile bays under the fuselage.

The Paveway series LGB demonstrated its value during attacks against the Thanh Hoa railway bridge that spanned the Song Ma River. In the *Rolling Thunder* bombing campaign in 1965–68, more than 700 missions were flown against this target, with little to show for them, and with eight US aircraft lost in the process. In April 1972, eight USAF F-4Es from the 8th Tactical Fighter Wing at Ubon, Thailand, carrying 2000lb LGBs, succeeded in putting the bridge out of action, even if it was still left standing. Finally, in May, 14 F-4s armed with a combination of 15 2000lb and nine 3000lb guided bombs, plus four-dozen 500lb conventional GP bombs, managed to destroy the bridge, taking the western span off its concrete abutments, and buckling the superstructure.

Another significant bridge target that was put out of action by Paveway LGBs was the Paul Doumer Bridge over the Red River, near Hanoi. Here, four of five major rail lines came together, and these

▼ GBU-8 HOBOS

First used during the Vietnam War, the GBU-8 was developed by Rockwell International. Based on a Mk 84 bomb body and using electro-optical technology, the HOBOS had the advantage over the Paveway I series in that it offered a fully autonomous fire-and-forget capability, with no requirement for laser illumination. However, it was considerably more costly than the Paveway.

Specifications

Length overall: 3630mm (11ft 11in)	Weight: 1027kg (2264lb)
Body diameter: 46cm (18in)	Guidance system: Electro-optical (TV) or IR
Stabilizer span: 1120mm (44in)	

U.S.AIR FORCE

▲ GBU-1 Paveway I

Also known as the 'BOLT-117', the GBU-1 was the initial expression of the successful Paveway family of LGBs. The weapon was based on a 750lb M117 bomb body. The laser guidance kit used was designated KMU-342. The first examples of the GBU-1 were used operationally in Southeast Asia in 1968.

Specifications

Length overall: n/a	Weight: 340kg (750lb)
Body diameter: n/a	Guidance system: Laser seeker
Stabilizer span: n/a	

Specifications

Length overall: 3840mm (14ft 4in)	Weight: 907kg (2000lb)
Body diameter: 460mm (18in)	Guidance system: laser seeker
Stabilizer span: 1700mm (67in)	

▲ GBU-10 Paveway I

The GBU-10 has been produced in both Paveway I and Paveway II variants, both with a 2000lb warhead. The GBU-10 provided the armament for F-4Ds of the USAF's 8th Tactical Fighter Wing 'Wolfpack', which attacked the notorious Paul Doumer Bridge in May 1972.

carried all supplies moved by rail from China and the port of Haiphong. A notoriously hard target, the bridge was defended by around 300 anti-aircraft artillery positions and 85 SAM sites. In the course of two separate attacks in May 1972, 16 F-4s struck the bridge, and two 2000lb GBU-10 LGBs were ultimately responsible for putting the bridge out of commission until the end of the war.

The HOBOS guided bomb was also employed by Phantoms in Vietnam, this weapon requiring the back-seater to lock the weapon on to the target by centring it in the crosshairs provided on a monitor screen in his cockpit. (Initially the rear-cockpit radar scope was used, before small TV screens were added in the rear cockpit.) Once locked on, the weapon could be dropped and the aircraft could turn away from the target. The first trials HOBOS weapons were delivered to F-4D units in Vietnam in the course of 1969. By the end of the conflict, the USAF had dropped around 700 GBU-8s, with the primary

operator being the 25th Tactical Fighter Squadron. An LGB specialist over Southeast Asia was the USAF's B-57G, which employed the 500lb Paveway I to great effect during highly successful night raids against the Ho Chi Minh Trail series of supply routes.

Naval operations

In total, over 25,000 Paveway I LGBs were dropped by USAF aircraft during the campaign in Southeast Asia, and the success of these weapons did much to establish the pre-eminence of precision-guided weapons for future conflicts. In contrast, the US Navy was less quick to adopt the LGB, and deployed only around a few hundred Paveway I bombs during the Vietnam War. The primary reason for this reluctance was one of cost. If an attack sortie launched by a carrier-based aircraft had to be cancelled, safety guidelines stipulated that ordnance should be jettisoned in the sea, and this was often judged unacceptably costly if LGBs were involved.

Guided bombs in *Desert Storm*

The 1991 Gulf War saw the LGB come of age. Although 'dumb' bombs continued to provide the bulk of ordnance used, guided weaponry demonstrated its key value in modern air warfare.

THE MEDIA CAMPAIGN that accompanied the 1991 Gulf War may have highlighted the contribution made by LGBs and other precision-guided ordnance, but the table on p.158 reveals the enduring importance of unguided 'dumb' bombs.

Operation *Desert Storm* did, however, mark the first occasion that LGBs had been utilized on such a large scale, with more than 9000 examples of these weapons being directed against various targets. The Paveway II family represented the numerically most important LGB of the conflict, with the 2000lb GBU-10, 1000lb GBU-16 and 500lb GBU-12 being the major types. The Paveway III was also employed, in the form of the 2000lb GBU-24, in which the Mk 84 warhead could be replaced with a BLU-109 hardened case penetrator warhead in order to attack reinforced targets.

The other member of the Paveway III family used in the Gulf War was the GBU-27, which was carried by the F-117A stealth fighters of the USAF's 37th Tactical Fighter Wing. This weapon was based on the GBU-24, but was adapted for internal carriage, with a redesigned tail assembly, and may also have been treated with radar-absorbent paint. The F-117/GBU-27 combination was directed against some of the most heavily defended Iraqi targets, which were illuminated using the aircraft's internal thermal imaging/laser tracking system. Another GBU-24 derivative that debuted in the Gulf was the GBU-28, codenamed 'Deep Throat'. This was an improvised

US GUIDED BOMBS IN OPERATION *DESERT STORM*

Name	Guidance	Bomb	Number used
GBU-10	laser	Mk 84	2637
GBU-12	laser	Mk 82	4493
GBU-15	EO/IR	Mk 84	71
GBU-16	laser	Mk 83	219
GBU-24	LL laser	Mk 84	284
GBU-24	LL laser	BLU-109	897
GBU-27	laser	BLU-109	739
GBU-28	laser	4000lb penetrator	2
		Total	**9342**

penetrating weapon with a warhead that weighed between 2045 and 2268kg (4500 and 5000lb). The warhead itself was created by welding a hardened nosecone to a bored-out section of 203mm (8in) gun barrel, which was in turn packed with explosive. Completed in a matter of weeks, a handful of GBU-28s were shipped to the Gulf, where two examples were used to destroy hardened Iraqi bunkers.

The British contingent employed the CPU-123 Paveway II laser guidance kit that was mated to the standard RAF 1000lb bomb, while French Jaguar tactical fighters made use of the Matra BGL kit allied to a 1000kg (2200lb) bomb. The Jaguars guided the BGL to their targets using the ATLIS targeting pod. British LGBs were dropped by both Buccaneers and Tornados, although in the latter case, guidance was

▼ GBU-27 Paveway III

The signature weapon of the F-117A stealth fighter over Iraq in 1991, the GBU-27 replaced the large fins of the GBU-24/B with a Paveway II-style airfoil section, which was more compact to allow carriage in the F-117's internal weapons bay. The GBU-27 series carries a penetrating warhead as standard.

Specifications
Length overall: 4200mm (13ft 10in)　　Weight: 907kg (2000lb)

Body diameter: 711mm (28in)　　Guidance system: Laser seeker

Stabilizer span: 1650mm (64.9in)

▲ GBU-12 Paveway II

the most numerous LGB employed during the 1991 Gulf War was the 500lb GBU-12. This is the US Navy's version, identified by its grey external protective coating, and using the BLU-111 filled with thermally insensitive explosive. During *Desert Storm* the GBU-12 was dropped by F-111Fs, F-15Es, and A-6s.

Specifications	
Length overall: 3270mm (10ft 9in)	Weight: 227kg (500lb)
Body diameter: 273mm (11in)	Guidance system: Laser seeker
Stabilizer span: 1490mm (4ft 11in)	

initially provided by Buccaneers, since the Tornado lacked the required Thermal Imaging Airborne Laser Designator (TIALD) pod. Using their Pave Spike daylight designator pods, the Buccaneers could provide 'buddy lasing' for the Tornados armed with LGBs. Generally, four Tornados would be supported by a pair of Buccaneers, with bombs released at medium level, beyond the reach of Iraqi anti-aircraft artillery. Ultimately, two TIALD pods were provided for combat use by the Tornado.

Alongside the US Navy's unpowered Walleye (discussed in Chapter 2), the GBU-15 glide-bomb was also employed in Operation *Desert Storm*. The USAF's GBU-15 was primarily launched by the F-111 and was used to attack bridges and other high-value hardened targets, including pumping stations that the Iraqis were using to dump crude oil into the Gulf. GBU-15s were used with both the daylight TV seeker head and the thermal imaging seeker.

The USAF F-111Fs of the 48th Tactical Fight Wing used the Pave Tack thermal imager/designator to deliver PGMs against targets that included airfields, transport bridges, bunkers and armour. Of the 375 Iraqi hardened aircraft shelters claimed destroyed during the war, the wing was credited with 245. When attacking bridges, the F-111s tended to opt for the GBU-15 and GBU-24 to attack the bridge supports, and accounted for 12 bridges destroyed out of 52 attacked. For pontoon bridges, the GBU-10 was favoured, while GBU-12s were the weapon of choice against armour. The 48th TFW eventually claimed 920 tanks and armoured vehicles destroyed, primarily using GBU-12s.

Making its debut in the Gulf was the F-15E, and the 4th Tactical Fighter Wing made use of early examples of the LANTIRN system. LANTIRN consists of a navigation pod with forward-looking infrared (FLIR) and terrain-following radar, together with a targeting pod with FLIR and a laser ranger/designator. Key targets for the F-15E included 'Scud' missiles and Iraqi armour.

▼ Safety check

A senior airman from the 2nd Aircraft Maintenance Squadron helps guide a GBU-12 onto a B-52 bomber, using normal loading procedures.

US AND UK UNGUIDED BOMBS IN OPERATION *DESERT STORM*

Name	Type	Number used
Mk 82 lo-drag	500lb GP	69,701
Mk 82 hi-drag	500lb GP	7952
Mk 83 lo-drag	1000lb GP	19,018
Mk 84 lo-drag	2000lb GP	9578
Mk 84 hi-drag	2000lb GP	2611
M117 lo-drag	750lb demolition	43,435
UK 1000lb	1000lb GP	288
	Total	152,583

Guided bombs in the Global War on Terror

Recent conflicts have seen changing requirements for guided bombs, with a new emphasis on all-weather operations and improved accuracy, and a drive towards lower-cost munitions.

THE AIR CAMPAIGNS fought in Afghanistan and Iraq in the first decade of the 21st century have seen significant changes in the way PGMs are used, a reflection of the changing nature of the target set and the requirement to limit collateral damage as well as reduce costs.

First employed by B-2s during Operation *Allied Force* over the former Yugoslavia in 1999, JDAM precision-guided bombs are now considered a standard air-to-ground weapon, having superseded 'dumb' bombs for most applications. When Coalition airpower returned to the Persian Gulf for Operation *Iraqi Freedom* in 2003, JDAMs constituted the majority of air-dropped ordnance.

The smaller GBU-38 JDAM was first used in combat in 2004, by USAF F-16s deployed during Operation *Iraqi Freedom*. The Laser JDAM, however, was first taken into battle in Iraq in 2008, when employed by F-16s of the USAF's 77th Expeditionary Fighter Squadron (EFS) against a moving enemy vehicle. The weapon was made operational in Afghanistan in 2010. Introduction of the Laser JDAM means that fighters can now carry one weapon where they previously had to carry two: formerly, a standard GBU-38 JDAM was typically complemented by a GBU-12 LGB, while the GBU-54 Laser JDAM now successfully combines the attributes of both of these weapons.

When faced by inclement weather or low cloud cover, standard LGBs were found to be less than effective during *Desert Storm* and in the air campaigns waged over the former Yugoslavia in the 1990s, driving the development of supplementary inertial/GPS guidance units. Such weapons are typified by the Paveway II EGBU, as employed by the RAF during operations in Afghanistan and Iraq.

Lightweight precision

The Viper Strike and SDB demonstrate the increasing importance of armed UAV operations and the shift towards using smaller munitions. The US Army began to deploy Viper Strike to Iraq in late 2004, with the weapon integrated on the MQ-5 Hunter UAV. Subsequently, the USAF has married the same weapon with the MQ-1 Predator UAV and the AC-130 gunship, and the USMC has selected it for use on its 'Harvest Hawk' KC-130J. The SDB saw its first combat use in 2006, when employed by F-15Es of the USAF's 494th EFS in Iraq. Involving close air support for ground troops, the debut mission for the SDB was typical of many more flown subsequently in both Iraq and Afghanistan.

▲ **GBU-39 SDB**

Seen here with its diamond-shaped wing folded, the SDB is carried on a Boeing-developed BRU-61 bomb rack, each of which carries four GBU-39 bombs. The same bomb rack can be employed for external carriage or can be loaded in internal weapon bays on the F-22, F-35 and B-2. The SDB's penetration capability is comparable to that of the much heavier 2000lb BLU-109 warhead.

Specifications

Length overall: 1800mm (5ft 11in)

Body diameter: 190mm (7.5in)

Weight: 129kg (285lb)

Warhead weight: 17kg (38lb)

Guidance system: Inertial and GPS

◄ **Weapons check**
US Air Force (USAF) aircraft munitions specialists assigned to the 48th Aircraft Maintenance Squadron (AMXS), conduct a final check of GBU-39 small diameter bombs (SDB) loaded on a USAF F-15E Strike Eagle aircraft at Royal Air Force (RAF) Lakenheath, United Kingdom. When released, the bombs rotate and deploy diamond-backed wings.

Non-US guided bombs

While the US established an early lead in the field of guided bombs through its prolific Paveway series, similar weapons have since also been developed and fielded by other countries.

INSPIRED BY GERMAN wartime efforts, and by US weapons fielded in Korea, the Soviet Union began the development of guided bombs in the early 1950s. The first two such weapons were the 5100kg (11,240lb) UB-5000F Condor and the 2240kg (4940lb) UB-2000F Chaika. While both were issued with line of sight radio command guidance and high-explosive warheads, the UB-5000F was also available with TV guidance, and was primarily intended for use against warships. These early weapons were soon superseded by guided missiles and it was not until the 1980s that a new generation of precision-guided bombs was developed in the USSR.

These weapons received the series designation KAB and were provided with either laser guidance (these receiving the suffix letter L), or with TV guidance (with the suffix Kr). In practice, the production versions of the weapons were initially based on 500kg (1102lb) and 1500kg (3306lb) bombs, resulting in the KAB-500L and KAB-500Kr, and the KAB-1500L and KAB-1500Kr, respectively. Sub-variants include versions equipped with

thermobaric, shaped-charge or armour-piercing warheads. The latest Russian precision-guided bombs include the rocket-boosted 1500kg UPAB-1500 glide-bomb intended to defeat hardened targets, the 250kg (551lb) LGB-250 laser-guided bomb, and the KAB-500S-E, which adds Global Navigation Satellite System (GLONASS) guidance.

In France, LGBs have developed since the late 1970s by both SAMP and Matra, who have fielded weapons that can be guided using the ATLIS pod for laser illumination. Although outwardly different from the American Paveway series, these French LGBs have used US seeker technology, with Rockwell guidance units being used in addition to the indigenous Thomson-CSF Elbis. French LGBs are similarly based on kits that can be added to existing free-fall GP bombs, with in-service LGBs being based upon 400kg (881lb) and 1000kg (2204lb) bombs.

More recently, France has developed an equivalent to the JDAM, with its AASM (Armament Air-Sol Modulaire, or Modular Air-to-Surface Weapon). Developed and produced by Sagem, the AASM

Specifications

Length overall: 3050mm (10ft)

Body diameter: 400m (15.7in)

Stabilizer span: 750mm (29.5in)

Weight: 525kg (1155lb)

Guidance system: Laser seeker

▲ KAB-500L

Compared to the heavier KAB-1500L, which is fitted with pop-out tailfins that deploy after leaving the pylon, the KAB-500L has a fixed tail unit. Like the Paveway (but unlike the French BGL), the seeker mounted on the gimbaled nose of the weapon is provided with a stabilizing ring.

Specifications

Length overall: 3100mm (10ft 2in)

Body diameter: n/a

Stabilizer span: n/a

Weight: 340kg (750lb)

Guidance system: Hybrid inertial/GPS (with IIR or semi-active laser homing in metric day/night version)

▲ AASM

France's AASM versions are designated in the Smart Bomb Unit (SBU) series. The SBU-38 is the inertial/GPS version, the SBU-54 is the laser-guided version, and the SBU-64 is the version with inertial/GPS and IR guidance. The AASM was first used in combat by a French Air Force Rafale over Afghanistan in 2008.

Specifications

Length overall: 4360mm (14ft 3.6in)

Body diameter: 1710mm (67.3in)

Stabilizer span: 1620mm (63.7in)

Weight: 1000kg (2205lb)

Guidance system: Laser seeker

▲ BGL-1000

Used in combat by the French Air Force over Bosnia and Kosovo in the 1990s, the BGL can be released at low or medium altitude at a distance of up to 10km (6.2 miles) from the target. General purpose or penetrating warheads can be fitted, and the typical launch aircraft are the Mirage 2000 and Rafale.

consists of a guidance and range-extension kit that can be attached to a standard bomb body. The modular design of the AASM allows 125kg, 250kg, 500kg and 1000kg bombs to be adapted. Depending on the mission, three different guidance kits can be added, comprising inertial/GPS, inertial/GPS with IR and inertial/GPS with a laser seeker. The version with an IR imager allows terminal correction prior to impact, while the laser version is optimized for attacks on mobile targets. The first version to enter

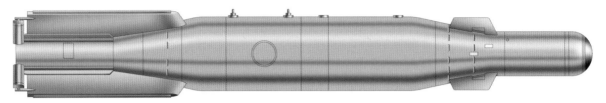

Specifications

Length overall: 3050mm (10ft)	Weight: 560kg (1234lb)
Body diameter: n/a	Guidance system: TV seeker
Stabilizer span: n/a	

▲ KAB-500Kr

In standard form, the TV-guided KAB-500Kr is provided with an armour-piercing warhead that can penetrate up to 1500mm (59in) of material, including targets that are buried. The weapon is also available with a fuel/air explosive warhead for use against area targets. The seeker consists of a daylight TV imaging sensor mounted in a gimbaled fairing in the nose.

French Air Force service was the 250kg AASM-250, which was first used in combat by the Rafale in 2008. New features planned for future variants or upgrades include an airburst setting and datalink.

In Germany, Diehl BGT Defence has developed a family of standoff precision weapons, known as HOPE and HOSBO. Both weapons use inertial/GPS guidance, but differ in their warheads: blast-fragmentation (HOSBO) or penetrator (HOPE). Although air-launched testing has been conducted, no orders have been forthcoming.

Israel's LGBs

Israel's precision-guided bomb inventory includes the Elbit Opher, a Paveway-type weapon with a passive IR homing seeker and canard flight control system. The Opher can be integrated with a range of standard free-fall GP bombs and allows fire-and-forget attacks on armour and other targets.

The Israel Aircraft Industries (IAI) Guillotine and Griffin represent LGBs developed primarily for the Israeli Defence Force/Air Force. Guillotine is similar to the Paveway, with a laser guidance package fitted as a modification to a conventional free-fall bomb. Guillotine kits are compatible with a range of low-drag bombs, including the US Mk 81, Mk 82 and Mk 83. The bomb's fin kit extends standoff range to some 30km (18.6 miles).

The Guillotine was superseded by the Griffin LGB, using a new laser seeker. The latest version of this weapon is the Griffin III, also known as the Next-Generation Laser-Guided Bomb (NGLGB). The latest variant is described as offering improved accuracy, and an enhanced ability to hit moving targets. The Griffin III also adds a trajectory shaping capability. Coupled with a penetrating warhead, this ensures optimum penetration of the target. Griffin III has an optional GPS guidance package, transforming it into a dual-guidance weapon. Export operators of the Griffin include the Chilean Air Force for its upgraded Mirage 50 Panteras, and the weapon is also associated with the Kfir, including export versions of this jet acquired by Colombia.

A follow-on IAI project was known as the Advanced Laser Guided Bomb (ALGB), with the objective of further increasing accuracy. The ALGB likely resulted in the Lizard LGB, which entered production for home and export use. The Whizzard LGB developed by Elbit aims to offer a range of different guidance options. In addition to the basic Lizard laser seeker, these comprise the Opher imaging IR fire-and-forget seeker combined with the laser seeker, and the GAL, or GPS-aided Lizard, which allies the laser seeker with an inertial/GPS package. A final option consists of an IR seeker coupled with inertial/GPS guidance. The Lizard has found notable export success, having been procured for use by Italian Air Force AMX fighter-bombers, and by the Peruvian Air Force for its Mirage 5P and Mirage 2000P fighters.

IAI's Medium Laser-Guided Bomb (MLGB) is closer in concept to the Laser JDAM, and offers dual-mode GPS and terminal laser guidance from the outset. The weapon carries an 80kg (176lb) warhead and a pop-out wing assembly. The light weight of the MLGB also allows carriage by UAVs.

Raptor at war

South Africa developed and fielded indigenous glide-bombs during its years of international isolation, and these saw limited combat use. The first of these

Very similar in appearance to the US-designed Paveway, development of the Israeli Griffin LGB was completed in 1990 and was initially optimized for use with standard Mk 80 series low-drag bombs. In Indian Air Force service, the Griffin guidance kit has been combined with British-type 1000lb GP bombs.

Specifications

Length overall: 1067mm (3ft 6in)	Weight: 20.4kg (45lb)
Body diameter: 140mm (5.5in)	Guidance system: Laser seeker
Stabilizer span: n/a	

weapons was the Kentron-developed Raptor, also known as the H-2. While the previous H-1 served as a technology demonstrator, the H-2 entered service, and was used during the campaign in Angola in the late 1980s. It was a modular glide bomb, initially produced with a command guidance system, although later versions introduced a range of new navigation options comprising autonomous, waypoint or inertial/GPS. For the terminal phase, the Raptor used a passive TV seeker, with imagery relayed to the launch aircraft via datalink for long-range engagements.

The Raptor was first used in anger by SAAF Buccaneers in 1987, during an attack on a bridge at Cuito Canavale. The first mission was unsuccessful, but a follow-up attack carried out in 1988 succeeded in damaging the target, despite the attentions of Angolan MiG-23s sent to intercept them.

After previously having procured Russian-made guided bombs, China is a more recent entrant in the field of PGMs, and has exhibited both LGBs and GPS-aided weapons. The first of these is the LT-2, exported as the GB-1. The LT-2 is in service with the PLA and was first identified in 2006, two to three years after its service entry. Based on a 500kg free-fall GP bomb, the weapon may be developed from the Russian-supplied KAB-500L. China's earlier efforts to field an indigenous LGB based on Paveway technology were thwarted by arms embargoes, and the original programme to develop weapons in this class likely began in the late 1980s. The LT-2 is to be used in conjunction with a range of locally designed targeting pods, including the Blue Sky.

China's LS-6 is a precision-guided glide-bomb in the class of the American JDAM. The weapon combines a standard 500kg GP bomb with guidance and range-extension packages. The former is based on an inertial/GPS guidance system, while the latter consists of a pair of folding wings that provide standoff range as well as increased manoeuvrability. The test program began in 2003, with a J-8B fighter used for the initial air launches.

Specifications

Length overall: 3530mm (11ft 7in)	Weight: 564kg (1243lb)
Body diameter: 377mm (14.8in)	Guidance system: Laser seeker
Stabilizer span: 950mm (37.4in)	

▼ LT-2
The LeiTing-2 (LT-2, or Thunder 2) is China's first LGB, and is externally similar to the Russian KAB-500L. The LT-2 entered PLA service in 2003–04 and reportedly offers a range of around 7km (4.3 miles), while the associated targeting pod has a range of 15km (9.3 miles).

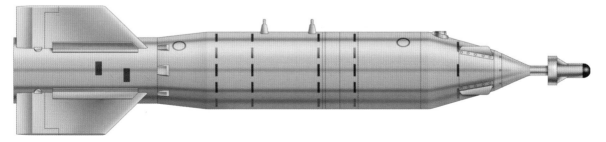

Chapter 6

Air-launched Rockets

Unguided rockets saw limited use as air-to-air weapons in World War I, but came of age in the interwar period, when they were enthusiastically adopted by the Soviet Union, primarily as air-to-ground weapons. The rocket saw widespread adoption by all the major powers in World War II, again mainly as an assault weapon, while after 1945 rocket projectiles served as a useful air-to-air stopgap until the arrival of the guided missile. Subsequently, unguided aerial rockets have been almost exclusively employed in the air-to-ground role, some now receiving precision guidance.

◀ **Cobra's venom**
A US Marine Corps AH-1W Cobra attack helicopter, assigned to Marine Light Attack Helicopter Squadron 369, fires off several rockets against a target during a close air support mission on a live-fire desert range at Marine Corps Air Station Yuma, Arizona, during a 2008 exercise. Unguided rockets remain a key weapon for attack helicopters, filling the gap between guns and costly guided air-to-ground missiles.

Early US rockets

The US began to employ air-to-ground rockets during World War II, with the USAAF and US Navy employing both tube-launched types and the popular Forward-Firing Aircraft Rocket (FFAR).

THE RESULT OF a US Navy programme, the 5in (127mm) FFAR was developed from 1943 as an air-to-ground weapon. It was originally schemed as a 3.5in (89mm) weapon for anti-submarine warfare, before being increased in size to accommodate a more powerful warhead suitable for attacking land targets and warships. Together with another Navy project, the 5in High-Velocity Aircraft Rocket (HVAR) of 1944, this weapon was one of the most important rockets used by the US and many allies in the immediate post-war period, including in Korea. Compared to the original 5in FFAR, the HVAR, or 'Holy Moses', had a more powerful motor for increased speed, and therefore greater destructive power. HVAR production continued into the mid 1950s, with post-war variants including shaped-charge AT and proximity fused warheads.

Alongside the 5in rockets, another wartime design, the 11.75in (298mm) Tiny Tim, saw limited post-war US Navy service. Also developed as an anti-ship weapon, it carried a 227kg (500lb) semi-armour piercing warhead, and saw active use in the Korean War. Another weapon employed in Korea was the Navy's 6.5in (165mm) Anti-Tank Aircraft Rocket (ATAR), or Ram, the result of a crash development programme launched in 1950. A more unusual rocket of the 1950s was the Bombardment Aircraft Rocket (BOAR), which propelled a 20 KT nuclear warhead from an AD Skyraider, using the loft-bombing technique to provide standoff range. The BOAR was in use from 1956 until 1963.

Mighty Mouse

In the air-to-air realm, development focused on the supersonic Mighty Mouse from the late 1940s, again originally a US Navy project. This was inspired by the wartime German R4/M and had a calibre of 2.75in – in metric nominally given as 70mm, but more accurately 69.85mm. This calibre would later become a recognized standard in this field. At the same time, the original FFAR designation was superseded by the Folding-Fin Aircraft Rocket (again FFAR), this indicating the introduction of pop-out tailfins to ensure stability, and permit carriage in launch pods.

Typically, the Mighty Mouse was used to arm early Air Defense Command interceptors, including the F-86D Sabre, F-89J Scorpion, F-94C Starfire and F-102A Delta Dagger. The rockets were carried in multi-tube launchers as bomber-destroyer weapons, to be launched in a collision-course attack under the command of a computerized fire-control system.

The AIR-2 Genie was a nuclear-armed unguided aerial rocket that armed F-89J, F-101B Voodoo and

▼ AIR-2 Genie

The world's first nuclear air-to-air weapon, the Douglas Genie was an unguided rocket, but thanks to its large lethal radius it could be fired in the general direction of a bomber formation using a firing solution provided by the aircraft fire-control system and a ground-based radar .

Specifications	
Length overall: 2950mm (9ft 8in)	Warhead weight: 99.8kg (220lb)
Calibre: 444.5mm (17.5in)	Range: 9.7km (6 miles)
Fin span: 900m (35.4in)	Guidance system: None
Launch weight: 372.9kg (822lb)	

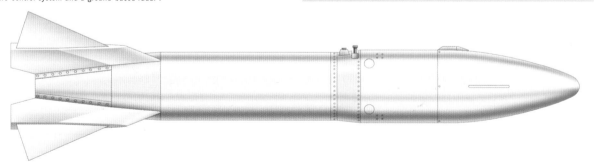

▼ Zuni

The 5in Zuni heavyweight Folding-Fin Aircraft Rocket was generally carried in a four-round external pod. Widely used in the Vietnam War, more recently the Zuni has been used by the USMC as a target-marking weapon for forward air control (and 'fast FAC') work.

Specifications

Length overall: 2769mm (109in)	Warhead weight: 18.1kg (40lb)
Calibre: 127mm (5in)	Range: 5.9km (3.67 miles)
Fin span: Not available	Guidance system: None
Launch weight: 68kg (150lb)	

F-106A Delta Dart interceptors. Developed from 1954, this became operational in 1957 under the original designation MB-1. The Genie was powered by a solid-fuel rocket motor, carried a 1.5 KT nuclear warhead and used pop-out tailfins for stability. The warhead was detonated by a timer that was set when the motor burnt out. Intended for launch against high-flying bombers, the Genie was redesignated AIR-2 in 1963 and remained in use (with the F-106) into the 1980s.

Successor to the 5in FFAR and HVAR was the Zuni series of 5in air-to-ground rockets, developed from the early 1950s. Various different types of warhead and fuse could be used in the Zuni rocket, including GP, shaped-charged, AT/anti-personnel and white phosphorous (smoke) warheads, and a delayed-action fuse. The Zuni entered service in 1957 and the most widespread pod became the four-round LAU-10. The definitive version of the Zuni arrived in the early 1970s and added a Mk 71 motor, and a new tailfin arrangement to form the Wrap-Around Fin Aerial Rocket (WAFAR).

▼ Vietnam rocket strike

The Zuni was widely used in Vietnam. Here a US Navy OV-10 Bronco close-support aircraft fires Zuni rockets at a target in the Mekong Delta in 1969.

Modern US rockets

The descendants of the air-to-air Mighty Mouse of the early Cold War period, the air-to-ground rockets in today's US arsenal comprise the 2.75in weapons of the Hydra family.

WHEN FIRST DEVELOPED by the US Navy in the late 1940s, the 2.75in unguided aerial rocket was envisaged as an air-to-air weapon. Inspired by the 5in FFAR and HVAR, however, the lighter 2.75in weapon was quickly adapted for air-to-ground applications and became the standard weapon of its type for US Army and Marine Corps attack helicopters and close-support aircraft.

The 2.75in rocket, now known as the Hydra, is a modular weapon that can accommodate various different warheads, and can be launched from a number of different pods for tactical aircraft and helicopters. Launch tube options include seven-tube or 19-tube rocket pods, while typical warheads include the M151 high-explosive, M229 high-explosive/ fragmentation, M247 high-explosive anti-tank (HEAT), M255 flechette, M261 dispenser (containing nine M73 AT/anti-personnel submunitions), M262 illuminating, M264 red smoke and M267 practice.

The warhead is attached to one of several types of rocket motor. The Mk 4 was the baseline motor, while the Mk 40 was developed for use from helicopters, and features increased spin to impart improved accuracy. The latest motor is the increased-thrust, smokeless Mk 66, developed from the early 1970s and intended for use from both fixed-wing aircraft and helicopters, and part of what is now designated as the Hydra 70 family of weapons. Depending whether the weapon is in use with a tactical fixed-wing aircraft or a helicopter, the basic seven- and 19-round launchers normally carry an LAU- or an M- series designation, respectively.

WAFAR Hydra

In its latest incarnation, with Mk 66 motor, the Hydra 70 rocket is fitted with a WAFAR tail kit, consisting of three fins. Unlike the earlier rocket motors, the Mk 66 starts to spin the missile while it is still in the tube, for increased accuracy. In addition to the earlier warheads mentioned above, the Hydra/Mk 66 combination is compatible with the M156 white phosphorus (smoke), M257 parachute-retarded battlefield illumination flare, M259 white phosphorus, M274 practice, M278 parachute-retarded IR illumination flare, Mk 67 white or red phosphorus smoke and WDU-4 flechette warheads.

The Mk 66 also forms the basis of the General Dynamics Advanced Precision Kill Weapon System (APKWS). This programme dates back to the mid 1990s, and originates in a US Army proposal to increase the accuracy of the Hydra 70, providing a lower-cost alternative to a guided AT missile such as the BGM-71 TOW or AGM-114 Hellfire. The new weapon would also be better suited for use against softer targets, or in situations where there was a particular risk of collateral damage.

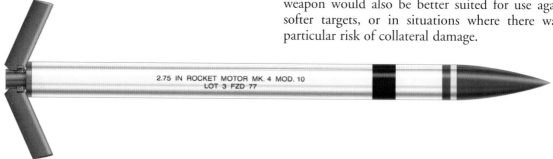

▲ 2.75in Hydra

Among the earliest motors used in the 2.75in series – now known as Hydra – are the Mk 4 and Mk 40. The Mk 4 illustrated here was intended for use by high-performance fixed-wing aircraft. The folding fins, which open to a diameter of 165mm (6.5in) are seen deployed.

Specifications	
Length overall: 1200mm (4ft)	Warhead weight: 2.7kg (6lb)
Calibre: 70mm (2.75in)	Range: 3400m (11,155ft)
Fin span: 165mm (6.5in)	Guidance system: None
Launch weight: 8.4kg (18.5lb)	

Specifications

Length overall: 1875mm (6ft 1.8in)	Warhead weight: 4.5kg (10lb)
Calibre: 70mm (2.75in)	Range: 5–11km (3.1–6.8 miles)
Launch weight: 14.5kg (32lb)	Guidance system: Semi-active laser homing

▲ **APKWS II**

BAE Systems' APKWS II is known by the designation WGU-59, and initial launches were carried out in 2010 from USMC AH-1W and US Army OH-58D(I) helicopters. Buddy designation was provided by AH-1Z and AV-8B aircraft.

The APKWS programme resulted in a guided version of the Hydra 70 rocket, to which was added a new warhead and guidance section. The dimensions were essentially similar, allowing the rocket to retain compatibility with previous launchers. The initial version of the APKWS (Block I) combined the Mk 66 motor with the established M151 warhead, and a low-cost semi-active laser seeker. In order to guide the weapon to the target, pop-out wings were provided towards the front of the rocket. The original APKWS programme was cancelled in 2005, and was reborn as the APKWS II. The prime contractor is BAE Systems with Northrop Grumman, and the rocket now features the Distributed Aperture Semi-Active Laser Seeker (DASALS) guidance package, located between the warhead and the motor, with laser seekers in the leading edges of the four pop-out control fins.

A similar effort to increase the accuracy of the Hydra family is being undertaken by the US Navy under the Low-Cost Guided Imaging Rocket (LOGIR) initiative. This adds a mid-course guidance package and an IIR terminal seeker.

Looking further ahead, the US Navy and the US Army are working on a successor to the Hydra, known as the Smart Munition/Advanced Rocket (SMARt) programme. This will consist of a new launcher that will serve as a digital interface between the launch aircraft and the APKWS rocket, allowing the pilot to select fusing options and launch modes in flight, and to assign targets to particular rockets.

▶ **Hydra at sea**

Enveloped in a cloud of smoke, a Mexican BO 105 helicopter fires 2.75in high-explosive rockets at a decommissioned US Navy destroyer during an exercise in the Atlantic.

Other Western rockets

Relatively simple to produce, unguided aerial rockets have been produced in a number of countries, although Canada, France and Sweden are arguably the leaders in this field.

THE HIGHEST-VELOCITY AERIAL rocket is the CRV-7 developed by Bristol Aerospace in Canada, and which is also used by the RAF. Key characteristics of the CRV-7 are its high-energy motor and flat trajectory, leading to an increased range and a much more powerful impact velocity. The CRV-7 can be fired from a 19-tube LAU-type launcher.

The primary developer of French aerial rockets was the former Thomson-Brandt Armaments, which produced a wide range of rockets in 68mm (2.68in) and 100mm (3.94in) calibres. As well as being compatible with the company's own 12- and 22-round launchers, which were optimized for helicopters, the SNEB 68mm projectiles can also be fired from launchers furnished by Matra (F1, F2 and F4 Type 155). For both 68mm SNEB and the 100mm type, the initial warhead options included high-explosive/fragmentation, hollow-charge and chaff. A second generation of warheads replaced the single charge with a multi-dart type, these carrying kinetic-energy penetrators designed for anti-armour applications.

In Sweden, rockets have been developed by the Bofors concern. These are provided primarily in two standard calibres: 75mm (2.95in) and 135mm (5.3in). For the 75mm weapon, carried in 19-round pods, high-explosive, AT and fragmentation warheads are provided. The 135mm rocket is carried in a six-tube launcher, with GP, anti-personnel/fragmentation and practice warheads.

Switzerland's Oerlikon has developed 81mm (3.19in) rockets, the major types being the SNORA and the SURA. The former is designed for tactical warplanes or helicopters, with a range of different launchers being available. The SURA uses a simpler installation, with the rockets being carried in external 'stacks', one above the other. This type of installation is suitable for use on helicopters, as well as lighter aircraft. Warheads for the SURA include hollow-charge and high-explosive/fragmentation.

▼ **SNEB 68mm**

The 68mm SNEB was adopted by a number of Western European tactical aircraft, including the RAF's Harrier and Jaguar. Among the most popular launchers for the SNEB is the Matra-designed Type 155, each of which carries 19 rockets.

Specifications

Length overall: 910mm (2ft 11.8in)	depending on warhead type
Calibre: 68mm (2.68in)	Warhead weight: Various
Fin span: 240mm (9.5in)	Range: 4km (2.5 miles)
Launch weight: 5kg (11lb) or 6.2kg (13.7lb)	Guidance system: None

▼ **CRV-7**

Offering very high velocity, the CRV-7 has been carried by a range of fixed-wing aircraft and helicopters, including Canadian Air Force CF-188 Hornets, RAF Harriers and Jaguars (both now retired) and British Army Air Corps Apache AH-1s.

Specifications

Length overall: 1042mm (3ft 5in) (no warhead)	Warhead weight: 3kg (6.6lb), 4.5kg (9.9lb) or 7kg
Calibre: 70mm (2.75in)	(15.4lb)
Fin span: Not available	Range: 6.5km (4 miles)
Weight: 6.6kg (14.6lb) without warhead	Guidance system: None

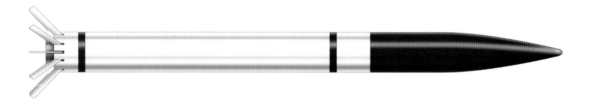

Soviet and Russian rockets

The USSR was one of the first nations to adopt aerial rockets, using these in combat during fighting against Japan in 1939. Post-war, the USSR fielded rockets in a range of calibres.

AMONG THE FIRST aerial rockets to be produced in quantity in the Soviet Union after 1945 was the 212mm (8.34in) ARS-212, or S-21, which was launched from a rail in the same manner as the American HVAR and which was derived from the popular RS-82 and RS-132 rockets used during World War II. Intended for air-to-ground and air-to-air use, the rocket's high-explosive/fragmentation warhead was detonated by an impact/proximity fuse, and it was carried in pairs by the MiG-15, MiG-17 and MiG-19. The improved ARS-212M version introduced revised tailfins and a new motor that imparted spin-stabilization, both of these features contributing to improved accuracy.

The ARS-212 was followed by another spin-stabilized development, the TS-212, or S-1, which was tube-launched from a single-shot launcher, and which was not fitted with fins. Unlike its predecessors, the TS-212 was only suitable for air-to-ground use, carrying a high-explosive/fragmentation warhead.

Armour-piercing weapon

The S-3K, or KARS-160, was a 160mm (6.3in) anti-armour weapon with a combined shaped-charge and high-explosive/fragmentation warhead, and was carried by the Su-7 fighter-bomber on a seven-round launcher. Based on the ARS-212, the S-3K carried a heavier warhead and tailfins of increased area. In addition to armoured vehicles, the S-3K could be employed against hardened structures, but also personnel, thanks to its fragmentation effect.

Conceived as a successor to the ARS-212, with greater range, destructive power and accuracy, the S-24 was a 240mm (9.44in) weapon introduced in the mid 1960s. An enlarged version of the ARS-212, the S-24 featured a more powerful motor and spin stabilization imparted by six rocket nozzles, with an

▲ **S-5**

The S-5 is likely the most numerous aerial rocket of the post-war period, and has seen action in conflicts across the globe. Each rocket is fitted with eight folding fins that are stowed against the jetpipe prior to launch. This is an example of the S-5M, with a more pointed nose.

Specifications

Length overall: 1400mm (4ft 6in)	Warhead weight: 1.16kg (2.56lb)
Calibre: 55mm (2.2in)	Range: 3–4km (1.9–2.6 miles)
Fin span: Not available	Guidance system: None
Launch weight: 5kg (11lb)	

▲ **S-8KOM**

While the earlier S-5 used spring-loaded fins, the six stabilizing fins of the S-8 are deployed using an actuating piston. The S-8KO version of this weapon is fitted with a combined fragmentation/anti-personnel warhead; the S-8KOM is an extended-range variant with a long-burn motor.

Specifications

Length overall: 1570mm (5ft 1.8in)	Warhead weight: 3.6kg (7.9lb)
Calibre: 80mm (3.1in)	Range: 1.3–4km (0.8–2.6 miles)
Fin span: 384mm (15.12in)	Guidance system: None
Launch weight: 11.3kg (25lb)	

Specifications

Length overall: 2540mm (8ft 4in)	Warhead weight: 21kg (46.3lb)
Calibre: 122mm (4.8in)	Range: 1.1–3km (0.68–1.86 miles)
Fin span: Not available	Guidance system: None
Launch weight: 57kg (126lb)	

▲ S-13

The S-13 is intended primarily for use against hardened targets, including bunkers, reinforced aircraft shelters and runways. The standard version is capable of penetrating 3m (10ft) of earth or up to 1m (3ft) of reinforced concrete, increased to 6m (20ft) of earth or 10m (32ft) of concrete for the S-13T version.

option for a radar proximity fuse in the S-24N version. The use of a proximity fuse ensured the rocket's warhead detonated above the target, for greater destructive effect. The S-24B was a concrete-piercing version for use against hardened structures, with a time-delay fuse, while the S-24BNK carried a shaped charge for the anti-armour mission and was similarly fitted with a delayed-action fuse. Carried singly on underwing launch rails, the S-24 series is compatible with the MiG-21, the Su-7 and Su-17 family, as well as the Su-25 and the Mi-24.

Ubiquitous Starling

Probably the most widespread aerial rocket of the post-war period is the S-5, a folding-fin rocket of 57mm (2.4in) calibre that was cleared for use on most Soviet tactical aircraft and assault helicopters. Early versions of the weapon were tested on the MiG-15, MiG-17 and MiG-19. In Soviet service, the rocket is known colloquially as the *Skvorets*, or Starling. First developed in the early 1950s, primarily for air-to-air applications, the S-5 was soon adapted for air-to-ground work. Fitted with eight forward-folding stabilizing fins, the S-5 rocket can be carried in standard pods that contain either eight (ORO-57K), 16 (UB-16-57) or 32 rounds (UB-32-57). An experimental installation on a MiG-17 consisted of four internal revolver-type launchers, each of which could carry six rounds. Warhead options for the S-5 include high-explosive/fragmentation (S-5M), armour-piercing shaped-charge (S-5K), enhanced fragmentation (S-5MO), flechette (S-5S), combined fragmentation/anti-personnel (S-5KO), illumination (S-5O) and chaff (S-5P). The last of these was intended to be used for defensive ECM, and could be launched ahead of an attacking formation to disable hostile air defence radars, and was notably carried by the Yak-28PP defence suppression aircraft.

The 80mm (3.15in) S-8 was developed as a successor to the S-5, offering longer range and a heavier warhead, such that it could be launched from outside the range of enemy air defences, and with greater destructive effect than the earlier S-5. Carried by tactical aircraft and combat helicopters, the S-8 has six stabilizing fins and is contained in the 20-round B-8 series launchers. These are provided in different versions optimized for use from supersonic jets or from rotary-winged aircraft. A multi-purpose fragmentation/armour-piercing warhead is carried as standard, but there are options for combined fragmentation/anti-personnel (S-8KO), concrete-piecing (S-8B), flechette (S-8S), flare (S-8O), chaff

▼ S-25L

The S-25L represents an innovative solution to providing a precision-guided weapon at relatively low cost. While the rocket's body and motor section are encased in a prefabricated launch tube, the larger warhead (and in the case of the S-25L, the guidance section) protrude from the front of the launcher.

Specifications

Length overall: 3310mm (10ft 10in)	Warhead weight: 190kg (419lb)
Calibre: 340mm (13.4in)	Range: 3km (1.86 miles)
Fin span: Not available	Guidance system: Semi-active laser homing
Launch weight: 480kg (1058lb)	

▲ **S-24**

A simple, heavy aerial rocket, the S-24 uses a rocket motor with six angled nozzles in order to impart spin. After the motor has burnt out, the four rear fins provide stabilization. The S-24 entered service on the Su-7 fighter-bomber.

Specifications

Length overall: 2330mm (7ft 8in)	Warhead weight: 123kg (271lb)
Calibre: 240mm (9.45in)	Range: 2–3km (1.3–1.8 miles)
Fin span: Not available	Guidance system: None
Launch weight: 235kg (518lb)	

(S-8P) or fuel/air explosive (S-8D) warhead types. As well as different warhead options, the S-8 can accept various types of motor that offer contrasting burn times and therefore different range parameters. Rockets with the suffix 'M' are equipped with a longer-burn motor.

The S-13 is a heavy aerial rocket intended to defeat robust targets such as bunkers, runways or hardened aircraft shelters, and is a 122mm (4.8in) weapon carried in a five-round B-13L pod. Based on an enlarged S-8 design, the primary warhead option is concrete-piercing, which can penetrate up to 1m (3ft) of concrete, but the same rocket can also be fitted with a high-explosive/fragmentation warhead (S-13OF) or an enhanced concrete-penetrating warhead (S-13T). In the latter, a tandem warhead is fitted, ensuring that the second charge detonates once the hardened structure has been breached. In service, the B-13L pod is mainly associated with the Su-25 and members of the extensive Su-27 family.

The 250mm (9.84in) S-25 heavyweight folding-fin rocket is carried in an individual launch tube. The rocket is loaded into the launch tube in the factory, the tube itself being fabricated from metal and wood. The rocket is similar in configuration to the S-8, and also features four stabilizing fins. Major warhead options comprise fragmentation (S-25O), high-explosive/fragmentation (S-25OF) for use against personnel, structures and light armoured vehicles, and 'bunker busting' types.

The latter, designated S-25OFM, represents an improvement of the basic high-explosive/fragmentation warhead, in order to defeat hardened structures. The warhead is designed to detonate once the structure has been breached. The S-25 is also available with laser guidance, as the S-25L, which is fitted with a laser seeker head and canard control fins for providing directional control. An alternative precision option for the S-25 adds a passive IR seeker, as the S-25TP.

Specifications

Length overall: 820mm (2ft 8.3in)	Warhead weight: 1.38kg (3.0lb)
Calibre: 57mm (2.24in)	Range: 5km (3.1 miles)
Fin span: 230mm (9.1in)	Guidance system: None
Launch weight: 3.86–3.97kg (8.5–8.7lb)	

▼ **Chinese 57mm**

The principal unguided aerial rockets operated by the People's Liberation Army are provided in 57mm (2.24in), 90mm (3.5in) and 130mm (5.1in) calibres. Of these, the 57mm rocket is apparently derived from the Soviet S-5. Illustrated is an 11-round pod for the Chinese 57mm rocket.

Chapter 7

Weapons Dispensers and Cluster Munitions

From the early days of air-launched bombs, it was clear that limitations in accuracy could be compensated for through the use of either a 'stick' of bombs, or by multiple warheads contained in a single device. The earliest cluster munitions comprised bundles of charges, or weapons that broke up in mid-air to produce a number of smaller bomblets. Modern cluster bombs and weapons dispensers are typically designed to attack specialized targets – armour, runways or personnel – and carry different payloads to meet these requirements. In order to provide further protection to the launch aircraft, some of the latest weapons dispensers are glide weapons that can be launched from standoff range.

◀ **Bomb loading**
US Navy aviation ordnanceman airmen (AOAN) move two Mk 6/7 Rockeye II multi-purpose cluster bombs on a dolly for aircraft loading aboard the aircraft carrier USS *Independence* (CV 62) during a deployment in the Persian Gulf in support of Operation *Southern Watch*.

US weapons dispensers and cluster munitions

The wide array of cluster munitions developed in the US extends to over 100 different weapons. The first such post-1945 weapons used the 'M'-series designation, or received a Mark number.

SUBSEQUENTLY, THE COMPLETE weapons were known as Cluster Bomb Units, or CBUs. A single CBU in turn requires the use of a dispenser, and this is designated as a Suspended Underwing Unit, or SUU. The same SUU can be used to carry a variety of different submunitions, resulting in a new CBU designation in each case, although the external appearance of the weapon remains similar. The submunitions themselves receive a designation in the BLU series, indicating Bomb Live Unit.

The first dedicated USAF submunitions dispenser was the SUU-7 series. Each SUU-7 contains 19 70mm (2.75in) tubes. The SUU-7 remains attached to the aircraft, with bomblets ejected rearwards. Cluster weapons based on the SUU-7 can be configured to carry anti-personnel bomblets and anti-materiel bomblets. An evolution of the SUU-7 is the SUU-10 series. This uses the same dispenser as the SUU-7, with some internal differences. The SUU-10 is used to carry various parachute-retarded anti-tank bomblets, as well as dummy fragmentation munitions. Another non-disposable dispenser was the SUU-13, with 40 downwards-ejecting tubes. The SUU-13 was used for the carriage of

▼ CBU-12

The CBU-12 consisted of the SUU-7 dispenser pod with a payload of 261 BLU-17 submunitions. A white phosphorus (WP) smoke bomblet, the BLU-17 was also carried in the CBU-13 dispenser, which again used the SUU-7, filled with both BLU-17 bomblets and BLU-16 smoke grenades. The bomblets were ejected rearwards from the tubes in the aft section of the SUU-7 pod.

Specifications (BLU-17)

Length overall: 145mm (5.73in)	Weight: 0.5kg (1.1lb)
Body diameter: 70mm (2.75in)	Guidance system: None
Stabilizer span: n/a	

Specifications

Length overall: 2600mm (8ft 7in)	Weight: Variable, depending on payload
Body diameter: 376mm (14.8in)	Guidance system: None
Height: 36.6cm (14.4in)	

▼ SUU-13

The SUU-13 was a non-expendable dispenser that was fitted with 40 downwards-ejecting submunitions tubes. Payloads included the BLU-18 (CBU-7), BLU-19 (CBU-15), BLU-20 (CBU-16), BDU-34 (CBU-17), BLU-25 (CBU-18), BLU-43 (CBU-28), BLU-39 (CBU-30), BLU-44 (CBU-37), BLU-49 (CBU-38), BLU-55 (CBU-47), BLU-60 (CBU-50) and the BLU-67 (CBU-51).

anti-personnel bomblets or mines, chemical bomblets, practice bomblets, mine submunitions, fragmentation bomblets and cratering bomblets.

Tube-type launcher

The SUU-14 dispenser consisted of six 70mm (2.75in) tubes, with rearwards ejection. It was used to carry various combinations of anti-materiel, smoke, fragmentation and incendiary. The SUU-30 was the USAF's first general-purpose submunition dispenser, meaning that it was dropped from the aircraft before its contents were released. In service from the 1970s to the 1990s, the SUU-30 was widely used to carry fragmentation bomblets (CBU-24, CBU-29, CBU-49, CBU-52, CBU-58, CBU-68 and CBU-71), incendiary bomblets (CBU-53 and CBU-54), fragmentation grenades (CBU-62 and CBU-63), and shaped-charge anti-vehicle bomblets (CBU-70).

Less common dispensers included the reusable SUU-36, used only to carry BLU-45 anti-vehicle mines as the CBU-33, and the SUU-37 that carries clusters of BLU-48 fragmentation bomblets as the CBU-43. Similar to the SUU-36 was the SUU-38, which carried either BLU-42 anti-personnel fragmentation bomblets (CBU-34) or BLU-48 fragmentation bomblets (CBU-42).

The SUU-41 dispenser was used to carry 'Gravel' mines, armament options including 1500 anti-personnel mines, or loads of 6500 or 7500 anti-intrusion mines. The SUU-49, meanwhile, was dedicated to the carriage of fuel/air explosive payloads, versions including the CBU-55 and CBU-72. The 340kg (750lb) SUU-51 dispenser could carry napalm bomblets, minelet canisters, anti-personnel fragmentation bomblets, or anti-material fragmentation/incendiary bomblets.

The successor to the SUU-30 series in USAF service is the expendable Tactical Munitions Dispenser (TMD) family consisting of the SUU-64, SUU-65 and SUU-66. Payloads are dispensed either

▲ **SUU-14**

The SUU-14 was only suitable for use by slow-flying aircraft, with submunitions ejected from the rear of the tubes (seen here on the right) using a mechanical piston. The SUU-14 was used to carry submunitions that included the BLU-3 (CBU-14), BLU-17 (CBU-22), BLU-24 (CBU-25) and BLU-69 (CBU-57).

Specifications

Length overall: 2040mm (6ft 8.4in)

Body diameter: 239mm (9.4in)

Stabilizer span: n/a

Weight: Variable, depending on payload

Guidance system: None

Specifications

Length overall: 2400mm (7ft 9.6in)

Body diameter: 406mm (16in)

Stabilizer span: Various, see text

Weight: Variable, depending on payload

Guidance system: None

▲ **SUU-30**

The widely used SUU-30 dispenser was released from the launch aircraft before it opened in two halves to release its submunitions. The basic version was the SUU-30/B, while sub-variants differed in their type of suspension, nose profile and tail units (options including larger fins or fintip plates).

▲ SUU-41

The SUU-41 series of dispensers was associated with 'Gravel' or 'Button' mines, which were carried on 10-cluster adapters within the pod. Mine options for the SUU-41 included XM41E1 anti-personnel mines, anti-intrusion mines, a combination of both, or dummy mines. 'Gravel' mines were delivered in cloth bags and were designed to detonate when put under pressure.

Specifications

Length overall: 3610mm (11ft 10in)

Body diameter: 389mm (15.3in)

Stabilizer span: 389mm (15.3in)

Weight: Variable, depending on payload

Guidance system: None

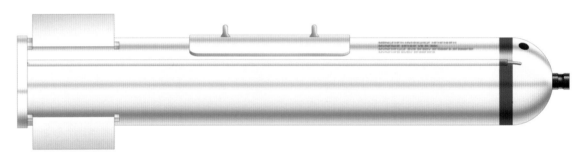

▲ SUU-49

The SUU-49 is a dedicated dispenser for fuel/air explosive (thermobaric) payloads. As such, it is primarily used to carry three BLU-73 FAE bomblets, with an option for three BLU-98 smoke bombs. Each BLU-73 carries 33kg (72lb) of ethylene oxide, detonated to form an aerosol cloud that is then ignited.

Specifications (SUU-49)

Length overall: 220mm (7ft 1.2in)

Body diameter: 356mm (14in)

Stabilizer span: 719mm (28.3in)

Weight: 59kg (130lb) (BLU-73 bomblet)

Guidance system: None

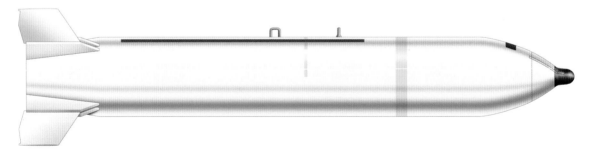

▲ CBU-100 Rockeye

The CBU-100 designation covers the SUU-76 expendable dispenser loaded with anti-tank bomblets. In total, the CBU-100 carries 247 Mk 118 bomblets. The SUU-75 and SUU-76 bomblet dispensers are both variants of the US Navy's Mk 7 Rockeye series. Note the tailfins seen in the extended position.

Specifications

Length overall: 2.31m (7.60ft)

Body diameter: 33.7cm (13.25in)

Stabilizer span: 87.6cm (34.5in) extended

Weight: 181kg (400lb)

Guidance system: None

at a set time after release, or at a particular altitude. The SUU-64 carries mines, as part of the Gator system (anti-armour and anti-personnel minelets), and can also be fitted with the Wind-Corrected Munitions Dispenser (WCMD) tail kit.

The SUU-65 submunitions dispenser has tailfins to impart spin after release, to improve munition accuracy. Contents include the Combined Effects Bomblet (CEB), anti-armour bomblets, Extended-Range Anti-Armor Munition (ERAM) and area-denial submunitions, and the WCMD kit can be fitted. The SUU-66 has the fins of the SUU-64, but no timer select switch, and a submunition ejection system. The SUU-66 can carry the Sensor Fused Munition (SFM) and can use the WCMD kit.

US Navy dispensers are based around the Mk 7 Rockeye series. This includes the SUU-58, part of the Gator system, carrying anti-armour or anti-personnel minelets. Versions include the CBU-78, CBU-82 and

US cluster bombs and dispensers in Operation *Desert Storm*

Name	Type	Number used
CBU-52/58/71	cluster bomb	17,831
CBU-87 CEM	cluster bomb	10,035
CBU-89 Gator	cluster bomb	1105
Mk 20 Rockeye II	cluster bomb	27,987
CBU-72	FAE	254
CBU-78 Gator	cluster bomb	209
		Total 57,421

CBU-83, all of which carry mixed loads of anti-armour/anti-vehicle and anti-personnel minelets. Other Rockeye variants are the SUU-75 and SUU-76 series. All are expendable dispensers, and the SUU-75 and SUU-76 carry anti-armour bomblets as the CBU-99 and CBU-100, respectively.

Specifications (SUU-58 Gator)

Length overall: 2400mm (7ft 9.6in)

Body diameter: 337mm (13.25in)

Stabilizer span: 87.6cm (34.5in)

Weight: 1.95kg (4.3lb) for each BLU-91 bomblet; 1.68kg (3.7lb) for each BLU-92 bomblet

Guidance system: None

▼ SUU-58

A member of the widely used Mk 7 Rockeye family, the US Navy's SUU-58 combines the dispenser with the Gator mine system, which employs BLU-91 anti-armour/anti-vehicle and BLU-92 anti-personnel minelets, plus a delay timer that sets the mines to self-destruct after a certain time.

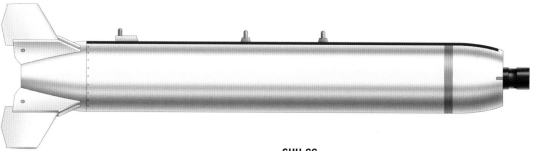

Specifications

Length overall: 2310mm (7ft 7.2in)

Body diameter: 397mm (15.62in)

Fin span: (retracted) 520mm (20.46in);

(extended) 1070mm (42in)

Weight: 29.5kg (65lb) for each BLU-108 SFM

Guidance system: IR for Skeet submunition

▼ SUU-66

The SUU-66 is part of the USAF's SUU-30 series of dispensers and employs a submunition ejection system that uses inflatable gas bags to force the bomblets out of the casing when it opens. The SUU-66 is used to carry the BLU-114 submunition, which is designed to disrupt electrical power grids, or, more commonly, the BLU-108 Sensor Fused Munition anti-armour munition, each of which carries four independent Skeet anti-armour submunitions.

European weapons dispensers and cluster munitions

Western European nations devised and fielded a number of cluster weapons during the Cold War, most of these emphasizing the vital anti-armour and runway-denial missions.

THE QUANTITATIVE SUPERIORITY possessed by Warsaw Pact forces on the Central Front during the Cold War drove Western European nations to develop a range of air-launched weapons designed to redress the balance. In particular, weapons dispensers were favoured as a means of maximizing the destructive effect of a single aircraft, whether directed against massed armour or mechanized formations, or against airfields and other key targets.

West Germany was the first country to introduce a dedicated multi-purpose weapons dispenser, in the form of the MBB-developed MW-1. First deployed in 1984, this was designed for carriage under the fuselage of a Tornado IDS strike aircraft. The MW-1 consisted of two sections, each of which contained 28 tubes that accepted various types of submunitions. The payload options comprised the KB44 sub-calibre armour-piercing hollow-charge bomblet (up to 4704

▼ BL755

The BL755 received a number of export orders, including from the West German *Bundesluftwaffe*, while the weapon also saw considerable use by Iran during the Iran–Iraq War. An improved version of the weapon was introduced in 1987, and this deployed more powerful anti-armour bomblets, these using a shaped charge that was designed to penetrate the target at a near-vertical attitude.

Specifications

Length overall: 2451mm (8ft 0.5in)	Weight: 264kg (582lb)
Body diameter: 419mm (16.in)	Guidance system: None
Stabilizer span: 566mm (22.3in)	

Specifications

Length overall: 3300mm (10ft 10in)	Weight: 305kg (672lb)
Body diameter: 360mm (14in)	Guidance system: None
Stabilizer span: 700mm (27.6in)	

▼ Belouga

Developed by Matra at Villacoublay, and by Thomson-Brandt, the BLG-66 Belouga is designed for use by supersonic tactical aircraft, and can be dropped at altitudes as low as 60m (200ft), and at speeds up to 1020km/h (634mph).

Although intended for carriage by a variety of aircraft and in different sizes, the JP233 was only adopted for service by the RAF's Tornado GR.Mk 1, and the Tornado IDS in its export version for Saudi Arabia. The Tornado carried two JP233 dispensers in a side-by-side installation under the fuselage.

Specifications

Length overall: 6550mm (21ft 6in)	Weight: 28.5kg (80lb) (munitions weight)
Body diameter: 840mm (33in)	Guidance system: None
Height: 600mm (23.6in)	

could be carried), MIFF anti-armour ground mine (total 872), MUSA fragmentation bomb (672), MUSPA area-denial mine with delay fuse (672), STABO runway-penetrating munition (244), and the ASW munition, which was designed to destroy hardened aircraft shelters (224). The MW-1 was withdrawn from use at the end of the Cold War.

French-developed cluster weapons include the BAT-120, carried in units of up to 18 bombs. The BAT-120 is designed to be used against air defence systems, vehicles and other 'softer' targets, and each 34kg (75lb) high-explosive/fragmentation bomblet is parachute retarded. The BM-400 developed by Thomson-Brandt is a bomb that breaks up into a number of smaller warheads that fall from the bomb casing. It is intended for use against hardened targets, and comprises a single container with three 100kg (220lb) submunitions that are ejected in a pre-set sequence, and are parachute-retarded. In addition to the basic anti-armour munitions, the BM-400 can also be adapted to dispense area-denial or cratering submunitions.

Developed from 1966, the Giboulée was a French bomblet dispenser designed for low-level use against armoured targets. Each dispenser consisted of a streamlined box containing 12 or 24 tubes, each of which accommodated five submunitions that were ejected towards the rear. The bomblets – either hollow-charge or fragmentation – were slowed by rear drag vanes. Successor to the Giboulée was the Matra Belouga, or BLG-66, a low-drag bomblet dispenser containing 151 1.3kg (2.9lb) grenades. Depending on the type of target to be attacked, the grenades can be of the general-purpose fragmentation, hollow-charge anti-armour or area-interdiction type. The Belouga is released at low level and at high speed, before deploying a parachute. Once slowed, the

Belouga releases its grenades in one of two pre-selected dispersal patterns.

In the UK, the Hunting BL755 became the standard cluster bomb of the RAF and Royal Navy, and also enjoyed notable export success. Introduced into service in 1972, the BL755, or Cluster Bomb No. 1, consists of a finned body containing seven compartments, each of which accommodates 21 submunitions. The submunitions carry a hollow charge for piercing armoured targets, although they also produce fragments on detonation, making the weapon suitable for the anti-personnel role. The Hunting Aerial Denial System (Hades) was a further development of the BL755, incorporating the HB876 area-denial minelet, and the SG357 shaped-charge runway-penetrating munition (for further details see below).

Runway denial weapon

A British equivalent to the MW-1 was the JP233, also developed by Hunting, and in service used exclusively by the Tornado. Carriage on this aircraft was similar to the MW-1, with two large pods being carried side-by-side under the fuselage. However, while the MW-1 was intended to undertake a range of missions, the JP233 was tailored for runway denial. For this purpose, each of the two dispensers was divided into two compartments, the forward section containing 215 small HB876 area-denial minelets, and the rear section accommodating 30 of the larger SG357 shaped-charge runway-penetrating munitions.

While the Cold War-era MW-1 and JP233 were based on submunitions dispensed from large containers carried by the aircraft, more recent developments provide standoff range to better protect the launch aircraft. (During Operation *Desert Storm*, low-level anti-runway missions flown by RAF

▲ **MW-1**

Germany withdrew the MW-1 from service after the Cold War, in line with the removal of cluster munitions from many inventories. Unlike the JP233, which was designed for runway denial, the MW-1 could be used for anti-armour, area-denial, runway attack and missions against soft-skinned vehicles and enemy personnel.

Specifications

Length overall: 5330mm (17ft 6in)	Weight: Up to 4700kg (10,362lb)
Width: 1320mm (52ft)	Guidance system: None
Height: 650mm (25.6in)	

Tornados with JP233s were considered among the most hazardous of the conflict.) Typical of standoff dispensers is the Dispenser Weapon System 39 (DWS 39), developed for carriage by the Swedish Air Force JAS 39 Gripen. This is a development of the DWS 24, itself an evolution of the MBB-designed Modular Dispenser System (MDS), which was offered in the 1980s as a lighter and more flexible counterpart to the MW-1. However, the MDS was intended to dispense its submunitions but retain the empty container aboard the aircraft.

Thor's hammer

Unpowered, the DWS 39 employs autonomous fire-and-forget guidance, gliding to its target after being launched. A range of 20km (6.2 miles) is possible from a high-altitude launch, or 10km (12.4 miles) after a launch at low altitude. The Swedish Air Force designation for the DWS 39 is BK 90 Mjölner

(Thor's hammer), with the dispenser manufactured by Germany's LFK (now part of MBDA), while the submunitions are the responsibility of Saab Bofors Dynamics. The guidance package is based on inertial navigation with a radar altimeter that also triggers release of the submunitions at the chosen altitude. Lift is generated by two fixed wings.

The dispenser system consists of 24 tubes (hence the original DWS 24 designation), each of which contains three charges. Two submunitions are available, the 4kg (9lb) MJ1 airburst explosive and the 18kg (40lb) MJ2 anti-armour charge. A mixture of both types can be carried, and these descend under parachutes.

Yugoslavia was a proponent of cluster weapons during the Cold War, and as well as acquiring the BL755, local industry developed the DPT-150, a 150kg (331lb) weapon that contained up to 54 fragmentation bomblets of various types.

▲ **BK-90 Mjölner**

When in service with the Swedish Air Force, the DWS 39 is known as the BK-90 (Bombkapsel 90). The manufacturer's designation changed from DWS 24 (indicating 24 submunitions tubes) to DWS 39, to signify its integration with the JAS 39 Gripen. Also offered are the 400kg (882lb) DWS 16, the 1000kg (2205lb) DWS 40, and the 1400kg (3086lb) DWS 60.

Specifications

Length overall: 3505mm (11ft 6in)	Weight: 600kg (1,323lb)
Width: 1000mm (39.4in)	Guidance system: INS and radar altimeter
Height: 630mm (24.8in)	

Soviet and Russian weapons dispensers and cluster munitions

The Soviet Union was long an exponent of air-launched cluster munitions, pioneering such weapons between the wars, and development continued during the Cold War years.

THE SOVIET UNION developed a series of fragmentation bombs under the designation AO, most of which were provided as smaller bomblets for carriage in cluster bombs. These were produced in a number of different sizes, up to and including 50kg (110lb). Among the AO family were the 1kg (2.2lb) AO-1, which was designed to fit nose to tail with other bomblets in order that more munitions could be accommodated in each dispenser. The O-1M was an air-delivered version of a landmine. The 2.5kg (5.5lb) AO-2.5 was also provided in the AO-2.5SCh version with a toughened semi-steel casing, and as the AO-2.5RT fragmentation munition. Another bomblet for carriage in a weapons dispenser was the ShOAB-0.5, which consisted of a spherical body containing 304 round anti-personnel pellets.

Also designed for carriage in dispensers were the MA series of submunitions. These comprised air-delivered mines, and included the MA-3 finless mine, which was intended to be used for laying barrier minefields across airfields and across transit routes. The MA-3's fuse was triggered when the mine hit the ground, and would be detonated by contact.

Soviet cluster bombs were produced under the RBK designation. The RBKs are disposable weapons, releasing their submunitions after they have been dropped by the launch aircraft. The outer casing contains a cassette-type carrier for various small-calibre submunitions, including anti-armour shaped-charge, pellet, fragmentation or incendiary types. The submunitions are delivered from the rear of the RBK when the cluster bomb reaches a pre-selected altitude and the fuse is triggered, gas forcing the munitions out of their cassettes once the tailcone and tailfin assembly have been released. Common versions of this weapon include the RBK-250 and RBK-500, which can carry AO-2.5 munitions, sub-BETAB concrete penetrators, PTAB-1M anti-armour munitions or SPBE anti-armour bomblets.

In the 500kg (1102lb) class, the RBK-500SPBE-D contains 15 larger anti-armour submunitions, of the sensor-fused type, which carry dual-mode IR seekers to target tanks and other armoured vehicles. The SPED-D is claimed to defeat all types of modern armour and can be dropped from altitudes of 400–5000m (1312–16,400ft).

▼ PROSAB-250

The Soviet Union began employing anti-bomber cluster munitions during World War II, and the concept was continued for some time after 1945. As jet bombers became more prevalent, the PROSAB was rendered redundant as a weapon for fighters, although it was retained in the inventory since it can also be used against conventional ground targets.

Specifications

Length overall: 1950mm (6ft 4.8in)	Weight: 250kg
Body diameter: 410mm (16.1in)	Guidance system: None
Stabilizer span: Not available	

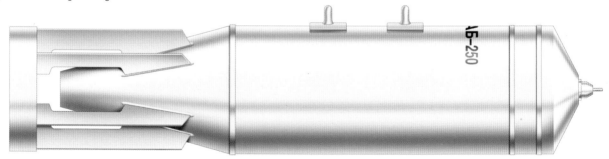

Specifications

Length overall: 1500mm (4ft 11.1in)	Weight: 250kg (551lb)
Body diameter: 325mm (12.8in)	Guidance system: None
Stabilizer span: 410mm (16.1in)	

▼ RBK-250

Unlike earlier Soviet cluster weapons, the RBK-250 and the RBK-500 cluster bombs were intended to withstand the strenuous g-forces and combat manoeuvres of high-speed tactical aircraft. The RBK-250 can also be configured to carry 48 ZAB-2.5 incendiary submunitions. The 500kg (1102lb) RBK-500 can carry 117 of the same submunitions.

The RBU-500U series can carry four different types of submunition. These include 10 concrete-penetrating BETAB-M submunitions used to crater runways. The anti-armour submunition is the PTAB-1M, with 352 carried in a single RBU-500U. For use against personnel and materiel, the RBK-500U carries 126 AO-2.5RTM bomblets primed to explode in the air. The RBK-500U can also accommodate 10 of the OFAB-50UD high-explosive/fragmentation submunitions, which can be set to detonate above the surface or after penetrating the ground.

Reusable dispenser

The KMGU-2 is a more modern reusable submunitions dispenser designed for carriage by high-speed tactical aircraft such as the MiG-29 and Su-25. It typically carries the AO-2.5 series fragmentation bombs. The munitions carried inside the KMGU-2 are delivered through rotary doors and can be directed downwards or to the side, depending on how the launcher is physically attached to the specific aircraft.

A particularly unusual cluster weapon developed in the Soviet Union was the PROSAB series. This comprised anti-aircraft bombs that were designed to be dropped into formations of enemy bombers by fighters flying at a higher altitude. The PROSAB-250 was introduced into service in the early 1950s, together with a smaller version, the 100kg (220lb) PROSAB-100, which was carried by the MiG-15. The PROSAB consists of a group of submunitions and a demolition charge within an outer casing. The detonation of the central charge breaks the casing and triggers the timed fuses on the smaller bomblets.

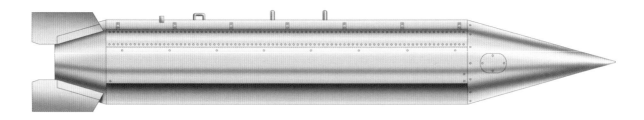

▲ KMGU-2

The streamlined, reusable KMGU-2 submunitions dispenser is normally associated with the AO-2.5 fragmentation bomblet, the PFM-1 anti-personnel mine and the PTAB-2.5 anti-armour bomblet. The weapon was used in combat in Afghanistan, and has also been cleared for carriage by helicopters, such as the Mi-24.

Specifications

Length overall: 3700mm (12ft 1.7in)	Weight: 450kg (992lb)
Body diameter: 480mm (18.9in)	Guidance system: None
Stabilizer span: 544mm (21.4in)	

Other weapons dispensers and cluster munitions

Cluster bombs are relatively simple to produce, and can be employed in a wide variety of applications. During the Cold War in particular, they found favour in various countries.

THE CARDOEN COMPANY of Chile developed a range of free-fall ordnance, including the CB-130 and CB-500 cluster munitions. The former contains 50 bomblets, while the larger CB-500 carries 240. In both cases, the bomblets are programmed to be dispensed according to a pre-determined pattern. Each bomblet is fitted with a standoff nose probe to ensure maximum armour penetration. Another Chilean cluster bomb system is that produced by Ferrimar, with a range of bombs carrying between 100 and 248 bomblets of the high-explosive anti-tank, high-explosive area-denial and armour-piercing type. Once launched, the Ferrimar cluster bomb deploys tailfins that impart spin on the container to help disperse the bomblets.

Israeli cluster bomb units include the TAL series, consisting of the identically sized TAL-1 and TAL-2. The first of these carries 279 0.5kg (1.1lb) bomblets, while the second accommodates 215 bomblets each of 0.4kg (0.9lb). After release from the aircraft, the cluster bombs are spun by the tailfins to dispense the contents over a wide area. The exact coverage is determined by the fusing option.

South Africa employed indigenously developed cluster bombs during its campaigns in the Border Wars, with the CB-470 being representative. This is an anti-personnel munition designed to make use of airburst. Instead of using a proximity fuse, the individual bomblets hit the ground and bounce before detonating. The bomblets, or Alphas, were first dropped from the bomb bay of Canberras, before the CB-470 container was produced, this being optimized for release at low level. Each of these units can carry a total of 40 Alphas. The CB-470 is programmed to release four salvoes of 10 munitions each, with distance separation to ensure maximum coverage. The bomblets are only armed after ejection.

Based on its hard experiences in the Iran–Iraq War, Iran has developed an indigenous standoff weapons dispenser. The Kite is a winged weapon system that is primarily intended for use against enemy air defence installations.

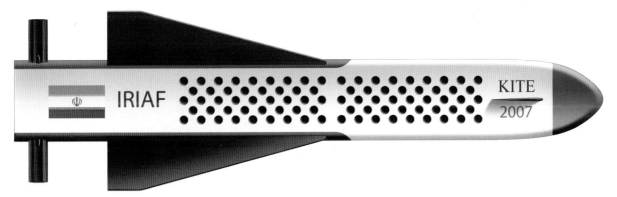

Specifications (estimated)

Length overall: 4100mm (13ft 5.4in)   Weight: 700kg (1543lb)

Width: 700mm (27.6in)   Guidance system: Inertial/GPS

Height: 500mm (19.7in)

▲ **Kite**

In service, the Kite is carried by F-4E Phantom IIs of the Islamic Republic of Iran Air Force. A low-altitude submunitions dispenser, the Kite has a range of 15km (9.3 miles), and can carry up to 200 submunitions. An improved version is available with a more sophisticated inertial/GPS guidance system.

Glossary of Terms

AAM	Air-to-Air Missile		JSF	Joint Strike Fighter
AARGM	Advanced Anti-Radiation Guided Missile		JSOW	Joint Standoff Weapon
AASM	Armament Air-Sol Modulair			
ACM	Advanced Cruise Missile		kT	Kiloton
AEW	Airborne Early Warning			
AGM	Air-to-Ground Missile		LACM	Land-Attack Cruise Missile
ALARM	Air-Launched Anti-Radiation Missile		LANTIRN	Low-Altitude, Navigation And Targeting by Infra-Red at Night
ALCM	Air-Launched Cruise Missile		LGB	Laser-Guided Bomb
AMRAAM	Advanced Medium-Range Air-to-Air Missile		LOAL	Lock On After Launch
APKWS	Advanced Precision Kill Weapon System		LOBL	Lock On Before Launch
ARM	Anti-Radiation Missile			
ASCC	Air Standardization Coordinating Committee		MAD	Magnetic Anomaly Detection
AShM	Anti-Ship Missile		MFD	Multi-Function Display
ASM	Air-to-Surface Missile		MICA	Missile d'Interception, de Combat et d'Autodéfense
ASMP-A	Air-Sol Moyenne Portée Amélioré		MMW	Millimetre-Wave
ASRAAM	Advanced Short-Range Air-to-Air Missile		MOAB	Massive Ordnance Air Blast
ASW	Anti-Submarine Warfare		MOP	Massive Ordnance Penetrator
ATGM	Anti-Tank Guided Missile		MT	Megaton
ATM	Anti-Tank Missile		MUPSOW	Multi-Purpose Standoff Weapon
AWACS	Airborne Warning And Control System			
			NSM	Naval Strike Missile
BLU	Bomb Live Unit		NVG	Night Vision Goggles
BROACH	Bomb Royal Ordnance Augmented Charge			
BVR	Beyond Visual Range		OCU	Operational Conversion Unit
			OTH	Over The Horizon
C2	Command and Control			
CALCM	Conventional Air-Launched Cruise Missile		PAF	Pakistan Air Force
CAP	Combat Air Patrol		PGM	Precision-Guided Munitions
CAS	Close Air Support		PLSS	Precision Location Strike System
CBU	Cluster Bomb Unit			
CCD	Charge Coupled Device		RAM	Radar Absorbent Material
CEB	Combined Effects Bomblet		RHAWS	Radar Homing And Warning System
CEM	Combined Effects Munition		RSAF	Royal Saudi Air Force
CNAF	Chinese Nationalist Air Force		RWR	Radar Warning Receiver
COIN	Counter-Insurgency			
			SAC	Strategic Air Command
DRAAF	Democratic Republic of Afghanistan Air Force		SACLOS	Semi-Automatic Command Line-Of-Sight
			SAM	Surface-to-Air Missile
ECCM	Electronic Counter-Countermeasures		SAR	Search And Rescue
ECM	Electronic Countermeasures		SARH	Semi-Active Radar Homing
ECR	Electronic Combat Reconnaissance		SATCOM	Satellite Communications
ERDL	Extended Range Data Link		SCALP EG	Système de Croisière conventionnel Autonome à Longue Portée et d'Emploi Général
FAA	Fleet Air Arm		SDB	Small Diameter Bomb
FAC	Forward Air Control		SEAD	Suppression of Enemy Air Defenses
FAE	Fuel/Air Explosive		SFW	Sensor Fused Munition
FFAR	Forward-Firing Aircraft Rocket/Folding-Fin Aircraft Rocket		SIGINT	Signals Intelligence
FLIR	Forward-Looking Infrared		SLAM	Stand-off Land Attack Missile
			SLAM-ER	Stand-off Land Attack Missile-Extended Range
GBU	Guided Bomb Unit		SLAR	Side-Looking Airborne Radar
GCI	Ground Control Intercept		SOM	Stand-Off Munitions
GP	General-Purpose (bomb)		SRAM	Short-Range Attack Missile
			SUU	Suspended Underwing Unit
HARM	High-speed Anti-Radiation Missile		SyAAF	Syrian Arab Air Force
HE	High Explosive			
HOBOS	Homing Bomb System		TALD	Tactical Air Launched Decoy
HOT	Hautsubsonique Optiquement Téleguidé Tiré d'un Tube		TAC	Tactical Air Command
HUD	Head-Up Display		TERCOM	Terrain Contour Matching
HVAR	High-Velocity Aircraft Rocket		TFR	Terrain-Following Radar
			TFW	Tactical Fighter Wing
IAF	Indian Air Force		TIALD	Thermal Imaging Airborne Laser Designator
IDF/AF	Israeli Defence Force/Air Force		TMD	Tactical Munitions Dispenser
IFF	identification fried or foe		TRIGAT	Third-Generation Anti-Tank
IIR	Imaging Infra-Red		TOW	Tube-launched, Optically-tracked, Wire-guided
INS	Inertial Navigation System			
IR	Infrared		UARAF	United Arab Republic Air Force
IrAF	Iraqi Air Force		UAV	Unmanned Aerial Vehicle
IRIAF	Imperial Iranian Air Force			
IRST	Infra-Red Search and Track		VHF	Very High Frequency
			VLF	Very Low Frequency
JASSM	Joint Air-to-Surface Standoff Missile		WAFAR	Wrap-Around Fin Aerial Rocket
JDAM	Joint Direct Air Munition		WCMD	Wind-Corrected Munitions Dispenser

Index